対訳

禅と
日本文化

Zen and Japanese Culture

対 訳

禅と日本文化
Zen and Japanese Culture

鈴木大拙
Daisetz T. Suzuki

北川桃雄 訳
Translated by Momo'o Kitagawa

KODANSHA INTERNATIONAL
Tokyo • New York • London

本書について

本対訳版の英文の原書は *Zen Buddhism and its Influence on Japanese Culture*
(1938年5月、京都の The Eastern Buddhist Society 刊)である。同書のパー
ト1の第6章まで収録している。日本文は、岩波新書「禅と日本文化」(岩
波書店刊、1940年9月に初版発行、1964年3月に改版発行) の定評ある
北川桃雄訳を用いた。この訳文は著者・鈴木大拙博士の校閲を経たもの
であり、著者の注釈も添えられている。同書第7章「禅と俳句」の英文
は原書に掲載されていないため、本対訳版には収めなかった。

写真
　「誕生釈迦仏立像・灌仏盤」東大寺所蔵
　「仏光国師（無学祖元）木像」円覚寺所蔵
　「枯木鳴鵙図」（宮本武蔵作）和泉市久保惣記念館所蔵
　講談社資料センター

Originally published in English as *Zen Buddhism and its Influence on
Japanese Culture* by The Eastern Buddhist Society in 1938, and originally
published in Japanese as *Zen to Nihon Bunka* by Iwanami Shoten publishers
in 1964.

CONTENTS
目次

Daisetz T. Suzuki at Matsugaoka Bunko in Kamakura.

著者（鎌倉の松ヶ岡文庫にて）

Preliminary to the Understanding of Zen

禅の予備知識

It goes without saying that most authorities, Japanese and foreign, who write at all impartially and intelligently on the moral or cultural or spiritual life of the Japanese people, agree on the importance of the influence which has been exercised by Zen Buddhism on the building-up of Japanese character. I have elsewhere quoted statements bearing upon this from the late Sir Charles Eliot and from Sir George Sansom as two most recent and authoritative foreign writers: the one on *Japanese Buddhism* and the other on *Japanese Culture**. It is more appropriate and necessary here to say a few words about Zen itself, as I imagine my readers have very little knowledge of it. This is, however, not a very easy task to do, for Zen is a difficult subject to comprehend for those who have no knowledge whatever of it either by hearsay or from reading, since Zen claims to be above logic and verbal interpretation, and again since it has never been made accessible to general readers. As to those who are especially interested in Zen, I would ask them to peruse some of my previous works on the subject. In the following, the barest possible sketch of it is given just enough perhaps to have a somewhat intelligent grasp of its influence on Japanese character and culture.

Zen is a form of Buddhism developed in China in early T'ang, that is, in the eighth century. Its real beginning is much earlier, it started with the

卍

　いまさらいうまでもないが、日本人の道徳的または修養的ないし精神的生活に関し、公明にかつ理解をもって、書いている内外権威者の多くは、禅宗が日本人の性格を築きあげる上にきわめて重要な役割を勤めたという点で、意見をひとしくしている。自分は最近のもっとも権威ある外国の二人の著述、サー・チャールズ・エリオットの「日本仏教」およびサー・ジョージ・サンソムの「日本文化史」からも、これに関する叙述を本書のどこかで引用しておいた。多数の読者は禅についてはあまりよく知らないものと見て、これについて、ここに何か二つ三つ述べることが適当であり、また必要であろう。しかし、これは容易なことではない。禅は、それに関して読んだり聞いたりして、概念的にでもなにか知識を持たぬ人には、これを理解するのが困難なのである。禅は理論と言語的解釈を超えることを要求し、また、これまで一般読者にはけっして近づきうるものではなかったからだ。とくに禅にたいして興味を持つ人々には、禅に関する余の著述の二、三を読まれることを希望する。とにかく、ここでは禅のごく大略を述べて、日本人の性格と文化におよぼしたその影響を多少なりとも読者に理解して欲しいのである。

　禅は初唐即ち八世紀に中国に発達した仏教の一形態である。その真の始まりはさらに早く、六世紀の初め、南インドから中国にきた

coming of Bodhi-Dharma to China from Southern India early in the sixth century. Its teaching is no other than the general teaching of Mahayana Buddhism, and what this teaches is of course that of Buddhism in general. Zen proposes, however, to teach the essential spirit of the Buddha himself discarding all the superficialities which have accumulated around the teaching of the founder during its course of development in India, in Central Asia, and in China itself. These "superficialities" may be ritualistic, doctrinal, and also due to racial psychology. Zen wants us to see directly into the spirit of Buddha.

What is this spirit? What is that which constitutes the essential teaching of Buddhism? This is Prajñā and Karunā. Prajñā and Karunā are Sanskrit terms. Prajñā may be translated "transcendental wisdom," and Karunā "love" or "compassion." Prajñā makes us look into the reality of things beyond their phenomenality, and, therefore, when Prajñā is attained we have an insight into the fundamental significance of life and of the world, and cease from worrying about merely individual interests and sufferings. Karunā is then free to work its own way, which means that love, unobstructed by its selfish encumbrances, is able to spread itself over all things. In Buddhism it extends even to inanimate beings, for Buddhism believes that all beings, regardless of the forms they take in their present states of existence, are ultimately destined to attain Buddhahood when love penetrates into them.

Zen undertakes to awaken Prajñā found generally slumbering in us under the thick clouds of Ignorance and Karma. Ignorance and Karma come from our unconditioned surrender to the intellect; Zen revolts against this state of affairs. And as intellection expresses itself in logic and words, Zen disdains logic and remains speechless when it is asked to express itself. The worth of the intellect is appreciated only after the essence of things is grasped. This means that Zen wants to reverse the ordinary course of knowledge and to resort to its own specific method of training our minds in the awakening of transcendental wisdom (*prajñā*).

The following story told by Goso Hoyen (Fa-yen; died 1104), of the Sung

菩提達磨から起ったのである。その教義は大乗仏教の一般教義と変りはない。その教えるところも、もちろん一般の仏教のそれである。しかし、禅の目的は、インド・中央アジア、そして中国においても、その発展するにしたがって建設者の教えの周囲に堆積したいっさいの皮相な見解を除去して、仏陀自身の根本精神を教えんというにある。これらの「皮相な見解」は儀礼的、教典的であり、かつ民族心理の特殊性にもとづくものといってよい。禅は仏陀の精神を直接に見ようと欲するのである。

　この精神はなんであるか。この仏教の真髄を成すものはなんであるか。これは般若（智慧）と大悲である。般若は「超越的智慧」、大悲は「愛」または「憐情」と訳すことができよう。般若によって、人は事物の現象的表現を超えてその実在を見得することができる。それゆえに、般若をえれば、われわれは生と世界との根本的の意義を洞徹しえて、たんなる個人的な利益や苦痛に思いわずらうことがなくなる。大悲がそのとき自在に作用する。それは「愛」がその利己的な妨げを受けずに、万物におよぶことができるという意味である。仏教では、愛は無生物にまでおよぶ。いっさいの存在は現在の生存状態のままで、いかなる形態をとろうとも、愛が彼らに滲透するときは、結局、成仏する定めになっていると信じられている。

　禅は、無明と業の密雲に包まれて、われわれのうちに睡っている般若を目ざまそうとするのである。無明と業は知性に無条件に屈伏するところから起るのだ。禅はこの状態に抗う。知的作用は論理と言葉となって現れるから、禅は自から論理を蔑視する。自分そのものを表現しなければならぬ場合には、無言の状態にいる。知識の価値は事物の真髄が把握せられた後に、始めてこれを知ることができる。これは、禅がわれわれの超越的智慧（般若）を目ざます場合に、認識の普通のコースを逆にした特別な方法で、われわれの精神をきたえるという意味である。
　宋代の五祖法演（1104 歿）によって説かれたつぎの説話は、知力・

dynasty, will help us greatly in our understanding the Zen method and Zen spirit which have been described as being against teaching based on intellect, logic, and verbalism.

"If people ask me what Zen is like, I will say that it is like learning the art of burglary. The son of a burglar saw his father growing older and thought, 'If he is unable to carry out his profession, who will be the bread-winner of this family, except myself? I must learn the trade.' He intimated the idea to his father, who approved of it. One night the father took the son to a big house, broke through the fence, entered the house, and, opening one of the large chests, told the son to go in and pick out the clothings. As soon as he got into it, the lid was dropped and the lock securely applied. The father now came out to the court-yard, and loudly knocking at the door woke up the whole family, whereas he himself quietly slipped away from the former hole in the fence. The residents got excited and lighted candles, but found that the burglar had already gone. The son who remained all the time in the chest securely confined thought of his cruel father. He was greatly morti-fied, when a fine idea flashed upon him. He made a noise which sounded like the gnawing of a rat. The family told the maid to take a candle and examine the chest. When the lid was unlocked, out came the prisoner, who blew out the light, pushed away the maid, and fled. The people ran after him. Noticing a well by the road, he picked up a large stone and threw it into the water. The pursuers all gathered around the well trying to find the burglar drowning himself in the dark hole. In the meantime he was safely back in his father's house. He blamed his father very much for his narrow escape. Said the father, 'Be not offended, my son. Just tell me how you got off.' When the son told him all about his adventures, the father remarked, 'There you are, you have learned the art.'"

This radical method of teaching the art of burglary aptly illustrates the methodology of Zen. When a disciple asks his master to be taught in Zen, the latter may slap his face and exclaim, "What a good-for-nothing fellow

論理・文字言語を基とする教説とは相反するものといわれる禅的方法と禅の精神を、われわれが理解する上に多大の助けとなろう。(註、原文は「五祖録」という禅宗語録に出ている)

『人が、禅とはいかなるものかと問えば、自分は禅とは夜盗の術をまなぶに似たるものと答えるであろう。ある夜盗の息子が自分の父の年老いたのを見て思った。「親父が商売をやれぬとすれば、この己より外に自家の稼ぎ手はないわけだ。己が商売をおぼえねばなるまい」。彼はこの考を父親にひそかにもらし、父親もこれを承知した。一夜、父は倅を伴い、ある豪家に至り、塀を破り、屋内に入り、大きな長持の一つを開き、息子に、このなかに入って衣服を取り出せと命じた。息子がなかに入るや否や、父はその蓋をおろして鍵をかたく掛けた。そして中庭にとびだし、泥棒だと大呼し、戸を叩いて、家中のものを起した上で、さて己はさきの塀の穴から悠々と逃げ去ってしまった。家人は立騒いで灯をつけたが、盗人はすでに逃げたことが判った。その間に長持のなかに固く閉込められた倅は、父親の無情をうらんだ。彼はひどく煩悶したあげく、名案が不意に浮んだ。鼠の物を嚙るような音を立てると、家人は下婢に灯を取って長持を調べよと命じた。蓋を開けるやいなや、ここに閉込められていた捕虜は飛びだした。灯を吹消した。下婢を突飛ばした。そして一目散に逃出した。人々は彼をおいかけた。彼は路傍に井戸を認めたので、大石を抱き上げてこれをその水中に投じた。すると、暗い井のなかに、盗人が入水したのだと思って、追手はことごとく井戸の周囲に集った。そのうちに彼は無事自家に戻った。彼は危機一髪のところだったといって、父親の非道を鳴らした。父親がいった。「マァ、憤るナ、どうして逃げてきたかちょっと話してみろ」

そこで倅がその冒険の一部始終を語り終った時、父親はいった。「それだ。お前は夜盗術の極意をおぼえ込んだ」』

この過激な夜盗術の教授法によって、禅の方法論が説明される。禅では弟子がその師匠に教えを求めると、師は弟子の面を打って一喝する。

you are!" When one approaches the master with the question, "I have a doubt about the truth which is said to liberate us from the bondage of the passions," or with some such questions, the master may take him before the entire congregation of the monks and declare, "Look, O monks, here is one who cherishes a doubt!" He may then push the poor monk away from his presence, while he himself nonchalantly retires to his own quarters. It appears as if doubting were criminal, or at least something one ought never to cherish where all is open for one's free and unobstructed inspection. If the master is asked whether he understands Buddhism, he will say. "No I do not." Further asked, "Who understands Buddhism then?" he will point at the pillar just outside his study.

When the Zen master makes a show of the logician, he goes altogether contrary to the usual method of reasoning and valuation. Not only in this case "Fair is foul and foul is fair," but "You are I and I am you." Facts so called are ignored, values become topsy-turvy.

The Japanese fencing master sometimes uses the Zen method of training. When a disciple came to a master to be disciplined in the art of fencing, the master, who was in retirement in his mountain hut, agreed to undertake the task. The pupil was made to help him gather kindlings, draw water from the nearby spring, split wood, make fire, cook rice, sweep the rooms and the garden, and generally look after his household affairs. There was no regular or technical teaching in the art. After some time the young man became dissatisfied, for he did not come to work as servant to the old gentleman, but to learn the art of swordsmanship. So one day he approached the master and asked him to teach him. The master agreed. The result was that the young man could not do any piece of work with any feeling of safety. For when he began to cook rice early in the morning, the master would appear and strike him from behind with a stick. When he was in the midst of his sweeping, he

『咄、この懶者奴。』また、一人の僧が『煩悩からわれわれを解脱させるという真理について一つの疑問がありますが』という類の問を持って師に近づいたとする。すると、師は法堂で、その僧を大衆の前に連れて行っていい放つ。『みなの衆、疑問を抱くものがここにいるぞ。』師はこんな風にして、この憐れむべき僧をその面前から突飛ばす。僧はほうほうの体で自分の室に退く。まるで疑問を抱くことが犯罪ででもあるかのようである。そうでないまでも、自在に自分で点検するにいいように一切が開放されている場所で、かえって何かうろうろして迷子になっているかのようにも思われる。弟子が師に対して、貴方は仏法を了解していられるか否か、などと尋ねると、彼はただちにいう。『いや、わしにゃなにも解らぬ。』さらに『それでは誰が仏法を会得しているのですか』と尋ねれば、師は書斎の前にある柱でも指すことであろう。

　禅匠が論理家らしい振舞をすることがあるとすれば、それは普通の推理法や評価標準をまったく逆にしたものである。シェクスピアが何かの戯曲中の一人物にいわせたように『美は醜であり、醜は美である』ばかりでなく、『汝は我であり、我は汝である』というのである。いわゆる事実なるものは無視され、価値は顛倒する。

　日本の剣匠たちはしばしば禅の鍛錬法を用いる。一人の熱心な弟子が剣術を習いたいというのでやってくる。山中の小庵に隠棲していた先師は、やむをえず、それを承知する。ところが、弟子の毎日の仕事は、師を助けて、薪を集め、渓流から水を汲み、材木を割り、火を起し、飯を炊ぎ、室や庭を掃くなど、家事一般の世話をさせられるのである。べつに規則正しく剣術の法を教えられることもない。日数がたつにつれて、若者は不満をおぼえてきた。自分は召使として働くため老先生の許にやってきたわけではなく、剣道の技をおぼえるためにやってきたのだ。そこである日、師の前にでて、不平をいって教えを乞うと、師匠は『うん、それなら』という。その結果、若者は何一つの仕事も安心の念を持ってすることができなくなった。なぜかというに、早朝飯を炊きだすと、師匠が現れて、背後から不意に棒で打ってかかるのだ。庭を掃いていると思ってい

would be feeling the same blow from somewhere, from an unknown direction. He had no peace of mind, he had to be always on the *qui vive*. Some years passed before he could successfully dodge the blow from whatever source it might come. But the master was not quite satisfied with him yet. One day the master was found cooking his own vegetables over an open fire. The pupil took it to his head to avail himself of this opportunity. Taking up his big stick, he let it fall over the head of the master, who was then stooping over the cooking pan to stir its contents. But the pupil's stick was caught by the master with the cover of the pan. This opened the pupil's mind to the secrets of the art, which had hitherto been kept away from him and to which he had yet been a stranger. He then for the first time really appreciated the unparalleled kindness of the master.

In this there is something of the Zen method of training, which consists in personally experiencing the truth whatever this may be, and not appealing to intellection or systemic theorisation. The latter busies itself with the detail of technique, and is consequently superficial and never leads to the central fact of the matter. Theorisation may be all very well when playing baseball, building factories, constructing fortresses, manufacturing industrial goods or murderous instruments of various kinds, but not with creating objects of art, or mastering arts which are the direct expressions of the human soul, or acquiring the art of living a life true to itself. Anything in fact which has to do with creation in its genuine sense is really "untransmittable," that is, beyond the ken of discursive understanding. Hence Zen's motto, "No reliance on words."

In this respect Zen is opposed to everything that goes by the name of science or scientific. Zen is personal while science is impersonal. What is impersonal is abstract and does not take notice of individual experiences. What is personal belongs altogether to the individual and has no signification without the backing of his own experience. Science means systematisation, and Zen is just its reverse. Words are needed in science and philosophy, but they are a hindrance in Zen. If words are needed in Zen, they are of

ると、何時何処からともなく、同じように棒が飛んでくる。若者は気が気でない。心の平和をまったく失った。何時も四方に眼を配っていなければならなかった。かようにして数年立つと、始めて、棒がどこから飛んでこようとも、これを無事に避けることができるようになった。しかし、師匠は、それでもまだ、彼を許さなかった。ある日、老師が炉で自分の菜を調理していたのを見て、弟子は好機逸すべからずと考え、大きな棒を取上げて、師匠の頭上にうちおろした。師匠はおりから、鍋の上に身を屈めて、なかのものを掻廻しているところだったが、弟子の棒は鍋の蓋で受けとめられた。この時弟子は、これまで到りえなかった、自分の知らない剣道の極意に対して、はじめて悟りを開いた。彼はそこで本当に師匠の比類なき親切さを味いえたということである。

　ここに禅の鍛錬法の一風変ったところがあるのだ。それは真理がどんなものであろうと、身をもって体験することであり、知的作用や体系的な学説に訴えぬということである。後者は技術の末にかかずらって、その結果皮相的になり、中心事実に到達せぬことになる。理論化ということは野球をやるときや、工場を建てるときや、各種工業製品を製造するときなどには、結構なことであるかも知れぬが、人間の魂の直接の表現である芸術品を創ったり、そういう技術に熟達したりする場合、また正しく生きる術をえんとする場合には、そういう訳にはゆかぬ。事実、純正の意味の創作に関連した事柄は、いかなる事でもみな、真に「伝え難き」もの、すなわち論議を主体とする悟性の限界を超えたものである。それゆえ、禅のモットーは「言葉に頼るな」（不立文字）というのである。

　この点において、禅は科学、または科学的の名によって行なわれる一切の事物とは反対である。禅は体験的であり、科学は非体験的である。非体験的なるものは抽象的であり、個人的経験に対してはあまり関心を持たぬ。体験的なるものはまったく個人に属し、その人の経験を背景としなくては意義を持たぬ。科学は系統化を意味し、禅はまさにその反対である。言葉は科学と哲学には要るが、禅の場合には妨げとなる。なぜであるか。言葉は代表するものであって、

the same value as coins in trading. We cannot wear coins to keep the cold away, we cannot eat coins to quench thirst or appease hunger. Coins are to be turned into real food, real wool, and real water when they are of real value to life. We are constantly forgetting this homely truth, and never cease hoarding money. In a similar manner we memorise words and play with concepts and think we are wise. "Wise" indeed we are, but this kind of wisdom never avails when, dealing with the realities of life. If it did is it not high time to have a millenium by now?

Roughly speaking, there are three kinds of knowledge.

The first is such as we gain from reading or hearsay, which we memorise and usually hold as an important possession; the bulk of knowledge so called is of this kind. We cannot walk all over the earth and personally survey it, and therefore for the knowledge of the world we depend upon a map which has been prepared for us by others. The second kind of knowledge is what is ordinarily known as scientific. It is the result of observation and experiment, analysis and speculation. It has a firmer foundation than the former, for here is something personal and experienced to a certain extent. The third kind of knowledge is the one attained by an intuitive mode of understanding. According to those who hold to the second form of knowledge, the intuitive kind is regarded as having no solid foundation in facts and therefore not so absolutely reliable. But as a matter of fact, scientific knowledge so called is not at all exhaustive and for that reason awaits further corrections, for it is confined to a sphere of its own limitation. When an emergence, especially of a personal nature, rises, science and logic may have no time to make use of its storage of knowledge and calculation, nor may memorised knowledge be available, for then the mind may fail to recall all the memories it has accu-mulated in the past. Intuitive knowledge on the other hand forms the basis

実体そのものではない、実体こそ、禅において最も高く評価される
ものなのである。禅において言葉が要るとしても、それは売買にお
ける貨幣と同じ価値のものである。寒さを防ぐために貨幣を着る訳
にゆかぬ。饑渇を充すために貨幣を飲む訳にゆかぬ。貨幣は、実際
の食物・実際の羊毛・実際の水が、生活に対して実際の価値を持つ時、
それらに換えられるべきものなのである。人々は始終この知れきっ
た事実を忘れていて、金を溜め込むことを止めようとせぬ。そんな
塩梅で、人々は言葉を記憶し、概念をもてあそび、それで自分は利
口だと考えている。なるほど、「利口」ではあるが、この種の利口
さは人生の諸事実を扱う場合には益するところはない。益するとこ
ろがあるならば、いまこそ黄金時代の千年期（訳註、キリスト再臨して
一千年間世を治めんという説より出る）を持つべき好機ではないか。

　大略すれば、知識には三種ある。

　第一は、読んだり聞いたりすることによってうるものである。わ
れわれはこれを記憶して、平素重要な所有物として持っているもの
で、いわゆる知識の大部分はこの種のものである。われわれは地球
上をくまなく歩きまわって、親しくこれを調査する訳にはゆかな
い。ゆえに、世界の知識については、他人が備えてくれた地図に頼
る。第二の種類の知識は、科学的と普通いわれているものである。
観察と実験・分析と推理の結果である。それは前者より強固な基礎
を持っているが、ある程度、体験的で経験的なところがあるからで
あろう。第三の種類の知識は直覚的な理解の方法によって達せられ
るものである。第二の形態の知識を重んずる人にしたがえば、直覚
的な知識は事実に確実な基礎を有せぬから、あまり絶対的な信頼を
置くことはできぬという。しかし、事実としては、いわゆる科学的
知識は完璧なものではなくて、それ自身限界性を有するものである
から、異変、とくに個人性異変の起った場合には、科学と論理はか
ねて貯えておいた知識と計較を利用する隙がない、記憶してい
る知識だけでは役に立たぬ。かかる場合には、精神はあまり咄嗟な
ので過去に貯蔵した記憶の一切を喚起することはできないからであ
る。しかるに一方、直覚的知識はあらゆる種類の信仰、とくに宗教

of all kinds of faith, specially religious, and most efficiently and successfully rises up to meet crises.

What Zen purposes to attain is the third form of knowledge which penetrates deeply down to the very foundation of existence, or, rather, which emerges from the depths of our own being.

I have been digressing; but from this fundamental attitude of Zen towards intellection in regard to the realisation of the spirit of Buddhism, we can see that there arise in the general atmosphere of Zen certain characteristic trends of thought and feeling towards things of the world, which are:

1. Its concentration on the spirit leads to the neglect of form;

2. Or, rather, it detects in form of any description the presence of the spirit;

3. Deficiency or imperfection of form is held to be more expressive of the spirit, because perfection of form is likely to attract one's attention to form and not to the inner truth itself;

4. The deprecation of formalism, conventionalism, or ritualism tends to make the spirit stand in all its nakedness or aloneness or solitariness;

5. This transcendental aloofness or the aloneness of the absolute is the spirit of asceticism, which means the doing-away with every possible trace of unessentials;

6. Aloneness translated in terms of the worldly life is non-attachment;

7. When aloneness is absolute in the Buddhist sense of the word, it deposits itself in all things from the meanest weeds of the field to the highest form of nature.

With this preliminary, I wish to treat in the following pages of the part Zen Buddhism has played in the moulding of Japanese culture and character, as especially exhibited in the arts generally, in the development of Bushido ("the way of the warrior"), in the study and propagation of Confucianism and general education, and in the rise of the tea-cult; while incidentally some other points will be touched upon.

的信仰の基礎を形成しており、最も能率的に危機に応じ能うのである。

　禅が呼びさまさんとするところは、この第三の形態の知識であって、それは深く存在の基礎にまで滲透している、というよりはむしろ、われわれの存在の深いところからでてくるものなのである。

　少しく枝葉に渉ったが、仏教精神の自覚に関し知的作用に対して持つ禅のこの根本的態度から察して、われわれは、禅の雰囲気のうちには一般に、世の事物に対するある特殊の考えかたと感じかたが存することを知るのである。それは、

　一、禅は精神に焦点をおく結果、形式（フォーム）を無視する。

　二、すなわち、禅はいかなる種類の形式のなかにも精神の厳存をさぐりあてる。

　三、形式の不十分、不完全なる事によって、精神がいっそう表われるとされる。形式の完全は人の注意を形式に向けやすくし、内部の真実そのものに向けがたくするからである。

　四、形式主義（フォーマリズム）、慣例主義（コンベンショナリズム）、儀礼主義（リチュアリズム）を否定する結果、精神はまったく裸出してきて、その孤絶性（アローンネス）、孤独性（ソリタリネス）に還る。

　五、超越的な孤高、または、この「絶対なるもの」（アブソルート）の孤絶がアスセチシズム（清貧主義、禁慾主義）の精神である。それはすべての必要ならざるものの痕跡を、いささかも止めないということである。

　六、孤絶とは世間的の言葉でいえば無執着ということである。

　七、孤絶なる語を仏教者の使う絶対という意味に解すれば、それは最も卑しと見られている野の雑草から、自然の最高の形態といわれているものにいたるまで、森羅万象のなかに沈んでいる。

　これだけの前置きをして、私はつぎに、一般諸美術・武士道の発展・儒教および一般教育の研究と普及・茶道の興隆などに見られるように、日本文化および日本的性格の形成上に、禅宗がつとめた役割を論じたいのである。他の点は機に触れていいおよぼすこととしよう。

A figure of the Infant Buddha.

誕生釈迦仏立像。

General Remarks on Japanese Art Culture

禅と美術

1

With these specifications, as detailed above, of the atmosphere emanating from Zen, we may now proceed to see what contributions Zen has made to the building-up of Japanese culture. It is a significant fact that all other schools of Buddhism have limited their sphere of influence almost to the spiritual life of the Japanese people; Zen has gone beyond it. Zen has internally entered into every phase of the cultural life of the people.

In China this was not necessarily the case. Zen united itself to a great extent with Taoist beliefs and practices, and also with the Confucian teaching of morality, but it did not affect the cultural life of the people so much as it did in Japan. (Is it due to the racial psychology of the Japanese people here that Zen has been taken up by them so intensely and deeply that it has intimately entered into their life?) In China, however, I ought not to omit to mention the noteworthy fact that Zen gave great impetus to the development of Chinese philosophy in the Sung dynasty and also to the growth of a certain school of painting. A large number of the latter were brought over to Japan beginning with the Kamakura era in the thirteenth century when there was constant travelling of the Zen monks between the two neighbouring countries. The paintings of Southern Sung thus came to find their ardent

卍

一

　禅から発する雰囲気を、上記のように略述したが、さらに進んで禅が日本文化の形成にいかなる寄与をなしたかを考えてみよう。禅以外の仏教各派が日本文化におよぼした影響の範囲は、ほとんど日本人の生活の宗教的方面に限られたようだが、ひとり禅はこの範囲を逸脱した。これは意義深い事実である。禅は国民の文化生活のあらゆる層のなかへ深くおよんでいる。

　中国においては、かならずしも事情は同じではなかった。禅は道教の信仰と実践、または儒教の道徳とも、広範囲に結びついたが、日本ほどにはその国民の文化生活に影響を与えなかった。（禅が日本人によって熱心に取上げられ、その生活に深く入り込んでいるのは、民族的心理に帰因するのであろうか。）しかし、中国の場合に注目しなければならぬ事実は、禅が宋学の発達およびある派の絵画の発展に非常に刺激を与えたということで、これははぶく訳にゆかぬ。後者は鎌倉時代の初期に、日中両国間を始終往来していた禅僧たちによって舶来された。南宋の絵画は、かくして、海のこなたにその熱心な歓美者を見出すことになったのである。それらは現にいま、日本の国宝となり、本土の中国においては、かえってこの種の階級の絵画はあまり見あたらない。

admirers on this side of the sea, and are now national treasures of Japan, while in China no specimens of this class of painting are to be found.

Before proceeding further, a few general remarks may be made about one of the peculiar features of Japanese art, which is closely related to and finally deducible from the world-conception of Zen.

Among things which strongly characterise Japanese artistic talents we may mention the so-called "one-corner" style which originated from Bayen (Ma Yüan), one of the greatest Southern Sung artists. This "one-corner" style is psychologically associated with the Japanese painters' "thrifty brush" tradition of retaining the barest possible number of lines or strokes which go to represent forms on silk or paper. Both are very much in accord with the spirit of Zen. A simple fishing boat in the midst of the rippling waters is enough to awaken in the mind of the beholder the sense of the vastness of the sea and at the same time that of peace and contentment—the Zen sense of the Alone. Apparently, the boat floats helplessly. It is a primitive structure with no mechanical device for stability and audacious steering over the turbulent waves, with no scientific apparatus for braving all kinds of weather—quite a contrast to the modern liner of so much tonnage. But this very helplessness is the virtue of the fishing canoe in contrast with which we feel the incomprehensibility of the Absolute encompassing the boat and all. Again, a solitary bird on a dead branch, in which not a line, not a shade, not a mass is wasted, is enough to show us the loneliness of an autumnal day when days become shorter and nature begins to roll up once more its gorgeous display of the luxurious summer vegetation. It makes one feel somewhat pensive but gives opportunity to withdraw the attention towards the inner life, which, when sufficiently inspected, spreads out all its rich treasures ungrudgingly before the eyes.

Here we have an appreciation of transcendental aloofness in the midst of multiplicities—which is known as *wabi* in the dictionary of Japanese cultural terms. *Wabi* really means "poverty," or, negatively, "not to be in or with fashionable society of the time." To be poor, that is, not to be depending on

さらにこの論を進める前に、日本芸術の一特徴につき、二、三の一般的な注意をしておこう。それは禅の世界概念と密接な関係があるし、結局、そこから類推することができるものである。

　日本人の芸術的才能のいちじるしい特色の一つとして、南宋大画家の一人馬遠に源を発した「一角」様式を挙げることができる。この「一角」様式は、心理的にみれば、日本の画家が「減筆体」といって、絹本や紙本にできるだけ少ない描線や筆触で物の形を表わすという伝統と結びついている。両者ともに禅の精神とはなはだ一致している。連たつ水の上の一介の漁舟は、観る人の心に海の茫漠たる広さの感じと同時に平和と満足の感じ、——「孤絶」の禅的感じを目ざめさすに十分である。（訳註、馬遠「寒江独釣図」）一見するところ、この小舟は頼りなげに浮いている。ごく原始的な構造で、安定に対する機械的工夫も、激浪を乗りこえる強い舵もない。あらゆる種類の天候をしのぐ科学的機具類もない。要するに、何万トンという現代の定期汽船（ライナー）とまったくいい対照（コントラスト）を見せている。しかし、この頼りなさこそ、この漁舟の美徳であって、これと対照してわれわれは小舟といっさいとを取りかこむ「絶対なるもの」の不可能を感じるのである。さらにまた、枯枝の上の孤独の鳥の図では、一本の線、一抹の影、一個の塊（マス）も無駄にされず、日がますます短くなって、自然が豪華に繰りひろげたゆたかな夏の繁茂を、ふたたび巻きおさめんとする秋の日の寂しさをわれわれに示してあまりある。（訳註、牧谿「叭々鳥」）それは人の気分を多少物思わしげにさせるが、内的生活に注意をむける機会を与えるものである。そして、もし内省の眼が十分に開けるときは、そのなかに蓄えられてある豊富な宝を、ことごとく惜みなくわれらの眼前に広げるのである。

　この点において、多様性のなかに超越的な孤絶性——日本の文化的用語辞典では、わびと呼んでいるものをわれわれは鑑賞するのである。わびの真意は「貧困」（ポヴァティー）、すなわち消極的にいえば「時流の社会のうちに、またそれと一緒に、おらぬ」ということである。貧

things worldly—wealth, power, and reputation, and yet to feel inwardly the presence in oneself of something which is of the highest value above time and social position—this is what essentially constitutes *wabi*. When it is stated in terms of practical everyday life, *wabi* is to be satisfied with a little hut, with a room of two or three tatami (mats), like the log-cabin of Thoreau, and with a dish of vegetables picked in the neighbouring fields, and perhaps to be listening to the patterings of a gentle spring rainfall. While later I will say something more about *wabi*, let me state this here that the cult of *wabi* has deeply entered into the cultural life of the Japanese people. It is in truth the worshipping of poverty—probably a most appropriate cult in a poor country like ours. With all the modern Western luxuries or comforts of life which have invaded us there is still an ineradicable longing in us for the cult of *wabi*. Even in the intellectual life, not richness of ideas, not brilliancy or solemnity in marshalling thoughts and building up a philosophical system is sought; but just to stay quietly contented with the mystical contemplation of Nature and to be satisfied with the world at large is a more inspiring business with us, at least with some of us.

However "civilised" and brought up in an artificial environment, we all seem to have an innate longing for primitive simplicity, not far from the natural state of living. Hence the city people's summer campings in the woods or travelling in the desert or opening an unbeaten track. We wish to go back once in a while to the bosom of Nature and directly to feel her pulsation. Zen's habit of mind to break through all forms of human artificiality and to take hold firmly of what lies behind them has helped the Japanese not to forget the soil but to be always friendly with Nature and to appreciate her unaffected simplicity. Life itself is simple enough, but when it is surveyed by the intellect it presents to the analysing mind a form of unparalleled intricacies. With all the apparatus in the control of science we have not yet fathomed the mysteries of life. But, once in its current, we seem to be able to understand it with all its apparent endlessness of pluralities and entanglements. Very likely, the most characteristic temperament of the

しいということ、すなわち世間的な事物——富・力・名に頼っていないこと、しかも、その人の心中には、なにか時代や社会的地位を超えた、最高の価値をもつものの存在を感じること——これがわびを本質的に組成するものである。日常生活の言葉でいえば、わびはソロー（訳註、十九世紀の米国の自然詩人）の丸太小屋にも似たわずか二、三畳の小屋に起臥して、裏の畠から摘んだ蔬菜の一皿で満足することであり、静かな春の雨の蕭々たるに耳を傾けることでもある。わびについてはさらに後に述べるとして、ここでは、ただ、わび道が日本人の文化生活に深く入っていることを述べておこう。それは事実、「貧困」の信仰、おそらくは日本のような国には極めてふさわしい道である。近代西欧の贅沢品や生活の慰安物がわが国を侵すようになっても、なお、わび道に対するわれわれの憧憬の念には根絶し難いものがある。知的生活の場合でも、観念の豊富化を求めないし、また、派手でもったいぶった思想の配列や哲学体系のたてかたも求めない。神秘的な「自然」の思索に心を安んじて静居し、そして環境全体と同化して、それで満足することの方が、われわれ、少くともわれわれのうちのある人々にとって、心ゆくまで楽しい事柄なのである。

　たといいかに「文明化」した人工的な環境に育つようになったとはいえ、私たちの心のなかには、みな自然の生活状態に遠くない原始的単純性に対して、生得の憧憬を持っているように思われる。それゆえに、市民は夏、森でキャンプをやったり、沙漠を旅行したり、人跡未踏の路をひらいたりするのである。しばらくでも、自然の懐に帰って、直接その鼓動を感じようと欲するのである。一切の人工による形式を破り、その背後によこたわるものを確実に把握しようという禅の心的習慣は、日本人が土を忘れず、いつも自然と親しみ、飾りけのない単純性を味うことを助けてきた。禅は生活の表面に存する複雑さを好まぬ。生命（ライフ）そのものははなはだ単純なものであるが、これを知力で量れば、分析的な眼には比類なき錯綜物の姿となってうつる。科学を支配するあらゆる手段を使っても、いまなお、生命の神秘は測り知れないのである。しかし、ひとたびその流れに身を

Eastern people is to grasp life from within and not from without. And Zen has just struck it.

Disregard of form results when too much attention or emphasis is given to the all-importance of the spirit. The "one-corner" style and the economising of the brush strokes also help to effect aloofness from conventional rules. Where you ordinarily expect a line or a mass or a balancing wing, you miss it, and yet this very fact awakens in you an unexpected feeling of pleasure. In spite of shortcomings or deficiencies which are apparent no doubt, you do not feel them so, indeed this imperfection itself becomes a form of perfection. Evidently, beauty does not necessarily spell perfection of form. This has been one of the favourite tricks of the Japanese artists—to embody beauty in a form of imperfection or even of ugliness.

When this beauty of imperfection is accompanied by antiquity or primitive uncouthness, we have a glimpse of *sabi*, so prized by Japanese connoisseurs. Antiquity and primitiveness may not be an actuality. If an object of art suggests even superficially the feeling of a historical period, there is *sabi* in it. *Sabi* consists in rustic unpretentiousness or archaic imperfection, apparent simplicity or effortlessness in execution, and richness in historical associations (which, however, may not always be present), and lastly, it contains inexplicable elements which raise the object in question to a rank of artistic production. These latter are generally regarded as derived from the appreciation of Zen. The utensils used in the tea-room are mostly of this nature.

The artistic element that goes into the constitution of *sabi* which literally means "loneliness" or "solitude," is poetically defined by a tea-master thus;

"As I come out
To this fishing village,
Late in the autumn day,

任せれば、生命というものが、その外見は無限の複数性と錯綜性を持つにもかかわらず、これを理解することができるように思える。おそらく東洋人の最も特異の気質（テンペラメント）は、生命を外からでなく、内から把握することであろう。禅は、まさに、それを掘りあてたのである。

　精神の重要さをあまりに注意・強調すれば、形式無視という結果をきたす。「一角」様式と筆触の経済化もまた、慣例的（コンベンショナル）な法則から孤絶するという効果を生ずるのである。普通なら一本の線、一つの塊（マス）、平衡翼（バランシング・ウィング）を予期するところにそれがない、しかもこの事実が予期せざる快感を心中に喚びおこすのである。それらはあきらかに短所や欠陥であるにかかわらず、そうは感じられない。事実、この不完全そのものが完全の形になる。いうまでもなく、美とはかならずしも形の完全を指していうのではない。この不完全どころか醜というべき形のなかに、美を体現することが日本の美術家の得意の妙技（トリック）の一つである。

　この不完全の美に古色や古拙味（原始的無骨さ）（プリミチヴ・アンクースネス）が伴えば、日本の鑑賞家が賞美するところのさびがあらわれる。古色と原始性とは現実味ではないかも知れぬ。美術品が表面的にでも史的時代感を示せば、そこにさびが存する。さびは鄙びた無虚飾や古拙な不完全に存する、見た目の単純さや無造作な仕事ぶりに存する、豊富な歴史的な連想（かならずしも現存しなくてもよい）に存する、そして、最後にそれはくだんの事物を芸術的作品の程度に引きあげるところの説明しがたき要素を含んでいる。これらの要素は禅の鑑賞から由来すると、一般に考えられている。茶室内に用いられる道具類は多くかかる性質のものである。

　さびは文字の上からいえば「孤絶」とか「孤独」とかを意味するが、これを構成している芸術的要素は、茶の宗匠によってつぎのように詩的に定義されている。

　　見わたせば
　　花も紅葉もなかりけり
　　浦のとまやの

No flowers in bloom I see,
Nor any tinted maple leaves.*"

Aloneness indeed appeals to contemplation and does not lend itself to spectacular demonstration. It may look most miserable, insignificant, and pity-provoking, especially when it is put up against the Western or modern setting. To be left alone, with no streamers flying, with no fire-works cracking, and this amidst a gorgeous display of infinitely varied forms and endlessly changing colours, is indeed no sight at all. Take one of those *sumiye* sketches, perhaps portraying Kanzan and Jittoku (Han-shan and Shiēte), and hang it in a European or an American art gallery, and see what effect it will produce in the minds of the visitors. The idea of aloneness belongs to the East and feels at home in the environment of its birth.

It is not only to the fishing village on the autumnal eve that aloneness gives birth, but also to a patch of green in the early spring—which latter is in all likelihood more expressive of the idea of *sabi* or *wabi* than the former. For in the green patch as we read in the following thirty-one syllable verse there is an indication of life-impulse amidst the wintery desolation;

"To those who only pray for the cherries to bloom,
How I wish to show the spring
That gleams from a patch of green
In the midst of the snow-covered mountain-village!*"

This is given by one of the old tea-masters as thoroughly expressive of *sabi* which is the principle governing the cult of tea, *cha-no-yu*. Here is just a feeble inception of life-power as asserted in the form of a little green patch, but in it those who have an eye can readily discern the Spring shooting out from underneath the forbidding snow. It may be said to be a mere suggestion that stirs his mind, but just the same it is life itself and not indeed its feeble indication. To the artist, life is here in its full strength as much as

秋の夕暮　　　　　　　　　〔藤原定家〕

　孤絶は実際、思索に訴える。目覚ましい示威(デモンストレーション)をやったりなどせぬ。一見はなはだみじめな、無意義な、憐憫を催させる底のものである。とくに西洋式や近代式の設備と対する時にはその感を深くする。次流しもひるがえらなければ、花火もあがらないようなところに、ただ独り残されているという事、そしてそれが色々と極りなく変りゆく物の形や物の色の華やかな眺めの真中であるとすると、実際見る影もない淋しさである。たとえば、寒山拾得かなにかの墨絵を欧米の美術館のなかに掛けて観衆の心にどんな効果を生ずるかを考えてみるがよい。孤絶の観念は東洋のものであり、これを生んだ環境のなかでこそ親しみを感ずるものなのである。
　孤絶が生むのは、秋の夕暮の漁村とばかりはかぎらない、早春のささやかな緑もある。このほうがさらに、さび、わびの観念を表現するのである。このささやかな緑に、つぎの三十一文字の詩で判るように、冬の荒涼たる最中(さなか)にも生の衝動(ライフ・インパルス)のあることが示されるのである。

　　花をのみ待つらむ人に
　　山里の雪まの
　　草の春を
　　見せばや　　　　　　　　〔藤原家隆〕

　これは昔の茶の宗匠が、茶の湯の指導原理たるさびを最もよくいい表すものとして、あげた歌である。ここにはささやかな草の形を借りてかすかながら生の力の萌(きざし)が主張されている。眼がある人ならば、そこに荒涼たる堆雪の下から春の芽ざしているのを、容易に認めることができよう。彼の心を動かすものは、暗示に過ぎぬというかも知れぬが、同時にそれは生命そのものであり、その微弱な指示だけではない。芸術家にとっては、野が緑にうもれ、花にうもれた

when the whole field is overlaid with verdure and even with flowers. One may call this the mystic sense of the artist.

Asymmetry is another of the features which distinguish Japanese art. The idea is doubtlessly derived from the "one corner" style of Bayen. The plainest and boldest example is given by the plan of Buddhist architecture. The principal structures such as the Tower Gate, the Dharma Hall, the Buddha Hall, and others may be laid along one straight line; but structures of secondary or supplementary importance, sometimes even those of major importance, are not arranged symmetrically as wings along either side of the main line. The latter may be found irregularly scattered over the grounds in accordance with the topographical peculiarities. You will readily be convinced of this fact if you visit some of the Buddhist temples in the mountains, for example, the Iyeyasu shrine at Nikko. We can say that asymmetry is quite characteristic of Japanese architecture of this class.

This can also be testified in the construction of the tea-room. Look at the ceiling which is constructed in at least three different styles, and at some of the utensils used in making and serving tea, and again at the grouping and laying of the stepping stones or flagstones in the garden. We find so many illustrations of asymmetry, or, in a way, of imperfection, or of the "one-corner" style.

Some Japanese moralists try to explain this liking of the Japanese artists for things not symmetrically formed and going against the conventional or rather geometrical rules of art, by the theory that the people have been morally trained not to be obtrusive but always to efface themselves and that the mental habit thus created of self-annihilation manifests itself now in art as when the artist leaves the important central space unoccupied. But to my mind this theory is not quite correct. Is it not a more plausible explanation to say that the artistic genius of the Japanese people has been inspired by the Zen way of looking at individual things as perfect in themselves and at the same time as embodying in them the nature of totality which belongs to the One?

時と同様に、ここにも力に充ちた生命が存するのである。これを芸術家の神秘感ということもできるであろう。

日本の芸術に著しいいま一つの特色は非相称性（アシンメトリー）である。この観念はあきらかに馬遠の「一角」様式に由来している。最も明白大胆な例は仏教寺院の建築物のプランである。山門、法堂（はっとう）、仏殿などの主要な建物は一直線に建っているが、二次的または従属的な建物、ときとすればさらに重要な建物ですら主要な線の両翼として相称的にならべられるということはない。後者は地勢の特徴に応じて、不規則に分散させられることもある。山間の寺、たとえば日光廟などを訪れれば、容易にこの事実を納得するであろう。非相称性がこの種の日本建築の特色だということができる。

この事はまた、茶室の構造に徴しても判る。少くとも三種の様式で構成されているその天井や、茶道具のあるものや、庭の飛石の打ちかた、沓脱（くつぬぎ）の据えかたなどを視よ。われわれは多くの非相称性や不完全性や「一角」様式の例を見出すのである。

日本のある道徳学者（モラリスト）たちは、日本の美術家たちがかように事物を非相称的に形成するのを好んで、慣例的な（コンベンショナル）（というより幾何学的な）美術上の諸法則を排する傾向のあることを説明して、日本人はでしゃばることなく、つねに己を卑くするような道徳に慣されてきたし、また、かくして創られた自己破却の心的習癖がしぜんと美術にもあらわれ、たとえば重要な中央の空間を余白のままに残しておく、というようになったのだと論じている。自分の考えるところでは、この説はまったく誤っている。日本人の芸術的天才が個々の事物をそれ自体で完全なるものとみると同時に、「一」に属する「多」の性質を体現するものとみる禅の方法に触発されたからだといった方がさらにもっともな説明ではないか。

The doctrine of ascetic estheticism is not so fundamental as that of Zen estheticism. Art impulses are more primitive, or more innate than those of morality. The appeal of art goes more directly into human nature. Morality is regulative, but art creative. The one is an imposition from without, but the other is an irrepressible expression from within. Zen finds its inevitable association with art but not with morality. Zen may remain unmoral but not without art. When the Japanese artists create imperfect objects from the point of view of form, and may even be willing to ascribe their art-motive to the current notion of moral asceticism; but their own interpretation together with that of the critics we need not give too much significance to it. Our consciousness is not after all a very reliable standard of judgment.

However this is, asymmetry is certainly characteristic of Japanese art, which is one of the reasons why lightness or prettiness also marks Japanese objects of art. Symmetry inspires a feeling of grace, solemnity, and impressiveness, which is again the case with logical formalism or the piling-up of abstract ideas. The Japanese are often thought not to be intellectual and philosophical, because of their general culture not being so thoroughly impregnated with intellectuality. This criticism I think has something to do with the Japanese love of asymmetry. The intellect primarily aspires for balancing while the Japanese are apt to ignore it with a strong inclination towards unbalancing.

Unbalancing, asymmetry, the "one-corner," poverty, simplification, *sabi* or *wabi*, aloneness, and other cognate ideas making up the most conspicuous characteristic features of Japanese art and culture—all those emanate from one central perception of the truth of Zen which is "the One in the Many and the Many in the One".

2

One of the reasons why Zen helped to stimulate the artistic impulses of the Japanese people and to colour their works with ideas characteristic of Zen is

超俗的美至上主義といえども、禅の「美」論ほどに根本的ではない。芸術衝動は道徳衝動より原始的であり、生得のものである。芸術の訴える力は端的に人間性に喰い込む。道徳は規範的だが芸術は創造的である。一は外部からの挿入で、一は内部からの抑えがたい表現である。禅はどうしても芸術と結びついて、道徳とは結びつかぬ。禅は無道徳であっても、無芸術ではありえない。日本の美術家が形態という見地からは不完全なものをつくり、しかもその芸術的動機を、しいて当代の道徳的観念に帰そうとするようなことがあるかもしれぬが、彼らが批評家に附和してくだす解釈などは、そう意義を認める必要はない。われわれの意識は結局、あまり頼りになる判断の標準とはならぬ。

　それはいずれにしても、非相称性はたしかに日本美術の特徴である。そしてまた、軽快性あるいは小綺麗さというものが日本美術の著しい特徴となっている一つの理由にもなる。相称性は優美・壮厳・重厚の惑情を起させるが、それはさきに述べた論理的な形式主義や抽象的観念の堆積の場合と同じことである。日本人はその一般教養に知性が十分に滲透していない故をもって、しばしば知的でなく、哲学的でないと思われている。この批評は日本人の非相称性愛好と多少関係がある、と自分は考える。知性はもともと均衡を欲するものであるが、日本人は不均衡を好む強い傾向によって、ややもすればそれを無視するのである。

　非均衡性・非相称性・「一角」性・貧乏性・単純性・さび・わび・孤絶性・その他、日本の芸術および文化の最も著しい特性となる同種の観念は、みなすべて「多即一、一即多」という禅の真理を中心から認識するところに発する。

二

　禅が日本人の芸術衝動を刺激し、禅独特の思想によってその作品を色づけることになった一つの理由は、つぎの諸事実に基づくので

due to the following facts; that the Zen monasteries were the repositories of learning and art at least during the Kamakura and the Muromachi era; that the Zen monks had constant opportunities to come in contact with foreign cultures; that the people generally, and the aristocrats especially, looked up to the Zen monks for cultural inspirations; that the latter themselves were artists, scholars, and mystics; that they were even encouraged by the political powers of the time to engage in commercial enterprises to bring foreign objects of art and industry to Japan; that the aristocrats and the politically influential classes of Japan were patrons of their institutions and willing to submit themselves to the discipline of Zen. Zen thus worked not only directly on the religious life of the Japanese but also most strongly on their general culture.

The Tendai, the Shingon, and the Jodo contributed greatly to make the Japanese thoroughly imbued with the spirit of Buddhism, and through their iconography developed their artistic instincts for sculpture, colour painting, architecture, textile fabrics, and metal works. But the philosophy of Tendai is too abstract and abstruse to be understood by the masses; the ritualism of Shingon is too elaborate and complicated and consequently too expensive for popularity. Shingon and Tendai produced fine sculpture and pictures and artistic utensils to be used in their daily worship. The most highly-prized "national treasures" belong to the Tempyo, the Nara, and the Heian periods when those two schools of Buddhism were in ascendency and intimately related to the cultured classes of the people. The Jodo teaches the Pure Land in all its magnificence with the Buddha of Infinite Light attended by his retinue of Bodhisattvas, and this inspired the artists to paint those splendid pictures of Amida preserved in the various Buddhist temples of Japan. The Nichiren and the Shin are the creation of the Japanese religious mind. The Nichiren gave no specifically artistic and cultural impetus to us; the Shin tended to be somewhat iconoclastic and produced nothing worth mentioning in the way of arts and literature except its hymns known as wasan and "letters" chiefly written by Rennyo (1415–99).

ある。鎌倉・室町時代に、禅院が少くとも学問芸術の貯蔵所になったこと、禅僧が終始、外国文化と接触する機会を有したこと、一般の人々、とくに貴族は禅僧を教養の鼓吹者として尊んだこと、禅僧それ自身芸術家であり、学者であり、神秘思想家であったこと、彼らが当代の政権者の奨励によって、当時の商企業に従事して、外国の芸術品や工芸品を日本にもたらしたこと、日本の貴族階級と政治的支配階級が禅門の後援者であり、喜んで禅の修業に服したこと、などである。禅はかくして日本の宗教生活に直接働きかけたのみならず、一般文化にもおよんだのである。

　天台・真言・浄土諸宗は日本人に仏教精神を深く滲透させる上に寄与するところが大きかった。仏徳具現を宗旨とすることにより、彼らは日本人の彫刻・絵画・建築・織物・金工などの発達を促進させた。しかし、天台の哲学は抽象煩瑣にすぎて大衆の理解するところとならず、真言の典儀は骨が折れて複雑で、結局、大衆には費用がかかりすぎた。真言・天台は彫刻・絵画およびその他日常の信仰に用いる美術的な器具を製作した。最もたかく評価される国宝はこの二宗派が栄えて、日本の文化階級と密接な関係をもった奈良・平安の二時代のものに多い。浄土宗は諸菩薩をうしろに従えた無量光の仏陀のいます壮厳極まりない極楽浄土を説くが、これに感得して、美術家は日本の各種寺院にいまなお保存されている壮厳なる仏画を描いた。日蓮宗と真宗は日本的宗教心理の創造したものである。日蓮宗はとくにわれわれに対して、芸術的・文化的刺激を与えはしなかった。真宗はやや仏像破毀主義に傾きすぎ、親鸞上人の和讃や蓮如上人の御文をのぞいて、美術・文学方面においてはとくに挙げるほどの作品はのこさなかった。

Zen came to Japan after Shingon and Tendai and was at once embraced by the military classes. It was more or less by historical accident that Zen was set against the aristocratic priesthood. The nobility too in the beginning felt a certain dislike for it and made use of their political advantages and mobilised a force in opposition to Zen. In the beginning of the Japanese history of Zen, therefore, Zen avoided Kyoto and established itself under the patronage of the Hōjō family in Kamakura. The latter, as the seat of the feudal government in those days, became the headquarters of Zen discipline. Many Zen monks from China settled in Kamakura and found the strongest supporters in Hōjō Tokiyori and Hōjō Tokimune and their successors and retainers.

The Chinese masters brought many objects of art and artists along with them and the Japanese who came back from China were also bearers of art and literature. Pictures of Mokkei (Mu-ch'i), Ryōkai (Liang-k'ai), Bayen (Ma-yuan), and others thus found their way to Japan. Handwritings of the noted Zen masters of China were also given shelter in the monasteries here. Calligraphy in the Far East is an art just as much as *sumiye* painting, and was cultivated almost universally among the intellectual classes in olden times. The spirit pervading the Zen pictures and calligraphy made a strong impression on them, and it was readily taken up and followed. In it there is something virile and unbending. A mild, gentle, and graceful air—almost feminine one might call it—which prevailed in the periods preceding the Kamakura, is now superseded by that of masculinity, expressing itself mostly in the sculptures and calligraphy of the period. The rugged virility which characterises the warriors of the Kwanto districts is proverbial, standing in good contrast to the grace and refinement of the courtiers in Kyoto. This soldierly quality emphasising its mysticism and aloofness from worldly affairs appeals to the will-power. Zen in this particular respect walks hand in hand with the spirit of Bushido.

There is another point in the discipline of Zen, or rather in the monastic life in which Zen carries out its scheme of teaching; as the monastery is usu-

禅は真言・天台の後に本邦に入ってきて、ただちに武門階級の支持をうけた。禅が貴族的僧侶階級に反するものとされたのは、多少、政治的・歴史的事情にもよるのであった。当初、貴族は禅にある反感をいだいて、政権を利用して反対の挙におよんだ。それゆえ、日本禅宗史の初めにあたって、禅は京都を避けて鎌倉の北条一族の庇護の下に興った。当時、幕府の所在地である鎌倉は禅修業の根拠地となり、中国から渡来した多数の禅僧たちは、鎌倉に居を定めて、北条時頼・北条時宗およびその後継者たちと家来から最も強く支持されることとなった。

　中国の禅師たちは多くの美術品と美術家をもたらし、中国から帰朝した日本人の僧もまた美術・文学を持ち帰った。牧谿・梁楷・馬遠・その他の絵画がかくして日本にきた。中国知名の禅僧の書（墨蹟）もまた日本の禅院に蔵された。極東の書は墨絵と同じく芸術であり、昔の知識階級の間ではほとんど普くその方面に教養が積まれた。禅の絵画と書を支配する精神は日本人に強い感銘を与えたので、ただちにこれを取上げて範としたのであった。そこにはなにか男性的で不屈のものがある。前代を支配していた温雅優美な風——女性的と称すべき——は、当代の彫刻や書体に表現される男性的な風にとってかえられた。関東武士の特色たる剛毅果断は諺にもなったくらいで、京都の朝臣たちの優美洗煉といい対照をなした。その神秘思想と俗事からの孤絶を強調する武士的気質は意志の力に訴える。この特殊の点から見て、禅は武士道精神と相提携するのである。

　禅の修業、というよりむしろ禅がその教義を実践する僧院生活には、さらにべつの点が存する。禅院は通例山林の間に在るので、そ

ally situated in the mountains, its inmates are in the most intimate touch with nature, they are close and sympathetic students of it. They observe plants, birds, animals, rocks, rivers, and other objects of nature which people of the town leave unnoticed. And what is specific of their observation is that it deeply reflects their philosophy or better their intuition. It is not that of a mere naturalist. It penetrates into the life itself of the objects the monks observe. Whatever they may paint of nature will inevitably be expressive of this intuition; the "spirit of the mountains" will be felt softly breathing in their works.

The fundamental intuition the Zen masters gain through their discipline seems to stir up their artistic instincts if they are at all susceptible to art. The intuition is apparently closely related to the feeling for art, which impels the masters to create things beautiful, that is, to express the sense of perfection through things ugly and imperfect. The Zen masters may not make good philosophers but very frequently fine masters of art, and even their technique is often of the first order; besides they know how to tell us about something unique and original. One of such examples is Muso the National Teacher (1275–1351) of "The Southern and the Northern Court," in the fourteenth century. He was a fine calligrapher and a great landscape gardener; wherever he resided, at quite a number of places in Japan, he designed splendid gardens some of which are still in existence, well preserved after so many years of changing times. Among the noted painters of Zen in the fourteenth and the fifteenth century we may mention Chō Densu (d. 1431), Reisai (op. 1435), Josetsu (cir. 1410), Shubun (op. 1414–1465), Sesshu (1421–1506), and others.

According to Georges Duthuit, the author of *Chinese Mysticism and Modern Painting*, who seems to understand the spirit of Zen mysticism, we have this:

"When the Chinese artist paints, what matters is the concentration of thought and the prompt and vigorous response of the hand to the directing

こに住むものは「自然」と密接な接触をする。そして、おのずから親しさと同情をもって「自然」にまなぶことになる。彼らは鳥や動物や岩や川やその他市井の人々が気づかぬままにある自然物を観察する。彼らの観察に特殊なところは、それが彼らの哲学、むしろ彼らの直観を深く反映することである。それは単なる博物学者の観察ではなくて、禅僧たちはその観察する対象の生命そのもののなかまで入りこまねばやまぬ。だから、いかなるものを描いても、かならず、彼らの直観を表現することになって、「山や雲の精神」が、その作品のなかにおだやかに息づいているのを、感じることができるのである。

　禅匠たちが、いやしくも、芸術に対して感受性をもつ以上は、その鍛錬によってえた根本的の直観は彼らの芸術的の本能を動かすにきまっている。直観は明らかに芸術感情と密接に関係しているからそれによって禅匠たちは美を創造する、すなわち醜や不完全なものを通して完全感を表現する。禅匠のなかには立派な哲学者にはなれなくても、すぐれた芸術家となれる者がしばしばある。その技術などもしばしば第一流のものがある。その上彼らはなにかしら特異でかつ独創的なものを表わす法に通じている。かかる好例の一つは吉野・室町時代の夢窓国師*である。国師は名筆家であり、偉大な造園家であった。国師は自分の滞在した日本各地に、立派な庭苑を計画し、そのあるものはいく変遷の年月をへて、現にいまも残っている。十四・十五世紀の知名の禅宗画家のなかでは、兆殿司（1431・歿）・霊彩（1435頃）・如拙（1410頃）・周文（1414-1465頃）・雪舟（1421-1506）らをあげることができる。

「中国の神秘思想と近代絵画」の著者ジョージ・ダスイットは禅的神秘思想の精神をよく理解しているようだが、彼に従えばこうである。
『中国の美術家が絵を描くとき大事なことは、思索の集中ということと、その意志の命に応じて一気呵成に手を下すことである。彼ら

will. Tradition ordains him to see, or rather to feel, as a whole the work to be executed, before embarking on anything. 'If the ideas of a man are confused, he will become the slave of exterior conditions.' And further on; 'He who deliberates and moves his brush intent on making a picture, misses to a still greater extent the art of painting.' This seems like a kind of automatic writing. Draw bamboos for ten years, become a bamboo, then forget all about bamboos when you are drawing. In possession of an infallible technique, the individual places himself at the mercy of inspiration." To become a bamboo and to forget that you are one with it while drawing—this is the Zen of a bamboo, this is the moving with the "rhythmic movement of the spirit" which resides in the bamboo as well as in the artist himself. What is now required of him is to have firm hold of the spirit and yet not to be conscious of the fact. This is a very difficult task only acquired after a long spiritual training.* The Eastern people have been taught since the early history of their civilisation to subject themselves to this kind of discipline if they wanted to achieve something in the world of art and religion. Zen in fact has given an articulation to it in the following phrase: "One in All and All in One." When this is thoroughly understood, there is creative genius.

It is of utmost importance here to interpret the phrase in its proper sense. People imagine that it means pantheism, and some students of Zen seem to agree with these critics. This is to be regretted, for pantheism is something entirely foreign to Zen and also to the artist's actual understanding of his work. When the Zen masters declare the One to be in the All and the All in the One, they do not mean that there is a thing to be known as the One or as the All and that the one is in the other and vice versa. As the One is in the All, they imagine, Zen is a pantheistic teaching. Far from it; Zen recognises neither the One nor the All as something distinct from each other. The phrase "One in All and All in One" is to be understood as a complete statement of absolute fact and not to be analysed into its component concepts. When we see the moon, we know that it is the moon, and that is enough. Those who proceed to analyse the experience and try to establish a theory of

の伝統は、まず仕事を始める前に、その描くものを全体として見る、というより感じるようになっている。「考が乱れていては外的状態の奴隷となる。」さらに曰く、「絵を作らんと意図して、熟思し、しかるのち筆を走らせるものは、絵画の術からはなはだしく外れる。」これは一種の自働器械的運動の類であるやにも見える。曰く、十年間、竹を描け、そして自身が一本の竹となって竹を描け、このようにして描く時、竹に関する一切を忘却せよと。間違いなき技術はすでに手にはいっているので、いまはただ天来の興に身を任せるのだ。』自分が竹となること、竹を描くとき竹と同一化したことさえ忘れること、これは竹の禅ではなかろうか。これは画家自身のなかにもあれば竹のなかにもあるところの、「精神の律動的な動き」とともに動くことである。彼に必要とするところは、この精神をしっかり把握して、しかもこの事実を意識しないことである。これこそ長い精神的鍛錬をへて始めてえられるはなはだ困難な仕事である。東洋人はその文明の初期より以来、芸術と宗教の世界でなにか成就せんと欲する場合には、まずこの種の修業に専心するように教えられてきた。禅は事実、つぎの言葉にそれをあらわしている。『一即多、多即一』これが十二分に理解されたとき創造の天才が生れる。

　ここでこの言葉を適当な意味に解釈することが極めて肝要である。この言葉は汎神論を意味すると想像されやすく、現に禅の研究者のなかにも、これらの批評家に同意するものがいる。これは遺憾なことである。汎神論は禅にはまったく縁遠いものである。また、芸術家が現に自分の仕事を理解することにもまったく縁遠いものである。禅匠が一が多にあり、多が一にあるという時、一なり多なりいうものが存して、それぞれ一方が他方のなかにあるという意味ではない。一が多のなかにあるという意味がはっきりせぬと、禅は汎神論だと想像される。が、禅では一といい、多というものが相互独立しているものとは認めぬのである。「一即多、多即一」というのは、それだけで絶対の事実を完全に叙述したものとして理解するべきである。それを分析して、また概念的に構成すべきではない。月を見て月と判れば、それで十分だ。この経験は絶対である。これを分析

knowledge, are not students of Zen. They cease to be so, if they ever were, at the very moment of their procedure as analysts. Zen always upholds its experience and refuses to commit itself to any system of philosophy.

Even when Zen indulges in intellection, it never subscribes to a pantheistic interpretation of the world. For one thing, there is no One in Zen. If it speaks at all of the One as if it recognised it, this is a kind of condescension to common parlance. To Zen students the One is the All and the All is the One. The one is always the same as the other, the two are never to be separated. Things are in and of *Sūnyatā* (Emptiness) with all their Suchness (*Tathatā*); this Suchness is Emptiness itself; *Tathatā* is *Sūnyatā*, and *Sūnyatā* is *Tathatā*.

The following *mondo* may help to illustrate the point I wish to make in regard to the Zen attitude towards the so-called pantheistic interpretation of Nature.

A monk asked Tōsu (T'ou-tzu), a Zen master of the T'ang period;

"I understand that all sounds are the voice of the Buddha; is this right?" The master said "That is right."

The monk then proceeded,

"Would not the master please stop making a noise which echoes the sound of a fermenting mass of filth?"

The master thereupon struck the monk.

The monk further asked Tōsu:

"Am I in the right when I understand the Buddha as asserting that all talk, however trivial or derogatory, belongs to ultimate truth?"

The master said, "Yes, you are in the right." The monk went on,

"May I then call you a donkey?"

The master thereupon struck him.

して認識論を打樹てんとする人は、その時、禅の学者でなくなる。禅学者であっても、分析学者としての方法をとったら、その時、彼は禅学者たる資格を放棄することとなる。禅は自分の経験を尊び、いかなる体系の哲学とも妥協することを拒むのである。

　禅が知的作用に一歩を譲る場合でも、汎神論的に世界を解釈することは避ける。いってみれば、禅では「一」と説く時でも、そんなものの存在を認めぬ。それを認めるかのごとく語る時でも、それはわれらが使い慣れた平常の言語文字に対して敬意を表したまでのことである。禅者にとってはいつも一即多、多即一である。二つのものはいつも同一性を持っていて、これが「一」、これが「多」と分けるべきではないのである。仏者の常套語でいえば、万物の姿は真如そのままである。真如とは無である。すなわち、万物は無のなかにある。無よりでて無にはいるのである。真如は無であり、無は真如である。

　つぎの問答は、いわゆる汎神論的世界観なるものに対する禅の態度を説明する助けとなろう。

　唐代に一僧あり、投子（大同禅師）に尋ねた。

『一切の音はみな仏陀の声であると思いますが、そう解してもいいでしょうか』

『それでいい』と和尚は答えた。

　僧はさらに一歩を進めて、

『それでは和尚さんの声も、ぶつぶつ醗酵するどぶ泥の音と違いないでしょうか』

　投子はこれを聞くや、かの僧に一棒を喰らわした。

　僧はまた尋ねた。

『悟った人にとっては、つまらぬ誹謗的な言葉でもみな究極の真理を表すものだと断定してよろしいでしょうか』

　師が答えた。

『よろしい』と。

　すると僧は進んで、

『では、和尚さんを驢馬だといってもよろしいでしょうか』

It may be necessary to explain these *mondo* in plain language. To conceive every sound, every noise, every talk one can make as issuing from the fountainhead of one Reality, that is, from one God, is pantheistic, I imagine. For "he giveth to all life, and breath, and all things" (Acts 17, 25); and again "In him we live and move and have our being" (Acts 17, 28). If this be the case, a Zen master's hoarse throat also echoes the melodious resonance of the voice flowing from the golden mouth of the Buddha, and even when a great teacher is decried as reminding one of an ass, the defamation must be regarded as reflecting something of ultimate truth. All forms of evil must be said somehow embodying what is true and good and beautiful, and to be a contribution to the perfection of Reality. To state more concretely, bad is good, ugly is beautiful, false is true, imperfect is perfect, and also conversely. This is indeed the kind of reasoning in which those indulge who conceive the God-nature to be immanent in all things. And Zen has often been criticised for a like tendency in its demonstrations.

But Tōsu put his foot down right against such intellectualist interpretations and struck his monk. The latter in all probability expected to see the master nonplussed by his remarks which logically follow from his first assertion. The master knew as all Zen masters do the uselessness of making any verbal demonstration against the monk. For verbalism leads from one complication to another and there is no end to it. The only effective way perhaps to make one like the monk in question here realise the falsehood of his conceptual understanding is to strike him and let him experience within himself the meaning of the statement, "One in All and All in One." It is required of him to awake from his logical somnolence. Hence Tōsu's radical measure.

Seccho (Hsüeh-tou) here gives his comments with the following lines:

"Pity that people without number try to play with the tide,
They are all ultimately swallowed up into it and die!
Let them suddenly awake [from the deadlock],

和尚は依然としてまた彼を打った。（註、この問答は碧巌集にでている）

　これらの問答を平易な言葉で説明する必要があろう。いっさいの響きも、音も、声も、一つの「実在」の源泉から、すなわち「唯一神」からでるものと考えるのは汎神論的であると自分は考える。「みづから凡ての人に生命と息と万の物とを与へ給へ」り（使徒行伝第十七章二五）また、「我らは神の中に生き、動きまた在るなり。」（同上第十七章二八）こうなると、禅者のしゃがれ声も、仏陀の黄金の口から流れでる抑揚に富んだ声となってひびくわけだ。立派な和尚さんも驢馬を思い出させると誹謗しても、その誹謗になにか究極真理を反映するものがあると見なければなるまい。一切の悪にも多少なり真・善・美を体現したものがあり、したがって実在の完成へ寄与するものといわねばならぬ。さらに具体的に述べれば、悪は善であり、醜は美であり、優は真であり、不完全は完全であり、またこれらの反対も同じである。これはじつに万物に神性が宿ると考える人々の陥る推論である。禅の説明にはこれとおなじような傾向があると従来しばしば批評されてきた。

　しかし、投子はかかる知的解釈をただちに斥けて、僧に一棒を喰らわしたのである。僧のほうでは自分の言葉は最初の断定から論理的に続いているのだから、和尚はおそらくこれに加えるところはあるまいと思ったのだ。和尚は、あらゆる禅匠と同じく、かかる僧に対しては言語的説明の無益なるを知った。言葉の上の詮議は一つの複雑から他の複雑に入って、終るところを知らぬからである。くだんの僧のごときに概念的理解の虚偽を悟らせる唯一有効な道は彼を打つことである、そして、「一即多、多即一」の意味を彼自身に体験せしめる事である。この僧にとっては論理的夢遊病（ロジカル・ソムノレンス）より醒めることが必要である。ゆえに投子は手荒い法にでたのである。

　雪竇はこれをつぎの詩をもって評している。

　　可㆑憐無㆑限弄㆑潮スルヲ人
　　畢竟還リテ落二潮－中一二死ス
　　忽然トシテ活シテ

And see that all the rivers run backward, swelling and surging."

What is needed here is an abrupt turning or awakening, with which one comes to the realisation of the truth of Zen—which is neither transcendentalism nor immanentism nor a combination of the two. The truth is as Tōsu declares in the following;

A monk asks, "What is the Buddha?"

Tōsu answers, "The Buddha. "

Monk; "What is the Tao?"

Tōsu; "The Tao."

Monk; "What is Zen?"

Tōsu; "Zen.*"

The master answers like a parrot, he is echo itself. In fact, there is no other way of illumining the monk's mind than affirming that what is is- which is the final fact of experience.

Another example is given to illustrate the point.

A monk asked Jōshū (Chao-chou), of the T'ang dynasty,

"It is stated that the Perfect Way knows no difficulties, only that it abhors discrimination. What is meant by No-discrimination?"

Jōshū said; "Above the heavens and below the heavens, I alone am the Honoured One."

The monk suggested, "Still a discrimination."

The master's retort was, "O this worthless fellow! Where is the discrimination?"

The monk remained without a word.

By discrimination the Zen masters mean not to accept facts as they are, but, by reflecting on them and analysing them into concepts, to go on with intellection and finally to commit themselves to a circulatory reasoning. Jōshū's affirmation is a final one, and allows no equivocation, no argumentation. We have to accept it on its face value and remain satisfied with it. In

百-川　倒-流<ruby>鬧<rt>ねう</rt></ruby><ruby>滐<rt>かつ</rt></ruby><ruby>滐<rt>かつ タラン</rt></ruby>　　　　　　　　　（碧巌集）

　ここで必要なことは、忽然として転換し覚醒することである。こ
れによって、人は禅の真理——超越論でも、内在論でも、両者の
結合でもない禅の真理を自覚するにいたる。この真理を投子はつぎ
のごとく述べる。

　一僧問う。『仏とは何ぞや。』

　投子答う。『仏』

　僧『道とは何ぞや。』

　投子『道』

　僧『禅とは何ぞや。』

　投子『禅』

　和尚は鸚鵡のごとく答える。彼は<ruby>谺<rt>こだま</rt></ruby>そのものである。事実、何ぞ
やというのは最後の体験事実だと断言するよりほかに、この僧の
心をてらす法はないのである。　　　　　　　　　（碧巌集）

　この点を解くために、いま一つの例を挙げよう。

　ある僧が唐代の禅僧<ruby>趙州<rt>じょうしゅう</rt></ruby>に尋ねた。

　『「完全な道」には別にむずかしいことはないが、ただ分別を嫌
うといわれています。「無分別」とはどういう意味ですか。』

　趙州がいった。

　『天上天下唯我独尊。』

　僧はまたいった。

　『それはなお一つの分別ではありませんか。』

　和尚の答は『咄、この愚かもの奴、分別なんていうものがどこに
あるかい。』

　僧は一語も返せなかった　　　　　　　　　　　（碧巌集）

　禅匠のいう分別とは、事実をそのままに受取ることではなくて、
これを反省し分析して概念となすことによって、知的作用を働かし
て、結局循環論法に陥るという意味である。趙州の断定は決定的の
もので、遁辞も争論も許さぬ。<ruby>額面高<rt>フェイス・ヴァリュー</rt></ruby>のままでこれを受取り、それ
で満足していなければならぬ。われわれがそれを受入れ損なった

case we somehow fail to accept it, we simply leave it alone, and go some-where else to seek our own enlightenment. The monk could not see where Jōshū was and went further on and remarked, "This is still a discrimina-tion!" The discrimination in point of fact was on the monk's side, and not on Jōshū's. Hence "the Honoured One" now turned into "a worthless fel-low."

As I said before, the phrase, "All in One and One in All " is not to be ana-lysed first to the concepts "One" and "All," and then to put the preposition between them; no discrimination is to be exercised here, but just to accept it and abide with it. This is all that is required here. The master strikes, or appears abusive, not because he is indignant or short-tempered, but because he wishes thereby to help his disciples out from the pit into which they have fallen. No amount of argument avails here, no verbal persuasion either. Only the master knows how to turn them away from a logical *impasse* and to open a new way for them; let them therefore simply follow him. By fol-lowing him they all come back to their Original Home.

What may be termed an intuitive or experiential understanding of fact—"All in One and One in All"—is the fundamental truth of Buddhism which is taught by all its various schools. In the terminology of the Prajñā school of Buddhism, *Sūnyatā* is *Tathatā* and *Tathatā* is *Sūnyatā*; *Sūnyatā*, Emptiness, is the world of the Absolute, and *Tathatā*, Suchness, is the world of particulars. One of the commonest sayings of Zen is; "Willows are green and flowers red." The world of particulars is asserted here, where, again, bamboos are straight and pine trees are gnarled. Facts of experience are accepted as they are, Zen is not nihilistic. But at the same time they are all of Emptiness, not indeed in its relative sense but in its absolute sense. Emptiness in its absolute sense is not a concept reached by the analytical process of reasoning, but a fact of experience as much as the straightness of a bamboo and the redness of a flower. For it is merely a statement of intuition or perception. When,

場合には、それはそのままにしておいて、どこか他に己の啓蒙を求めねばならぬ。この僧は趙州が何処にいるかを解することができぬものだから、さらに進んでいったのであった。『それはなお一つの分別ではありませんか。』事実上から見れば、分別は僧の側にあって趙州には無い。ゆえに、『唯我独尊』はここでは『この愚かもの奴』に変った。

　前にいったように、『一即多、多即一』という句は、まず「一」と「多」という二概念に分析して、両者の間に「即」をおくのではない。ここでは分別を働かしてはならぬ。それはそのまま受取って、そこに腰を落ちつけねばならぬ。これがここで必要ないっさいである。和尚が打ったり、罵ったりするのは、いたずらに憤りを発したり、短気だからではない、それによって弟子たちを陥穽から助けだしてやりたいとの老婆心からである。ここではいくら議論しても利益はないし、またいくら言葉の上で説服しようとしても無駄である。ただ師家（しけ）だけが、それを論理的袋小路（ロジカル・アンパス）から転じて、新しい道を開く法を知っている。それゆえに、われらはただ彼にしたがえばよいのである。彼にしたがって行くことによって、われらはみな「本住地」に戻るのである。

「一即多、多即一」という事実の直観的または体験的理解と名づけていいものは、どの仏教各派でも教える仏法の根本義である。般若経の語でいえば、「空即是色、色即是空」である。空は「絶対」の世界であり、色は特殊の世界である。禅の最も普通の文句の一つに「柳は緑に、花は紅」というのがある。ここでは特殊の世界を直説しているので、この世界では、また竹は直く、松は曲っているのである。体験の諸事実がそのままに受取られる。禅は否定的、虚無説的ではない。しかし、同時に特殊世界の経験諸事実は相対的の意味でなく、絶対的の意味において、いっさい空である。絶対的意味における空とは、分析的な論理の方法で達しうる概念ではなくて、竹の直き、花の紅などという体験事実そのままを指すのである。直観または知覚の事実を素直に認めることである。知的作用という外側のものに向わずに、心がその注意を内部に向ける時、一切は空か

instead of going outwardly towards intellection, the mind directs its attention inwardly, it perceives that all things go out of Emptiness and return to it and that this going-out and returning is just one movement though we have to describe it as if it were two. This dynamic identification as it were is the basis of our experience, and on it are displayed all our life-activities. Zen teaches us to dig down to this basis. It is from this point of view that when asked "What is Zen?" the master sometimes answers, "Zen," and sometimes "Not-Zen."

We can see now that the principle of *sumiye* painting is derived from this Zen experience, and that Directness, Simplicity, Movement, Spirituality, Completeness, and such qualities as we observe in the *sumiye* class of Oriental painting have organic relationship to Zen. There is no pantheism in *sumiye* as there is none in Zen.

らでて、空に帰することを知覚するのである。而してここに往還といえば往くと還るとの二つの方向があるかのごとく考えなければならぬが、その実はただ一つの動きであることを知って欲しい。この動態的同一作用<ruby>ダイナミック・アイデンチフィケーション</ruby>ともいうべきものは、われわれ体験の基礎であって、一切の生活活動はその上に展示されるのである。禅はわれわれにこの基礎まで掘りさげるべきことを教える。『禅とは何ですか。』と問われると、『禅だ。』とか、『非禅だ。』などと禅者が答えるのは、じつにこの見地からである。（章末の註参照）

　われわれは今や水墨画の原理がこの禅体験から発していること、直接性・単純性・運動性・精神性・完全性・等々の東洋水墨画にみられる諸性質は、禅と有機的な関係をもつことを知るのである。水墨画には禅の場合と同様、汎神論は存せぬのである。

　（著者註）原書講演の頃から考えていた禅経験の論理ともいうべきものを附けておきたい。それは般若経に『諸心皆為非心、是名為心』（taccittam accittam yaccittam）というので、要約して『即非の論理』としておく。つまり『心は心に非らざるが故に心なり』で、否定がすなわち肯定で、否定と肯定とは相互に『非』の立場にある、絶対に相向い立っているが、この『非』の立場が、ただちに『即』である。自分はこれを禅の論理というのである。『即非』はまた『無分別の分別』、『無意識の意識』でもある。これ以上は哲学者に譲る。

A statue of Bukkō Kokushi (Mugaku Sogen).

仏光国師（無学祖元）木像。

卍

Zen and the Samurai

禅と武士

It may be considered strange that Zen has in any way been affiliated with the spirit of the military classes of Japan. Whatever form Buddhism takes in different countries where it flourishes, it is a religion of compassion, and in its varied history it has never been found engaged in warlike activities. How is it then that Zen has come to activate the fighting spirit of the Japanese warrior?

In Japan Zen was intimately related from the beginning of its history to the life of the samurai. Although it has never actively incited the latter to carry on their bloody profession, it has passively sustained them when they have for any reason once entered into it. Zen has sustained them in two ways, morally and philosophically. Morally, because Zen is a religion which teaches not to look backward once the course is decided upon; philosophically, because it treats life and death indifferently. This not turning backward ultimately comes from the philosophical conviction, but being a religion of the will Zen appeals to the samurai spirit more morally than philosophically. From the philosophical point of view, Zen upholds intuition against intellection, for intuition is the more direct way of reaching the Truth. Therefore, morally and philosophically, there is in Zen a great deal of attraction for the military classes whose mind being comparatively simple

なにかの関係でもよいが、禅が、日本の武門階級と交渉があった
といえば、不思議に考えられるかもしれぬ。各国において仏教は
いかなる形態をとって栄えたにせよ、それは慈悲の宗教であり、そ
の歴史に変化はあったが、けっして好戦的な活動に従ったことはな
かった。それでは、どうして禅が日本武士の戦闘精神をはげますこ
とになったのだろうか。

　日本においては、禅は当初から武士の生活と密接な関係があった。
もっともそれはけっして彼らの血なまぐさい職業を実行するように
示唆したのではない。武士がなにかの理由で一たび禅に入った時は、
禅は受動的に彼らを支持したのであった。禅は道徳的および哲学的
二つの方面から彼らを支援した。道徳的というのは、禅は、一たび
その進路を決定した以上は、振返らぬことを教える宗教だからで、
哲学的というのは生と死とを無差別的に取扱うからである。この振
返らないということは、結局、哲学的確信からくるのであるが、元
来、禅は意志の宗教であるから、哲学的より道徳的に武士精神に訴
えるのである。哲学的見地からは、禅は知性主義に対立して直覚を
重んじる。直覚の方が真理に到達する直接的な道であるからだ。そ
れゆえ、道徳的にも哲学的にも、禅は武門階級にとって非常に魅力
がある。武門階級の精神は比較的に単純で哲学的思索に耽けるとい

and not at all addicted to philosophizing—and this is one of the essential qualities of the fighter—naturally finds a congenial spirit in Zen. This is probably one of the main reasons for the close relationship between Zen and the samurai.

Secondly, Zen discipline is simple, direct, self-reliant, self-denying, and this ascetic tendency goes well with the fighting spirit. The fighter is to be always single-minded with just one object in view which is to fight and not to look either backward or sidewise. To go straightforward in order to crush the enemy is all that is necessary for him. He is therefore not to be encumbered in any possible way, be it physical, emotional, or intellectual. Intellectual doubts, if they are at all cherished in the mind of the fighter, are great obstructions to his onward movement, while emotionalities and physical possessions are the heaviest encumbrances he may have to suffer if he wants to behave himself most efficiently in his business. Good fighters are generally ascetics or stoics, which means to have an iron will. When needed Zen supplies them with this.

Thirdly, there is an historical connection between Zen and the military classes of Japan. Eisai (1141–1215) is generally regarded as the first Buddhist priest who introduced Zen into Japan. But his activities were more or less restricted to Kyoto, and Kyoto was at the time the headquarters of the older schools of Buddhism. The inauguration of any new faith here was almost impossible owing to the strong opposition offered by them. Eisai had to compromise to some extent by assuming a reconciliatory attitude towards the Tendai and the Shingon. Whereas, in Kamakura which was the seat of the Hōjō government, there were no such historical difficulties. Besides, the Hōjō regime was militaristic, as it succeeded the Minamoto family who rose against the Taira family and the court nobles. The latter lost their efficacy as a governing power because of their over-culture and effeminacy and consequent degeneration. The Hōjō regime is noted for its severe frugality and moral discipline and also for its powerful administrative and militaristic equipments. The directing heads of such a strong governing machine

うようなことは全然ないから――これが武人の根本的資質の一つであるが――当然、禅において似あいの精神を見いだすのである。おそらくこれが禅と武士との間に密接な関係が生じた主なる理由の一つであろう。

　つぎに、禅の修業は単純・直截・自恃・克己的であり、この戒律的な傾向が戦闘精神とよく一致する。戦闘者はつねに闘うべき目前の対象にひたすら心を向けていればよいので、振返ったり傍見をしてはならぬ。敵を粉砕するためにまっすぐに進むということが彼にとって必要な一切である。ゆえに彼は物質的・情愛的・知的いずれの方面からも、邪魔があってはならぬ。もし戦闘者の心に知的な疑惑が少しでも浮んだならば、それは彼の進行に大きな妨げとなる。もろもろの情愛と物質的な所有物は、彼が最も有効的に進退せんと欲する場合には、この上ない邪魔物になる。立派な武人は総じて禁慾的戒行者（アセティクス）か自粛的修道者（ストイック）である。という意味は鉄の意志を持っているということである。そうして必要あるとき、禅は彼にこれを授ける。

　第三に、禅と日本の武門階級とは歴史的つながりがある。栄西（えいさい）（1141-1215）は一般に禅を日本に紹介した最初の僧侶と見られている。しかし、彼の活動は多かれ少なかれ京都にかぎられていた。京都は当時旧仏教の本拠であった。この地に新宗教創建は彼らの強硬な反対のためほとんど不可能であった。栄西はある程度まで天台や真言と妥協して調和的な態度をとらなければならなかった。しかるに北条氏の居を定めた鎌倉は、かかる歴史的の難問題はなかった。そのうえ、平氏および公卿たちに抗って起った源氏の後をついだ北条時代は武門的であった。平氏および宮廷貴族は、その過度の文化と、優柔不断と、その結果たる堕落のために、支配者としての権力を失った。北条時代はその厳格な節倹と道徳的修養とで、またその強力な行政的および軍事的整備とで聞えている。かかる強い政治機関の指揮者たちは、宗教に関してはその伝統を無視して、禅を彼らの精神的な指南として抱懐した。禅は十三世紀以来、足利時代を通し、徳川時代においてさえ、日本人の一般文化的生活に種々な影響をおよぼしえた。

embraced Zen as their spiritual guide, ignoring tradition in this matter of religion; Zen could not fail to exercise its varied influence in the general cultural life of the Japanese ever since the thirteenth century and throughout the Ashikaga and even in the Tokugawa period.

Zen has no special doctrine or philosophy with a set of concepts and intellectual formulas, except that it tries to release one from the bondage of birth and death and this by means of certain intuitive modes of understanding peculiar to itself. It is, therefore, extremely flexible to adapt itself almost to any philosophy and moral doctrine as long as its intuitive teaching is not interfered with. It may be found wedded to anarchism or fascism, communism or democracy, atheism or idealism, or any political and economical dogmatism. It is, however, generally animated with a certain revolutionary spirit, and when things come to a deadlock which is the case when we are overloaded with conventionalism, formalism, and other cognate isms, Zen asserts itself and proves to be a destructive force. The spirit of the Kamakura era was in this respect in resonance with the virile spirit of Zen.

We have the saying in Japan; "The Tendai is for the royal family, the Shingon for the nobility, the Zen for the warrior classes, and the Jōdō for the masses." This saying fitly characterises each sect of Buddhism in Japan. The Tendai and the Shingon are rich in ritualism and their ceremonies are conducted in a most elaborate and pompous style appropriate to the taste of the refined classes. The Jōdō appeals naturally more to plebeian requirements because of the simpleness of its faith and teaching. Besides its direct method of reaching final faith, Zen is a religion of will-power, and will-power is what is urgently needed by the warriors, though it ought to be enlightened by intuition.

The first Zen follower of the Hōjō family was Tokiyori (1227–1263) who succeeded his father Yasutoki in the Hōjō regency. He invited to Kamakura the Japanese Zen masters in Kyoto and also some Chinese masters directly from Southern Sung, under whom he earnestly devoted himself to the study of Zen. Finally, he succeeded in mastering it and this fact must have given

禅には、一揃いの概念や知的公式を持つ特別な理論や哲学があるわけではない。ただそれは人を生死の羈絆から解こうとするのである。しかも、これをするために、それ自身に特有な、ある直覚的な理解方法によるのである。それゆえに、その直覚的な教えが妨げられぬ限り、いかなる哲学にも道徳論にも、応用自在の弾力性を持っていて、極めて抑揚に富んだものである。禅は無政府主義やファシズムにも、共産主義や民主主義にも、無神論や唯心論にも、またいかなる政治的、経済的な教説にも結びついている。ある意味では、禅はいつも、革命的精神の鼓吹者ともいえる。また過激な叛逆者にもなれば頑固な守旧派にもなりうるものを、そのなかに貯えている。なんでも危機——いかなる意味でもよいが、それに瀕した時は、禅は本来の鋭鋒を現して、左右いずれとも現状打破の革新力となる。鎌倉時代の精神はこの点において、禅の男性的精神と相呼応していた。

　日本につぎのいい表しがある。『天台は宮家、真言は公卿、禅は武家、浄土は平民』と。この言葉は日本の仏教各宗の特色をよく表している。天台と真言は儀礼主義に富んでいて、その諸儀式を行うや、なかなか煩雑で、手のこんだ華麗豪奢なものがあるので、それが洗煉された階級の嗜好に投ずるのである。浄土宗はその信仰と教義が単純であるから、おのずから平民の要求に応じている。禅では究極の信仰に到着するために、最も直接な方法をえらんだほかに、これを遂行するに異常な意力を要求する宗教である。そして、意力は武人のぜひとも必要とするところのものである。もっとも禅は意力だけではなく、最後は直覚によって解決をつけるべきものではあるが。

　北条氏の最初の禅の修行者は、執権泰時の後を継いだ時頼（1227-1263）であった。彼は京都から禅匠たちを、また直接、中国南宋からも禅匠たちを、鎌倉にまねいて、その許で禅の研究に熱心に没頭

great impetus to all his retainers to imitate the example of their master.

Gottan, the Chinese Zen master, under whom Tokiyori had his final enlightenment after twenty-one years' constant application, on the occasion composed the following verse for his illustrious disciple:

"I have no Buddhism about which I can this moment talk to you,
Nor have you any mind with which you listen to me hoping for an attainment:
Where there is neither preaching nor attainment nor mind
There Shakyamuni has a most intimate interview with Buddha Dipankara."

After a very successful regency, Tokiyori died in 1263 when he was only thirty-seven years old. When he realised that the time for departure was approaching he put on his Buddhist robe and sat on a straw seat of meditation and writing his farewell-song passed away quietly. The song reads:

"The karma-mirror raised high
These thirty-seven years:
'Tis broken now with one hammer blow,
The Great Way remains ever serene."

Hōjō Tokimune (1251–1284) was his only son and when his father's mantle fell on him in 1268 he was only eighteen years old. He proved himself to be one of the greatest personages to which Japan has given birth. Without him, indeed, the history of this country would not be what it actually is. He it was who most effectively crushed the Mongolian invasions lasting several years, in fact during the whole length of his regency, 1268–1284. It almost seems that Tokimune was a heaven-sent agency to stave off the direst calamity that might have befallen the nation, for he passed away with the termination of the greatest event in the history of Japan. His short life

した。ついに彼は、その奥義を会得した。この事実は彼の家人たちに非常に刺激を与え、彼らはこぞって主君の範にならった。

時頼は、二十一年間の絶えざる努力によって、ついに中国の禅匠兀庵＊の許で悟りをえた。

その際この著名な弟子のために、兀庵は、つぎの詩偈を作った。

```
我  無  仏  法  一  時  説
子  亦  無  心  無  所  得
無  説  無  得  無  心  中
釈  迦  親  見  燃  燈  仏
```

時頼はりっぱに執政の役を勤め、1263年にわずか三十七歳にして死んだ。彼は死期の迫るを悟るや、袈裟を着け坐禅を組んで、辞世の詩をしたためて心静かに逝った。

```
業  鏡  高  懸
三  十  七  年
一  槌  打  砕
大  道  坦  然
```

北条時宗（1251-1284）は時頼の独り子であり、1268年父の後をついだときはわずかに十八歳であった。彼は日本が生みだした最大の人物の一人となった。彼がいなかったなら、わが国の歴史は現在のごとくではなかったかもしれぬ。1268年から1284年までの執政の間、数年にわたって続いた蒙古人の侵入（元寇）を最もみごとに粉砕したのは彼であった。時宗は日本国家の上に振りかかろうとした大災害を除くため天から遣わされた使者であったかのごとくに思われる。彼は日本歴史における最大の事件の終末をつけるとともに逝ったのである。彼の短い生涯は単純であった。その全部はこの事

was simply and wholly devoted to this affair. He was then the body and soul of the whole nation. His indomitable spirit controlled the whole situation, and his body in the form of a most strongly consolidated army stood like a solid rock against the tumultously raging waves of the Western sea.

What is, however, a still more wonderful thing about this almost super-human figure, was that he had time and energy and aspiration to devote himself to the study of Zen under the masters from China. He erected temples for them and one especially for Bukko Kokushi*, which was also meant to console the departed spirits both Japanese and Chinese at the time of the Mongolian invasions. Tokimune's grave is still in this last-mentioned temple known as Engakuji. Some letters are still preserved which were sent to him by his several spiritual masters, and from which we know how studiously and vigorously he applied himself to Zen. The following story though not quite authenticated gives support to our imaginative reconstruction of his attitude towards Zen. Tokimune is said to have once asked Bukko the National Teacher:

> † When he was threatened by the Mongolian soldiers while still in South China, he uttered this:
>> "Throughout heaven and earth there is not a piece of ground where a single stick could be inserted;
>> I am glad that all things are void, myself and the world:
>> Honoured be the sword, three feet long, wielded by the great Yüan swords-men;
>> For it is like cutting a spring breeze in a flash of lightning."

"The worst enemy of our life is cowardice, and how can I escape it?"

Bukko answered, "Cut off the source whence cowardice comes."

Tokimune: "Where does it come from?"

Bukko: "It comes from Tokimune himself."

Tokimune: "Above all things, cowardice is what I hate most, and how can it come out of myself?"

件にささげられた。彼はそのとき、全国民の唯一の頼みであった。彼の不屈不撓の精神は全国民を支配した。彼の全存在は、一致団結した軍隊の形となって、西海の狂瀾怒濤に対する絶壁のごとく突立った。

　しかし、さらにそれ以上、このほとんど超人的な人物について驚嘆すべきことは、中国からきた諸禅匠の許で、禅をまなぶ時間と精力と向上心を持ったことであった。彼はとくに仏光国師*（註）のために一寺を建立した。それはまた、元寇で亡くなった日中両国軍民の霊を弔うためでもあった。時宗の廟はいまなお鎌倉の円覚寺にある。彼の精神上の師たちから送られた書翰はまだ保存されてあるが、それによってわれわれは彼がいかに禅に丹誠したかを知る。つぎの話は史的に確証がある訳ではないが、彼の禅に対する態度を、われらの想像の上に再現する助けとなろう。時宗は、ある時、仏光国師にたずねた。

（註）国師がまだ南宋時代に兵乱を避けて雁山の能仁寺にいた時、元の兵士たちが暴れ込んできたが、自若として下の一偈を唱えた。

乾坤無レ地スルニ卓二孤笻ヲ一
且喜人空法亦タ空ノ
珍重ス大元三尺ノ剣
電光影裏斬ニ春風ヲ一

時宗『われわれの生涯の大敵は、臆病という事です。どうしたらこれを避けることができましょうか。』
仏光『その病のよってくるところを断ち切れ。』
時宗『その病は何処からくるか。』
仏光『時宗自身からくる。』
時宗『臆病は、諸病のうちで私の最も憎むところです。どうして

Bukko: "See how you feel when you throw overboard your cherished self known as Tokimune. I will see you again when you have done that. "

Tokimune: "How can this be done?"

Bukko: "Shut out all your thoughts."

Tokimune: "How can my thoughts be shut out of consciousness?"

Bukko: "Sit cross-legged in meditation and see into the source of all your thoughts which you imagine as belonging to Tokimune."

Tokimune: "I have so much of worldly affairs to look after and it is difficult to find spare moments for meditation."

Bukko: "Whatever worldly affairs you are engaged in, take them up as occasions for your inner reflection, and some day you will find out who is this beloved Tokimune of yours."

Something like the above must have taken place sometime between Tokimune and Bukko. When he received definite reports about the Mongolian invaders coming over the sea of Tsukushi, he appeared before Bukko the National Teacher and said,

"The greatest event of my life is at last here."

Bukko asked "How would you face it?"

Tokimune uttered "*Kwatsu!*" as if he were frightening away all his enemies actually before him.

Bukko was pleased and said, "Truly, a lion's child roars like a lion."

This was the courage of Tokimune with which he faced the overwhelming enemies coming over from the continent, and successfully drove them back.

Historically speaking, however, it was not his courage alone that accomplished the greatest deed in the history of Japan. He planned out everything that was needed for the task, and his ideas were carried out by the armies engaged in the different parts of the country to resist the powerful invaders. He never moved out of Kamakura but his armies far out in the western parts of Japan executed his orders promptly and effectively. This is really

私自身からそれがでてくるでしょうか。』

仏光『汝の抱ける時宗という自己を投げ棄てた時、どんな感じが
　　するか。それを果しえた時、余はふたたび会おう。』

時宗『いかにしたらそれができますか。』

仏光『いっさいの汝の妄念思慮を断ち切れ。』

時宗『いかにしたら、わがもろもろの思念と意識を断ち切れます
　　か。』

仏光『坐禅を組むのだ。そして時宗自身に属すると思ういっさい
　　の思念の源に徹底せよ。』

時宗『私には面倒を見なければならぬ俗事が沢山あります。瞑想
　　する暇がなかなか見つかりませぬ。』

仏光『いかなる俗事に携ろうとも、それを汝の内省する機会とし
　　て取上げよ。いつかは汝の内なる時宗の誰なるかを悟るであろ
　　う。』

　上述のごとき対話が時宗と仏光との間に或時あったに違いない。
筑紫の海を渡って蒙古襲来の確報を受けた時、彼は仏光国師のまえ
に現れていった。

『生涯の一大事が到頭やって参りました。』

　仏光が尋ねた『いかにしてかそれに向われる所存か。』

　時宗は威を振って『喝!!(カーツ)』と叫んだ。あたかも目前に群がりく
る数万の敵を叱咤し去ったかのように。

　仏光は悦んでいった。『真に獅子児なり、能く獅子吼す。』

　これこそ時宗の勇気であり、それにより彼は大陸から渡ってきた
圧倒的の敵軍に立向ってみごとこれを撃退したのである。

　しかし、歴史の事実から見ると、時宗が日本歴史上最大の行為を
成就したのは彼の勇気だけではなかった。彼はその仕事に要するあ
らゆる事項を計画した。強力な侵入者に反抗するために、全国各地
方から集めた軍勢によって、彼の考は実行された。彼は鎌倉からけっ
して動かなかったが、彼の軍勢は遠く西国にあって機敏かつ有効に
その命令を行なった。通信方法といっても継立(つぎたて)の馬より速いものも

marvellous in these remote days when there was no speedier method of communication than relaying horses. Unless he had the perfect confidence of all his subordinates, it was impossible for him to achieve such a feat.

Bukko's eulogy of Tokimune at his funeral ceremony sums up his personality: "There were ten wonders in his life which was really the actualisation of a Bodhisattva's great Pranidhana (vows); He was a filial son to his mother; he was a loyal subject to his Emperor; he sincerely looked after the welfare of the people; studying Zen he grasped its ultimate truth; wielding an actual power in the Empire for twenty years, he betrayed no signs of joy or anger; sweeping away by virtue of a gale the threatening clouds raised by the barbarians, he showed no feeling of elation; establishing the Engakuji monastery, he planned for the spiritual consolation of the dead [both Japanese and Mongolian]*;1 paying homage to the teachers and fathers [of Buddhism] he sought for enlightenment—all this proves that his coming among us was solely for the sake of the Dharma. And then when he was about to depart, he managed to rise from his bed, put the Buddhist robe I gave him over his enfeebled body, and wrote his death-song in full possession of his spirit. Such a one as he must be said to be really an enlightened being, or a Bodhisattva incarnate. . . ."

Tokimune was born great, no doubt, but his study of Zen must have helped him a great deal in his dealing with state affairs and also in his private life. His wife was also a devout Zen follower and after his death she founded a nunnery in the hills just opposite the Engakuji.

When we say that Zen is for the warrior, this statement has a particular signification for the Kamakura period. Tokimune was not merely a fighting general, but a great statesman whose object was peace. His prayer offered to the Buddha at the time of a great religious ceremony performed at the Kenchoji under the leadership of the abbot, when the intimation of the first Mongolian invasion was received, runs as follows:

"The only prayer Tokimune a Buddhist disciple cherishes is: That the time to come he may be the guardian of the Buddha's doctrine; That the

ないようなそんな遠い時代に、これは真に驚嘆すべきことである。彼にしたがうもののすべての完全な信頼がなかったなら、彼はかかる放れ業を成就することは不可能であった。

　時宗の葬式にさいして作った仏光国師の弔詞は時宗の人格を要約し尽している。曰く、

　　『故迩大檀那果公禅門、大願力に乗じて来り、利那種に依て住す。此の所以を視、其の所由を観ずるに、十種の不可思議あり。何をか十種と謂ふ。母に事へて考を尽し、君に事へて忠を尽し、民に事へて恵に牧し、禅に参じて宗を悟る。二十年乾坤を握定して、喜慍の色あるを見ず。一風蛮烟を掃蕩して、略矜誇の状あらず。円覚を造りて以て幽魂を済し、祖師を礼して以て明悟を求む。此れ乃ち人天転振して法の為に来る。乃至臨終の時、死を忍んで以て老僧の衣法を受け、了々として偈を書して長へに行く。此は是れ世間了事の凡夫、亦菩薩の応世と名く…』

　時宗が生れながらにして偉かったことは疑いもないが、禅をまなんだことが公私の生活において大いに助けとなったに違いない。彼の夫人も熱心な修禅者であり夫の死後、円覚寺の真向いの山中に松ヶ岡東慶寺という尼寺を創建した。

　禅は武人に適するといったが、この言葉は鎌倉時代には特別な意味がある。時宗は武人であるのみならず、また大政治家であり、その目的は平和であった。第一回の元寇の報が達した時、時宗は建長寺において、無学祖元を導師として法儀を営んだが、その際の彼の祈願文はつぎのごとくである。

　　『専ら祈るらくは、弟子時宗、永く帝祚を扶け、久しく宗乗を護り、一箭を施さずして、四海安和に、一鋒を露はさずして、群魔

four seas remain unruffled without an arrow being shot; That all evil spirits be kept under subjection without a spear-head being unsheathed; That the masses be benefitted by means of a benevolent administration so that they could enjoy a long life in happiness more than ever; That the darkness of the human mind be illumined by the touch of transcendental wisdom which should be raised high; That the needy be properly ministered to and those in danger be saved by the heart of compassion being widely open. May all the gods come and protect us, all the sages extending their quiet help, and every hour of the day there be a great gathering of auspicious signs!. . ."

Tokimune was a great Buddhist spirit and a sincere follower of Zen, and it was due to his encouragement that Zen came to be firmly established in Kamakura and then in Kyoto and began to spread its moral and spiritual influence among the warrior classes. The constant stream of intercourse thus started between the Japanese and the Chinese Zen monks went even beyond the boundaries of their common cause; for books, paintings, porcelains, textiles, and many other objects of art were brought from China; even carpenters, masons, architects, and cooks came along with their masters. Thus the trading with China which later developed in the Ashikaga period had its initiation in the Kamakura.

Led by such strong characters as Tokiyori and Tokimune, Zen was auspiciously initiated into the Japanese life, especially into the life of the samurai. As Zen gained more and more influence in Kamakura it spread over to Kyoto where it was strongly supported by Japanese Zen masters. The latter soon found strong followers among members of the Imperial family headed by Emperors Godaigo, Hanazono, and others. Large monasteries were built in Kyoto and masters noted for their virtue, wisdom, and learning were asked to be founders and successive abbots of such institutions. Shōguns of the Ashikaga regime were also great advocates of Zen Buddhism, and most generals under them naturally followed suit. In those days we can say that the Japanese genius went either to priesthood or to soldiery. The spiritual cooperation of these two could not help but contribute to the creation of

頓に急み、徳仁普く利し、寿福弥々堅く、慧炬を秉つて、昏衢を
燭し、慈心を剖いて、危乏を賑さん、諸天匡護し、衆聖密に扶け、
二六時中吉祥駢び集らんことを云云』

　時宗には偉大な仏教精神が宿っていて、真摯な禅の修行者であっ
た。禅が鎌倉および京都に固く樹立されるようになり、武人階級の
間に道徳的・精神的影響をおよぼし始めたことはじつに彼の奨励に
よる。日本と中国の禅僧間に端を発した不断の交渉は、両者のとも
に関心する精神的事項のみにかぎらなくなった。なぜかというに、
書物・絵画・陶瓷・織物・その他多くの美術品が、中国からもたらさ
れたり、また大工・石工・建築家・料理人などがその主人たちととも
に日本に渡ってきたからである。かようにして、後に室町時代に
発達した中国との貿易は、その端をすでに鎌倉時代に発したのであ
る。
　時頼・時宗のごとき強い人格に導かれて、禅は日本人の生活に、
とくに武士の生活に著しく浸潤してきた。禅が鎌倉にますます影
響をおよぼすにしたがって、それはまた京都にも波及した。そこで
は日本人の禅匠たちによってつよく支持された。それはやがて後醍
醐天皇、花園天皇をはじめ、その他の皇族のあいだにふかい信奉を
えた。多くの禅院が京都に建てられ、学徳をもって鳴る禅匠がその
開山となり、一山の師道となった。足利幕府の将軍もまた禅の尊崇
者であり、そのしたの多くの武将も自然これにならった。当時の日
本の天才たちは僧侶か武人になった。この両者の精神的協力は、一
般に「武士道」として知られているものの創造に貢献せざるをえな
かった。

what is now generally known as Bushido, "the way of the warrior."

At this juncture, let me touch upon one of the inner relationships that exist between the samurai mode of feeling and Zen. What finally came to constitute Bushido as we generally understand it now is to be an unflinching guardian-god of the dignity of the samurai, and this dignity consisted in loyalty, filial piety, and benevolent spirit. But to fulfil these duties successfully two things are needed; the one is to train oneself in moral asceticism, not only in its practical aspect but in its philosophical preparation; and the other is to be always ready to face death, that is, to sacrifice oneself unhesitatingly when occasion arises. To do this, much mental and spiritual training is needed.

There is a document recently talked very much about in connection with the military operations in China. It is known as the *Hagakure* which literally means "Hidden under the Leaves," for it is one of the virtues of the samurai not to display himself, not to blow his horn, but to keep himself away from the public eye and be doing good for his fellow-beings. To the compilation of this book which consists of various notes, anecdotes, moral sayings, etc., a Zen monk had his part to contribute. The work started in the middle part of the seventeenth century under Nabeshima Naoshige, the feudal lord of Saga in the island of Kyushu. The book emphasises very much the samurai's readiness to give his life away at any moment, for it states that no great work has ever been accomplished without going mad, that is, when expressed in modern terms, without breaking through the ordinary level of consciousness and letting loose one's hidden powers lying further below. These powers may be devilish sometimes, but there is no doubt that they are superhuman and work wonders. When the Unconscious is tapped, it rises above individual limitations. Death now loses its sting altogether, and this is where the samurai training joins hands with Zen.

To quote one of the stories cited in the *Hagakure*; Yagyū Tajima-no-kami was a great swordsman and teacher in the art to the Shōgun of the time, Tokugawa Iyemitsu. One of the personal guards of the Shōgun one

ここで武士の感じかたと禅との内的関係の一つに触れておこう。われわれがいま一般に武士道として理解するものを作りあげるようになった中心思想は、武士たるものの威厳を不断にたゆむことなく擁護するということである。この威厳とは、忠孝仁義の精神である。しかし、これらの義務を立派に果すためには、二つの事が要る。一は実践的な方面のみにあらず、哲学的な方面でも、一種の鍛錬主義を抱持することであり、一は常住死を覚悟すること、すなわち、その機に臨めば、躊躇なく身命を放擲することである。これがためには、多くの精神上の修養が大いに必要である。

　最近⻆国における軍事行動に関連して、やかましくいわれた一つの文書（ドキュメント）がある。「葉隠（はがくれ）」＊というのであるが、それは文字通り「葉の陰に隠れる」意で、わが身を誇示せず、角笛を吹いて廻らず、世間の眼から遠ざかって、そうして社会同胞のために深情を尽すのが、武士の徳の一つだというのである。この書は種々の記録・逸話・訓言などから成っているが、その編纂は、ある禅僧が担当したのである。この仕事は十七世紀の中葉に佐賀藩主の鍋島直重の下で着手された。この書はいつにても身命を捧げる武士の覚悟を極めて強調し、いかなる偉大な仕事も、狂気にならずしては、すなわち、現代語で表現すれば、意識の普通の水準を破ってその下に横たわる隠れた力を解放するのでなければ、成就されたためしはないと述べている。この力はときとして、悪魔的（デビリシュ）であるかも知れぬが、超人間的であり、すばらしい働きをすることは疑えぬ。無意識状態が口を切られると、それは個人的の限度を超えて立ちのぼる。死はまったくその毒刺を失う。武士の修養が禅と提携するのはじつにこの点である。

　「葉隠」に引用されている話の一つを引こう。柳生但馬守＊は偉大な剣道家でときの将軍徳川家光の指南番であった。一日旗本の一人が但馬守のところにやってきて剣道指南を頼んだ。

day came to Tajima-no-kami wishing to be trained in fencing.

The master said, "As I observe, you seem to be a master of fencing yourself; pray tell me to what school you belong, before we enter into the relationship of teacher and pupil."

The guardsman said, "I am ashamed to confess that I have never learned the art."

"Are you going to fool me? I am teacher to the honourable Shōgun himself, and I know my judging eye never fails."

"I am sorry to defy your honour, but I really know nothing."

This resolute denial on the part of the visitor made the swordsmaster think for a while, and he finally said, "If you say so, that must be so; but still I am sure of your being master of something, though I know not just of what."

"Yes, if you insist, I will tell you this. There is one thing of which I can say I am complete master. When I was still a boy, the thought came upon me that as a samurai I ought in no circumstances to be afraid of death, and ever since I have grappled with the problem of death now for some years, and finally the problem has entirely ceased to worry me. May this be at what you hint?"

"Exactly!" exclaimed Tajima-no-kami, "That is what I mean. I am glad that I made no mistake in my judgment. For the ultimate secrets of swordsmanship also lie in being released from the thought of death. I have trained ever so many hundreds of my pupils along this line, but so far none of them really deserve the final certificate for swordsmanship. You need no technical training, you are already a master."

The problem of death is a great problem with every one of us; it is, however, more pressing for the samurai, for the soldier, whose life is exclusively devoted to fighting, and fighting means death to either side of fighters. In feudal days nobody could predict when this deadly encounter might take place, and the samurai worth his name was always to be on the alert. A warrior-writer of the seventeenth century, Daidōji Yūzan, therefore, writes in the beginning of his book to be called a "Primer of Bushido," to the following effect:

師が云つた、『お見受する所、貴殿は既に剣道の師のやうであるが、吾等師弟の契りを結ぶ前は何流で御座つたか話されい。』

　其旗本は答へた『お恥しき儀なれど剣道を習ひしことは御座いませぬ。』
　『拙者をお戯れになる積りか。拙者は将軍御指南役で御座るぞ、この眼に狂ひは御座らぬ。』
　『御意に逆らひて恐れ入りますが、拙者は何にも知り申しません。』
　客の否定があまり、きっぱりしてゐるので、師は少し考へてゐたが遂に云つた『貴殿がさう云はれる以上、左様に違ひ御座るまい。しかし、何とは判然申し難いが何かの師匠であつたに違ひ御座らぬ。』
　『断つてと云はるるならば申し上げませう。実は完全に習得したと申しえらるる一事が御座います。某未だ年少の頃、武士として如何なる場合にも死を恐れるべきに非らずとの念を発し、爾来数年、死の問題と組討いたし、漸くにして其こと全く煩ふに及ばなくなりました。この事でも先生は指されるので御座いませうか。』
　『確かに』と但馬守は叫んだ『その通りで御座る。拙者の判断に間違ひはなかつた。剣道の極意は死を恐れざることで御座る。某は当流において幾百の門弟を指南してをりますが、一人として誠それ程に免許皆伝に及んだものは御座らぬ。貴殿は技を学ぶには及ばぬ、立派に師範で御座る。』　　　　　　　　　　（葉隠第十一巻）
　死の問題はわれわれの誰にも大問題である。しかし、もっぱら戦闘に生命を捧げる武士にとってはさらに逼迫している。戦闘は闘うもの双方の側にとって死を意味する。封建時代には誰もこの死的遭遇がいつ起るか予言できなかった。その名に背かぬ武士は常住不断に注意を怠らなかった。それゆえに十七世紀の武人著者の大導寺友山＊は彼の著「武道初心集」の初めに、つぎのような意味のことを書いている。

"The idea most vital and essential to the samurai is that of death which he ought to have before his mind day and night, night and day, from the dawn of the first day of the year till the last minute of the last day of it. When this notion takes firm hold of you, you are able to discharge your duties to their fullest extent; you are loyal to your master, filial to your parents, and naturally can avoid all kinds of disasters. Not only is your life itself thereby prolonged, but your personal dignity is enhanced. Think what a frail thing life is, especially that of a samurai. This being so, you will come to consider every day of your life your last and dedicate it to the fulfilment of your obligations. Do never let the thought of a long life seize upon you, for then you are apt to indulge in all kinds of dissipation, and close up your days in dire disgrace. This was the reason why Masashige is said to have told his son Masatsura to keep the idea of death all the time before his mind."

The writer of this "Primer" has rightly given expression to what has been unconsciously going on in the mind of the samurai generally. The notion of death, on the one hand, makes one's thought extend beyond the limitations of this finite life, and, on the other hand, screws it up so as to take daily life seriously. It was, therefore, natural for every sober-minded samurai to approach Zen with the idea of mastering death. Zen's claim to handle this problem without appealing either to learning or to moral training or to ritualism, must have been a great attraction, to the comparatively unsophisticated mind of the samurai. There was a kind of logical relationship between his psychological outlook and the direct practical teaching of Zen.

Further, we read the following in the *Hagakure*:
"Bushido means the determined will to die. When you are at the parting of the ways, do not hesitate to choose the way to death. No special reason for this except that your mind is thus made up and ready to see to the business. Some may say that if you die without attaining the object, it is a useless death, dying like a dog. But when you are at the parting of the ways, you need not plan for attaining the object. We all prefer life to death and our planning and reasoning will be naturally for life. If then you miss the object

『武士に取って最も肝要な考は、元旦の暁より大晦日の終りの一刻まで日夜念頭に持たなければならぬは死という観念である。この念を固く身に体した時、汝は十二分に汝の義務を果しうるであろう。主に忠、親に孝、而して当然一切の災難を避けることができる。汝は長命をうるのみならず、威徳も具わるであろう。人の命の常なきを、取りわけて、武士の命の常なきを考えよ。かくして、汝は日々是れ汝の最期と考え、汝の義務を充さんがために、日々を捧げるに至るであろう。命長しと思うこと勿れ。何となれば汝は一切の浪費に耽り易く、汚名の間に汝の生を閉じ易いからである。正成の其子正行に絶えず死を覚悟させたのも、このゆえなりという。』

「武道初心集」の著者は一般に武士の心中に無意識に起っていたところのものを正しく表現したのであった。死の念は、一方においては、人の考をこの固定した生命の有限を超えさせ、他方においては、日常生活を真面目に考えさせるように引締める。それゆえ、真面目な武士が死を克服せんとする考をもって、禅に近づくのは当然である。禅がこの問題を、学問や道徳的修養や儀礼に訴えることなく取扱うことを主張するのは、比較的に思弁を事とせぬ武士の心には、大きな魅力であったに違いない。武士の心構えと禅の直接的・実践的教義との間には一種の論理的な関係があった。

さらに「葉隠」にはつぎの一節がある。
『武士道といふは、死ぬ事と見附けたり。二つ二つの場にて、早く死ぬ方に片附くばかりなり。別に仔細なし。胸すわつて進むなり。図に当らぬは、犬死などといふ事は、上方風の打上りたる武士道なるべし。二つ二つの場にて、図に当るやうにするは及ばぬことなり。我人、生くる方好きなり。多分好きな方に理が附くべし。若し図にはづれて生きたらば腰抜なり。この境危ふきなり。図にはづれて死にたらば、犬死気違なり。恥にはならず。これが

and are alive, you are really a coward. This is an important consideration. In case you die without achieving the object, it may be a dog-death—the deed of madness, but there is no reflection here on your honour. In Bushido honour comes first. Therefore, every morning and every evening, have the idea of death vividly impressed in your mind. When your determination to die at any moment is thoroughly established, you attain to perfect mastery of Bushido, your life will be faultless, and your duties are fully discharged."

A commentator adds a verse by Tsukahara Bokuden [One of the greatest swordsmen, 1490–1572.]—"The ultimate end of all discipline for the samurai, whatever form it may take, is one and one only, that is, not to flinch in the face of death."

According to Nagahama Inosuke as told in the *Hagakure*,

"The essence of swordsmanship consists in giving yourself up altogether to the business of striking down the opponent. [As long as you are considerate about your own safety you can never win in the fight.] If the enemy too is ready to give his life to it, you are then well-matched. The final outcome will depend on faith and fate." The commentary notes here read:

"Araki Matayemon [a great swordsman of the early Tokugawa era] gave this instruction to his nephew, Watanabe Kazuma, when they were about to engage in the deadly fight with their enemy; 'Let the enemy touch your skin and you cut into his flesh; let him cut into your flesh and you pierce into his bones; let him pierce into your bones and you take his life!'

In another place, Araki advises: 'When you are to measure swords with your enemy, be ready at once to lay down your life before him. As long as you are the least concerned with your escaping safely you are doomed.'"

Further, the *Hagakure* state:

"The samurai is good for nothing unless he can go beyond life and death. When it is said that all things are of one mind, you may think that there is such a thing as to be known as mind. But the fact is that a mind attached to life and death must be abandoned, when you can execute wonderful deeds." This is to say that all things are accomplished when one attains a mind

武道には丈夫なり。毎朝毎夕、改めて死に死に、常住死身になりて居る時は、武道に自由を得、一生落度なく、家職を仕果すべきなり。』　　　　　　　　　　　　　　　　　　　（葉隠第一巻）

註釈者は塚原卜伝＊の歌を加えている。
武士の学ぶ教へは押なべて
そのきはめには死の一つなり

「葉隠」のなかに長浜猪之助が語るところによれば、
『兵法の要は、唯身を捨てて、敵を討つべし。対手も身を捨てて討つとき、此時はじめて、対になるなり。其の時勝つは、信心運命にあるなり。……』　　　　　　　　　　　　（同書第十一巻）

註釈者はつぎのように附記している。
荒木又右衛門が、伊賀上野の仇討の時、甥の渡辺数馬に訓えた言葉として、「皮を斬らして肉を斬れ、肉を斬らして骨を斬れ、骨を斬らして命を取れ」と伝えられている。

また、荒木は他のところで（「一刀流聞書」）「真剣の勝負に当りては、我身を殺されに行くと思ふべし。左すれば鋭く丈夫なものに相成候。真剣には我が身を殺されに行くと思はねば勝つこと出来申さず候。爰の所意味深し。」
さらに、「葉隠」には、
『生死を離るべき事、武士たるものは、生死を離れねば何事も役に立たず、万能一心と云ふも、有心のやうに聞ゆれども、実は生死を離れたることなり。その上にて、如何様の手柄もさるるものなり。芸能などは道に引入るる縁迄なり。』　　　　　　（同前）
これは沢庵禅師に拠る「無心」の心に達すればいっさいが成就す

of "no-mind-ness" according to the great Zen master, Takuan, as quoted below. It is a state of mind which is no more troubled with the question of death or that of immortality.

As Tsukahara Bokuden was mentioned just now who is one of those swordsmen who really understood the mission of the sword not as a weapon of murder but as an instrument of spiritual self-discipline, let me cite here the two best-known incidents in his life.*

Takeda Shingen (1521–1573) and Uesugi Kenshin (1530–1578) were two great generals of the sixteenth century when Japan was in warring state within its own boundaries. The two are generally mentioned together, for their provinces—the one in the north and the other in central Japan—lay closely together, and they had on several occasions to fight for supremacy. They were well matched as able soldiers and good rulers, and were also students of Zen. When Kenshin once learned of Shingen's suffering very much from lack of salt for his people, Kenshin was generous enough to supply his enemy with the needed material from his own province. Facing the Japan Sea Echigo produced enough salt. In one of the pitched battles at Kawanaka-jima Kenshin grew impatient, it is said, of the slow progress of his army, and, wishing to decide at once the fate of the day, he personally rode into the camp of Shingen. Seeing the general of the opposing force quietly sitting on a camp-chair with a few of his guards, Kenshin drew his sword and let it fall squarely over the head of Shingen, saying, "What would you say at this moment?"—a regular Zen question. Shingen was not disturbed at all and answering, "A snow-flake on the blazing stove," warded the threatening weapon with at iron fan which was at the time in his hand. The *mondo* probably never took place, but the story illustrates well how the two intrepid head-shaven warriors were lovers of Zen.

The way Kenshin came to study Zen in all earnest under Yekiwō was this: When Yekiwō once gave his sermon on Bodhi-Dharma's "I know not," Kenshin was among the audience. He knew something of Zen and wished to test this monk. He appeared in the dress of an ordinary samurai indis-

ることをいうのである。それは死とか不死とかの問題に煩わされぬ心の状態である。

　塚原卜伝の名がいまでたが、彼は殺人の武器としてではなく、精神的な自己鍛錬の器具としての剣の使命を真に理解した剣士の一人である。彼の伝記には有名な二つの挿話がある。一つは大言壮語する一武士を孤島に置き去りにした無手勝流の話で、他は彼の三人の息子の剣技の熟達振りを試みた話であるが、いずれも広く人口に膾炙している。

　武田信玄（1521-1573）と上杉謙信（1530-1578）とは日本が戦国時代に在った十六世紀の二名将であった。二人はその領地が――一は日本の北部・一は中部で――相接していたので、一般にならび称せられ、彼らは幾度かその優越を争わねばならなかった。彼らは武人としても、支配者としても、相伯仲した。また、禅を学ぶ点でも同じであった。謙信はかつて信玄が領民のための塩の欠乏にいたく悩んでいるのを知った時、寛大にも自分の領地からその必要な物資を敵に供給した。日本海に臨んでいるので越後は塩を十分産した。川中島の対陣戦の一つでは謙信は敵の出方の遅いのに業を煮やして、一挙に勝敗を決せんものと単身信玄の陣に乗り込んだ。謙信は敵将が数人の幕下とともに悠然と椅子に腰かけているのを見るや、剣を抜いて信玄の頭上真向から切りつけて『いかなるかこれ剣刃上の事』と禅問を発した。信玄は少しも騒がず、その時彼の手にしていた鉄扇で襲いくる武器をかわして『紅炉上一点の雪』と答えたという。この問答、おそらくは真実でなかったでもあろう。が、この話は二人の入道武士が禅の愛好者であったことをよく説明している。

　謙信が益翁の許で極めて熱心に禅を研究するようになった次第はこうである。益翁がかつて菩提達磨の「不識」について説教をしていた時、謙信は聴衆の一人だった。彼は禅について多少知っていたのでこの僧を試さんと思った。他の士分の者と変りない服装をして

tinguishable from the test, and waited for the opportunity, but the monk suddenly turned towards Kenshin and demanded: "O Lord General! What is the meaning of Dharma's 'I know not'?" Kenshin was taken by surprise and did not know what to say. Thereupon, Yekiwō continued, "O Lord General, why not give me an answer today when you talk so glibly about Zen on all other occasions?"* Kenshin's pride gave way. He began to study Zen now most seriously under the leadership of this monk, who used to tell him this, "If you are really desirous of mastering Zen, it is necessary for you once to give up your life and to plunge right into the pit of death."

Kenshin later left the following admonition for his retainers:

"Those who cling to life die, and those who defy death live. The essential thing is the mind. Look into this mind and firmly take hold of it and you will understand that there is something in you which is above birth-and-death and which is neither drowned in water nor burned by fire. I have myself gained an insight into this Samadhi and know what I am telling you. Those who are reluctant to give up their lives and embrace death are not true warriors."

Shingen also made reference to Zen and death in his "Constitution":

"Pay proper reverence to the gods and the Buddha. When your thoughts are in accord with the Buddha's, you will gain more power. If your domination over others issues from your evil thoughts, you will be exposed, you are doomed. Next, devote yourselves to the study of Zen. Zen has no secrets other than seriously thinking of birth-and-death."

From those statements we can in an unmistakable manner see that there is an inner necessary relationship between Zen and the warrior's life. This is also readily explained from the behaviour of the Zen masters themselves who sometimes even seem to make sport of death. Shingen's Zen teacher was Kwaisen, abbot of Yerin-ji, in the province of Kai. After Shingen's death, the monastery was besieged by the soldiers of Oda Nobunaga on the third of April, 1582, because the abbot refused to give up Nobunaga's enemies who took refuge in it. The soldiers forced all the monks including Kwaisen

聴衆のなかにかくれ、その機を待った。しかし、この僧は不意に謙信の方を向いて尋ねた『殿、達磨不識の意味は如何。』謙信は呆気にとられ、いうところを知らなかった。益翁さらに畳みかけて『殿、貴方は他の場合にはいつも禅を喋々するのに今日はなぜお答あらぬ。』謙信の誇りはくじかれた。彼はこの僧の指導のもとに極めて真面目に禅を学び始めた。師僧はつねに彼にこういった。『貴方が真に禅を会得せんと欲せらるるならば、命を捨てて直下に死の穴へ飛び込むことが必要です。』

謙信は後に彼の家臣たちにつぎのような訓戒をのこした。
『生を必する者は死し、死を必する者は生く。要はただ心志の如何にあり。よく此の心を得て、守持する所堅ければ、火に入りて焼けず、水に陥つて溺れず、何ぞ生死に関せんや。予、常に此の理を明かにして三昧に入れり。生を惜しみ死を厭ふが如きは、未だ武士の心胆にあらず。』

信玄もまた彼の「信玄家法」に禅と死にいいおよんでいる。
『仏心を信ずべきこと。曰ふ、仏心に叶へば、則ち時々力を添へ、横心を以て人に勝てば、則ち露はれて亡ぶべし。伝に云ふ、神は非礼を享けずと。
参禅嗜むべきこと。語に曰く、参禅は別に秘訣なし、唯だ生死の切なるを思ふと。』

これらの言説よりして、われわれは禅と武士の生活との間に内的な必然的関係があることを誤りなく見ることができる。これは時として死をもてあそぶかとさえ思われる禅匠の振舞からも、容易に説明されることである。信玄の師は甲斐国恵林寺の快川和尚であった。信玄の死後、この禅院はそこに逃げ込んだ敵兵を引渡すのを拒んだという理由で、1582年4月3日（天正十年）、織田信長の兵卒によって包囲された。兵卒たちは快川および一山の衆徒をことごとく山門の楼上に上らせた。建物全体に火を放って、反抗者を生きながらに焼

himself to go up to the top story of the monastery gate. The plan was to burn the recalcitrants alive by setting the whole edifice on fire. The monks headed by the abbot quietly gathered and sat cross-legged taking their seats in due order in front of the Buddha-image. The abbot gave his last sermon in his usual manner, saying, "We are now encircled by the flames, and how would you revolve your Wheel of the Dharma at this critical moment? Let each one of you say a word." Thereupon, each expressed himself according to his light of understanding. When all were finished, the abbot gave his view and all entered into the fire-Samadhi. The abbot's words were this:

"For a peaceful meditation, we need not go to the mountains and streams; When thoughts are quieted down, fire itself is cool and refreshing."

The Japan of the sixteenth century from a certain point of view produced many fine specimens of humanity. The country was torn to pieces, as it were, politically and socially. The feudal lords were at war with one another all over Japan. The masses must have suffered very much, but this deadly competition for supremacy military and political among the military classes helped to strain to the utmost end the mental and moral powers in every possible way. Virility asserted itself in various quarters of life, and we can say that most of the virtues composing Bushido were formed in this period, and that Shingen and Kenshin were typical representatives of the samurai-lords. They both were personally brave and never flinched in the face of death; they were wise and thoughtful and resourceful not only in war but in governing the people under them; they were not mere fighters, ignorant and callous, they were accomplished in literature and highly religious.

It is interesting that both Shingen and Kenshin were great Buddhists. Shingen's secular name is Harunobu and Kenshin's Terutora, but they are better known by their Buddhist titles. They were both educated while young at Buddhist monasteries, and had their heads shaven in their middle ages calling themselves "Nyūdō" of Buddhism. Kenshin was a celibate and

殺そうという企てであった。禅僧たちは和尚を頭に静かに集って、仏像の前に席次正しく結跏趺坐した。和尚は平素の通りに説教を与えて、いった。『われわれはいま、焰に囲まれている。この危機に臨んで、諸子はいかに達磨の禅輪を転ぜんとするか。各々一句をいえ。』そこで、めいめい自分の悟達に応じて自己を表現した。みなが終った時、和尚は自分の意見を述べた。そして、すべての者は火定三昧に入った。和尚の偈はこうである。

安　禅　不　必　須　山　水
滅　却　心　頭　火　自　涼

　ある観点からすれば、十六世紀の日本は多くの立派な人間の標本を造りだした。国家はいわば政治的にも社会的にも寸断された。封建諸侯が日本中で互いに戦った。庶民ははなはだ苦しんだに違いないが、この武門階級の間における政治的・軍事的の覇権の争奪戦はあらゆる方法を尽して精神的・道徳的の力を極度に緊張する助けとなった。生活のいろいろな方面に剛毅の気風が現れて、武士道を作る徳の大部分はこの時期に形成され、信玄と謙信は武門諸侯の典型的な代表者であったということができよう。彼らはともに勇気があって、死に面して怯まず、戦闘のみならず領民を支配する点でも賢明にして思慮ふかく智慧があった。無智鈍感な一介の武人ではなくて、諸芸に通じ宗教心に富んでいた。

　信玄も謙信もともにすぐれた仏教徒であったことは興味深いことだ。信玄の俗名は晴信、謙信は輝虎である。が、法名の方が知られている。彼らは若い時禅院で教育をうけ、中年にして剃髪して入道を称した。謙信は仏教僧侶と同様に肉食妻帯をしなかった。

vegetarian like the Buddhist monk.

Like most Japanese of culture, they loved Nature and composed poems both in Japanese and Chinese. One of the poems by Kenshin while engaged in a campaign in the neighbouring provinces, reads in substance:

"The bracing frosty autumnal air descends upon the soldiers in bivouac; the night is advancing, the wild geese in orderly formation are seen flying in the moonlight; the mountains of Ecchu are silhouetted over against the dreamy waves of Noto Bay—[What a splendid view this is, and how entranced I am!] albeit that we are far away from the home-people, who may be thinking of our expedition [in view of the same moonlight]."

Shingen's appreciation of Nature was by no means behind that of his rival in Echigo. When he once visited a Buddhist temple in the remoter part of his province, where Achala (Fudō Myōwō) was enshrined, the abbot of the monastery near-by requested of him to pass by it on his way home. Shingen first declined the invitation saying that he was busily preparing for a campaign taking place in a few days and would not have time to call on the abbot this time, and added that when he came back from the engagement, he would surely visit the monastery. But the abbot, who by the way was the one who allowed himself to be burned alive in the hands of Oda Nobunaga's soldiers afterwards, insisted:

"The cherries are just beginning to bloom, and I have already set up a fine seat for you where you can enjoy the glorious Spring. I hope you will not fail to appreciate the flowers."

Shingen acquiesced:

"It would not do to set my face against the cherries and then I ought also to mind the pressing invitation of the abbot."

In appreciation of the fine opportunity to enjoy the flowers and an

多くの教養ある日本人と同様に、二人は自然を愛し、詩歌を作った。謙信が隣国における出陣にしたがっているさい作った詩に大要つぎのごとき作がある。

『爽やかな霜を含んだ秋気が陣営の兵達（つわもの）の上に降りる。夜は更けゆき、雁が列を作って飛んでゆくのが月光のなかに見える。越中の山々が、能登湾の夢のような波の上にシルエットを作っている。——（なんという美観、なんという魅惑的な眺めであろう）遠く離れている家郷、その家郷の人々は（この同じ月明に接して）わが遠征軍を想っているかも知れない。（註）』

（註）上は下の有名な詩を指す。

霜満テ軍営ニ秋気清　　数行過ル雁月三更
越山併セ得タリ能州景　遮莫（サモアラバアレ）家郷懐フ遠征

　信玄の自然を味う心はけっしてその越後の敵将におくれをとるものではなかった。彼がかつて領内僻遠の地の不動明王を祠ったある寺を訪ねた折、その近くの禅寺の住持が、帰途に立寄らんことを求めた。信玄は始めその招きを断って、二、三日後に起る戦の準備に忙しいから今度は貴寺を訪ねる暇がないだろうといった。さらに附加えて、従軍から戻ったらかならず貴寺を訪ねようといった。この和尚は後に織田信長の兵卒たちの手で焚殺された一人であったが、なお強いていった。

『桜はいまちょうど開き始めました。拙僧は貴方が麗しい春を賞美されるように立派な席を設けております。ぜひ、花を賞（め）でにおいで下さい。』

　信玄は黙従した。
『桜に対面せぬのもよろしくあるまいし、和尚のたっての招きも疎かにする訳にゆくまい。』と。
　花を賞する好機に恵まれ、和尚と塵外の語らいを楽んだ信玄は、

unworldly conversation with the abbot, Shingen composed the following verse in Japanese:

"If I did not have this invitation from my friend, how greatly I should have missed this magnificent sight of the cherry-blossoms! The monastery might be found all swathed in snow next spring when I proposed to visit it."*

Such a disinterested enjoyment of Nature as shown by Shingen and Kenshin even in the midst of warlike activities, is known as *fūryū*, and those without this feeling of *fūryū* are classed among the most uncultured in Japan. The feeling is not merely esthetical, it has also a religious signification. It is perhaps due to the same mental attitude that has created the custom among cultured Japanese of various accomplishments of writing a verse either in Japanese or Chinese at the last moment of death. The verse is known as the "parting-with-life-verse." The Japanese have been taught and trained to be able to find a moment's leisure to detach themselves from the intensest excitements in which they may happen to be placed. Death is the most serious affair absorbing all one's attention, but the cultured Japanese think they ought to be able to transcend it and view it objectively. The custom of leaving a farewell song, though not mecessarily universally observed by the cultured even in the feudal days, started in all likelihood in the Kamakura period with the Zen monks and their followers. When the Buddha passed into Nirvana, he had his disciples about him and gave them his farewell exhortation. This must have been imitated by the Chinese Buddhists, especially by the Zen Buddhists, who, instead of leaving a farewell instruction for their followers, expressed their own views of life.

Takeda Shingen's farewell words were a quotation from Zen literature:

"It is largely left to her own natural bodily perfection, and she has no special need to resort to artificial colouring and powdering in order to look beautiful."

This refers to the absolute perfection of Reality from which we all come and to which we all return and in which we all are; a world of multitudes

つぎのような和歌を作った。
　　さそはずば
　　くやしからまし桜花
　　さてこん春は
　　雪のふるてら

　戦の真最中に、信玄や謙信が示した、かかる利害を超越した「自然」の享楽は「風流」と呼ばれている。この風流の感情なきものは、日本では最も教養のないもののなかに入れられている。この感情は単に美的のみならず宗教的な意義をもっている。諸芸に通じた教養ある日本人の間に、臨終に際して詩歌をかく習慣を創始したのも、おそらくは同じ心的態度にもとづく。かかる詩歌は「辞世の詩や歌」として知られている。日本人は自分たちが最も激しい興奮の状に置かれることがあっても、そこから自己を引離す一瞬の余裕を見つけうるように教えられ、また、鍛錬されてきた。死は一切の注意力を集注させる最も厳粛な出来事であるが、教養ある日本人はそれを超越して、客観的に視なければならぬと考えている。辞世の歌をのこすということも、封建時代でさえかならずしも教養ある者の一般が行なった訳ではなかった。おそらくは鎌倉時代に禅僧の一派から始まったのであろう。仏陀が涅槃に入った時、弟子をまわりに集めて別れの訓戒を与えた。これに倣ったのが中国の仏教徒、とくに禅宗僧侶であって、門弟に別れの訓辞をのこすかわりに、自己の人生観を表白した。

　武田信玄の別辞（偈）は禅文学からの引用であった。
　　大　底　還ル他　肌　骨　好
　　不レ　塗ニ　紅　粉ヲ　自　風　流

　これはわれわれ凡てがそこからきたり、そこに還り、そこに住するところの「実在」の絶対的完全性のことを言っているのである。

passes away and comes again, but what is at the back of it always retains its perfect beauty unchangingly.

Uyesugi Kenshin composed his own, the one in Chinese and the other in Japanese, thus:

"Even a life-long prosperity is but one cup of *saké*;
A life of forty-nine years is passed in a dream;
I know not what life is, nor death.
Year in year out—all but a dream."

"Both Heaven and Hell are left behind;
I stand in the moonlit dawn,
Free from clouds of attachment."

The following are the deaths of the Kamakura warriors as recorded in the Taiheiki (compiled late in the fourteenth century), which will clarify, side by side with those of the Yerin-ji monks, the attitude towards death.

Among the retainers of Hōjō Takatoki, who was the last of the Hōjō family, there was one Shiaku Shinsakon Nyūdō, not very high in the official rank of the samurai hierarchy of Kamakura. When he was about to commit suicide to follow his master whose destiny was going to be sealed, he called in his eldest son Saburozaemon and said to him; "Kamakura is doomed as it is surrounded by enemies on all sides, and I am going to share the fate of the master as his loyal follower. But you are still young and have not yet been in active service and are not so intimately related to the master as I have been. You somehow manage to escape the approaching tragedy, and after saving your life become a monk and serve the Buddha and look after the spiritual welfare of us all. Nobody will blame you for doing this."

Saburozaemon, however, showed no inclination to follow his father's rational advice, for he said,"Even though I have not yet been actively and personally connected with our master I have as your son been brought up

多様の世界は過ぎさり、また、還る、しかし、その背後にあるもの
は変らぬままにその完全な美をとどめる。

　上杉謙信は、べつに和歌と漢詩を作った。

一　期　栄　花　一　盃　酒
四　十　九　年　一　睡　夢
生ハ不レ知ラ死亦不レ知ラ
歳　月　只　是　如二夢　中一

極楽も地獄も先づは
有明の月の
心にかかる雲もなし　　　（謙信家記）

　つぎに示すのは「太平記」（十四世紀末に編纂された）に記録されて
いる鎌倉武士の死であるが、それはかの恵林寺の禅僧と相ならんで、
武士道とくに死にたいする彼らの態度におよぼした影響を明らかに
するものであろう。

　北条高時の家臣の一人に塩飽新左近入道という鎌倉の武士階級の
なかではあまり身分の高くないものがあった。運つきたる主君に殉
じて自害せんとした時、

　　『嫡子三郎左衛門忠頼を呼び、諸方の攻口悉く破れ、御一門達大
　　略腹切らせ給ふと聞えければ、入道も守殿に先立ちまゐらせて、
　　其忠義を知られ奉らんと思ふなり。されば御辺は未私眷養にて、
　　公方の御恩をも蒙らねば、縦令一所にて今命を捨てずとも、人あ
　　ながち義を知らぬものとはよも思はじ。然ればいづくにも暫く身
　　を隠し、出家遁世の身ともなり、我後世を訪らひ、心安く一身の
　　生涯をくらせかしと、泪の中に宣ひければ、三郎左衛門忠頼も両
　　眼に泪を浮め、しばしば物も申されざりけるが、良ありて、是こ
　　そ仰セともおぼえ候はね、忠頼直に公方の御恩を蒙むりたることは
　　候はねども、一家の続命悉く是れ武恩にあらずといふ事なし。其

under the benevolent protection of his grace. If I already followed the life of monkhood, it would be a different matter. Having been born into the family of a samurai, how can I leave you and our master and save myself to become a monk? No shame is greater than this. If you are to share the destiny of our master, let me be your guide to the next world." Even before he finished his last sentence, he disembowled himself and gave up the ghost.

His brother Shiro observing this was seen hastily preparing to follow the example. But the father Nyūdō stopped this and said; "Do not be so hasty. You must follow order and wait for me." Shiro put his dagger back into its scabbard and sat meekly before his father waiting the latter's further command. The father now told him to bring him a chair. He sat in it cross-legged in the fashion of a Zen monk, and quietly making ink dipped his brush into it and wrote his song of death on a piece of paper;

"Holding forth this sword,
cut vacuity in twain;
In the midst of the great fire,
A stream of refreshing breeze!"

When he finished writing, he committed suicide like the brave samurai that he was, and Shiro completed the deed by cutting off his father's head in accordance with the samurai code of honour. As to himself, using the same sword he pierced his own body with it up to the hilt and fell forward on the ground dead.

There was another Zen warrior called Nagasaki Jiro Takashige at the time of the Hōjō downfall. He called on his Zen master who also happened to be the teacher of Hōjō Takatoki, and asked; "How should a brave warrior behave at a moment like this?" The Zen teacher at once gave this: "Go straightforward with your sword wielding!" The warrior at once perceived what it meant. He fought most gallantly until, exhausted, he fell before his master, Takatoki.

上忠頼幼少より釈門に至る身ならば、恩を棄てて無為に入る道も
しかなるべし。苟くも弓矢の家に生れ名を此門葉にかけながら、
武運の傾くを見て、時の難を遁れんがために、出塵の身となり
て、天下の人に指をさされん事、是に過ぎたる耻辱や候べき。御
腹召され候はば、冥途の御道しるべ仕り候はんといひも終てず、
袖の下より刀を抜きて偸かに腹に突き立てて、畏りたる体にて死
にける。其弟塩飽四郎是を見て、続きて腹を切らんとしけるを、
父の入道大いに諫めて、暫く吾を先立て、順次の孝専にし、其後
自害せよと申しければ、塩飽四郎抜きたる刀を収めて、父の入道
が前に畏りてぞ候ひける。是を見て、快げに打笑ひ、閑々と中門
に曲彔をかざらせて、其上に結跏趺坐し、硯取り寄せて、自ら
筆を染め辞世の頌をぞ書きたりける。

提‐持　吹‐毛
截‐断　虚‐空
大　火　聚　裏
一　道　清　風

と書きて、叉手して頭を伸べて、子息四郎に其討てと下知しけ
れば、大膚脱になりて、父の頭をうち落して、其太刀を取り直し
て、鐔本まで己が腹に突き貫きて、うつぶしさまにぞ臥したりけ
る。郎等三人是を見て走り寄り、同じ太刀に貫かれて、串に指し
たる魚肉の如く、頭を連ねて伏したりける。』

(太平記巻十)

　北条氏滅亡のとき、いま一人長崎次郎高重という禅武士がいた。
彼は彼の師で北条高時の師でもあった禅匠を訪ねて問うた。『如何
なるか是勇士恁麼の事。』（このような大事のとき勇士はいかに振
舞ったらいいでしょうか。）禅師はただちに答えた。『吹毛急に用ひ
て前まんに如かず。』（刀を振りまわして真直ぐに進め。）この武士
はただちにその意を悟った。彼は最も勇敢に闘い、ついに力尽きて、

This was indeed the kind of spirit Zen cultivated among its warrior-followers. Zen did not necessarily argue with them about immortality of soul, or about righteousness of the divine way, or about ethical conduct, but it simply urged to go ahead with whatever conclusion rational or irrational a man has arrived at. Philosophy may safely be left with intellectual minds; Zen wants to act, and the most effective act is, once the mind is made up, to go on without looking backward. In this respect, Zen is indeed the religion of the samurai warrior.

"To die *isagi-yoku*" is one of the thoughts very dear to the Japanese heart. In some deaths, if this characteristic is present, crimes committed by the offenders are judged even charitably. *Isagi-yoku* means "leaving no regrets," "with a clear conscience," "like a brave man," "with no reluctance," "in full possession of mind," and so on. The Japanese hate to see a death irresolutely and lingeringly met with, they desire to be blown away like the cherries before the wind, and no doubt this Japanese attitude towards death must have gone very well with the teaching of Zen. The Japanese may not have any specific philosophy of life, but they have decidedly one of death which may sometimes appear to be that of recklessness. The spirit of the samurai deeply breathing Zen into itself propagated its philosophy even among the masses. The latter, even when they are not particularly trained in the way of the warrior, have imbibed his spirit and are ready to sacrifice their lives for any cause they think worthy. This has repeatedly been proved in the wars Japan has so far had to go through for one reason or another. A foreign writer on Japanese Buddhism aptly remarks that Zen is the Japanese character.

主君高時の前に倒れた。

　この種の精神が、じつに、禅が武士修禅者の間に養ったものであった。禅はかならずしも霊魂の不滅や神の道の義しさや倫理的行為については彼らと議論をしなかったが、ただ合理・非合理いかなる結論にもせよ、人がそれに達したものをもって突進することを説いた。哲学は知的精神の所有者によって安全に保存せられてよい。禅は行動することを欲する。最も有効な行動は、ひとたび決心した以上、振りかえらずに進むことである。この点において禅はじつに武士の宗教である。

「潔く死ぬ」ということは、日本人の心に最も親しい思想の一つである、死にようにはさまざまあることだが、この特性が存するときは罪人の犯した罪さえ寛大に裁かれる傾きがある。「潔く」は「悔を残さずに」「明らかな良心をもって」「勇士らしく」「ためらうことなく」「落着払って」などの意味である。日本人は思い切りわるくぐずぐずして死を迎えるのを嫌う。風に吹かれる桜のように散り逝くことを欲する。たしかに日本人のこの死に対する態度は禅の教えと一致したに違いない。日本人は別段、生の哲学は持たないかもしれぬが、たしかに死の哲学は持っている。時とするとそれは一見、向う見ずの哲学であるようにも思われよう。禅を深く吸込んでいる武士の精神はその哲学をまた庶民の間にまで拡げた。庶民は自分たちがとくに武士の仕方で鍛錬されていないときでもその精神を吸込んでいて、正しいと考えるいかなる理由のためにも、自分の命を犠牲にする覚悟をしている。これは従来、日本がなにかの理由で飛込まねばならなかった諸戦争で、しばしば証明せられてきたことである。日本の仏教に関して書いている外国の一記者は、禅は日本的性格だと適切な言を吐いている。

（註、サー・チャーレス・エリオット大使著「日本仏教」）

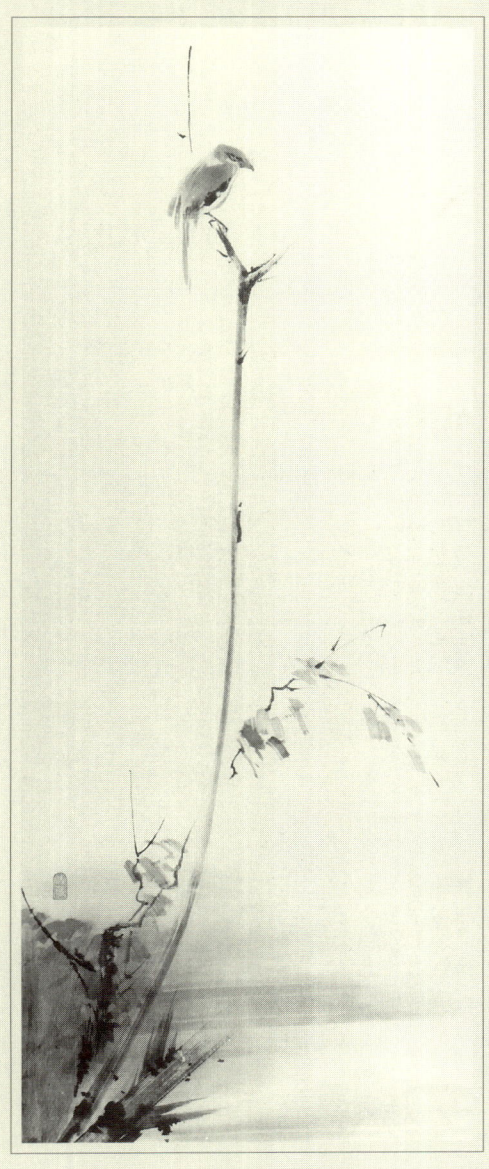

"A Singing Bird on a Dead Branch" by Miyamoto Musashi.

宮本武蔵作「枯木鳴鵙図」。

Zen and Swordsmanship
禅と剣道

卍

1

"The sword is the soul of the samurai": therefore, when the samurai is the subject of a talk of any kind, the sword inevitably comes with it. The samurai is asked, when he wishes to be faithful to his vocation, to rise above the question of birth and death, and to be ready at any moment to lay down his life, which means either to expose himself before the striking sword of the enemy or to direct his own towards himself. The sword thus comes most intimately connected with the life of the samurai, and has become the symbol of loyalty and self-sacrifice. The reverence paid universally to it in various ways proves it.

The sword has thus a double office to perform: the one is to destroy anything that opposes the will of its owner, and the other is to sacrifice all the impulses that arise from the instinct of self-preservation. The former relates itself with the spirit of patriotism or militarism, while the other has a religious connotation of loyalty and self-sacrifice. In the case of the former very frequently the sword may mean destruction pure and simple, it is then the symbol of force, sometimes perhaps devilish. It must therefore be controlled and consecrated by the second function. Its conscientious owner has been always mindful of this truth. For then destruction is tuned against the

卍

一

「刀は武士の魂である。」それゆえ、武士がなにかの話題になる時
にはきっと、刀がこれに伴う。武士がその務めに忠実たらんと欲す
る時は、生死の問題を乗りこえ、いつでも自分の命を投げだす覚悟
が要る。それは敵の白刃に身を曝らすか、あるいはまた、己の刀を
己に擬することを意味する。刀はかく武士の生命と最も密接に結び
つくこととなり、忠と自己犠牲の象徴となった。日本人がいろいろ
の仕方で、ひろく刀に対して尊敬を払うということが、それを証拠
立てている。

　刀には、かくして、果すべき二重の務めがある。一は持主の意志
に反するいかなるものをも、破壊することであり、一は自己保存の
本能から起る一切の衝動を犠牲にすることである。前者は愛国主義
や軍国三義の精神と関係し、後者は忠と自己犠牲という宗教的な意
義を持つ。前者の場合、しばしば刀は単純に破壊を意味する。その
ときは力、時として悪魔的な力の象徴である。それゆえそれは第二
の機能によって抑制され、聖化されなければならぬ。良心的な持主
はいつもこの真理を心掛けてきた。そうする時には破壊は悪魔の方
に転じられるからである。刀は平和・正義・進歩・人道の妨げをな

evil spirit. The sword comes to be identified with the annihilation of things which lie in the way of peace, justice, progress, and humanity. It stands for all that is desirable for the spiritual welfare of the world at large. It is now the embodiment of life and not of death.

Zen speaks of the sword of life and the sword of death, and it is the work of a great Zen master to know when and how to wield either of them. Mañjusrī carries a sword in his right hand and a sūtra in his left. This may remind us of the prophet Mahomet, but the sacred sword of Mañjusrī is not to murder any sentient beings, but our own Greed, Anger, and Folly. It is directed towards ourselves, for when this is done the outside world which is the reflection of what is within us becomes also free from Greed, Anger, and Folly. Achala (Fudō Myōwō) also carries a sword, and will destroy all the enemies who oppose the prevalence of the Buddhist virtues. Mañjusrī is positive while Achala is negative. Achala's anger burns like a fire and will not be put down until it burns up the last camp of the enemy: he will then assume his original features and be Vairochana Buddha again whose servant and manifestation he is. Vairochana holds no sword, he is the sword itself, sitting alone with all the worlds within himself. In the following *mondo*," the one sword" signifies this; Kusunoki Masashige (1294–1336) came to a Zen monastery at Hyogo when he was about to meet the overwhelming army of Ashikaga Takauji at the Minatogawa, and asked the master: "When a man is at the parting of the ways between life and death, how would be behave?" Answered the master," Cut off your dualism, and let the one sword stand serenely by itself against the sky!" This absolute"one sword"is neither the sword of life nor the sword of death, it is the sword from which this world of dualities issues and in which they all have their being, it is Vairochana Buddha himself. You take hold of him, and you know how to behave where the ways part.

The sword now represents the force or the straight-forwardness of the

す諸物を全滅させることと同一だ、ということになる。ひろく世界の精神的安寧のために望ましい一切のものに味方する。それはいまや、生の体現であって死の体現ではない。

　禅は活人剣と殺人刀ということを語る。そのいずれを、いつ、いかなる風に、使うべきかを知るのは、すぐれた禅匠の働きである。文珠菩薩は、右手に剣を、左手に経典をもつ。これは予言者マホメットを想起させる。しかし、文珠菩薩の聖なる剣は、生きものを殺すためではなくて、われわれ自身の貪慾・瞋恚・愚癡を殺すためである。それはゎれわれに向って擬せられる。こうするのは、われわれの内部にあるものの反映であるところの外界の世界も、また、貪慾・瞋恚・愚癡から自由にされるからである。不動明王もまた、剣を持って、仏徳の流行を阻むいっさいの敵を滅さんとする。文珠は積極的で、不動は消極的である。不動の憤怒は火のごとく燃え、敵の最後の陣営を焼き尽すまでは消えない。しかる後にふたたび元の容相をとり、彼がその侍者であり、示顕であるところの盧舎那仏となる。盧舎那仏は剣を持たぬ。彼は剣そのもので、その内に全世界を容れつつ、寂然として不動なのである。つぎの「一剣」問答がこれを意味する。楠正成（1294–1336）が湊川で足利尊氏の大軍を迎えようとしたとき、兵庫のある禅院にきて、和尚に尋ねた。
　『生死交謝の時如何』（人が生死の岐路に立った時はいかにしたらいいでしょうか。）
　和尚が答えた。
　『両頭ともに截断すれば、一剣天に倚つて寒し。』（お前の二元論を断切れ。一本の剣だけを静かに天に向って立たせよ。）
　この絶対的な「一剣」は、生の剣でも、死の剣でもない。そこから二元の世界が生じ、また、そこにおいて生死一切がその存在を持つところの、剣である。それは盧舎那仏自体である。これを把握するならば、路の岐れるところにおいて、いかに振舞うべきかを知るのである。
　剣は、いまや、宗教的直観の力や直進をあらわす。この直観は智

religious intuition, which, unlike the intellect, does not divide itself so as to block up its own passageway. It marches onward without looking backward or sideways. It is like Chwang-tsu's dissecting knife which cuts through the joints as if the latter were waiting for it to be separated. Chwang-tsu would say then: The joints separate by themselves, and then the knife, even after many years of usage, is as sharp as when it first came from the hands of the grinder. The One Sword of Reality never wears out after cutting up ever so many victims of selfishness.

The sword is also connected with Shinto in which, however, I do not think as in Buddhism it has attained a highly developed spiritual signification. It still betrays its naturalistic origin. It is not a symbol, but an object endowed with some spiritualistic power. In the feudal days of Japan the samurai class cherished this kind of idea towards the sword, although it is difficult to define exactly what was going on in their minds. At least they paid the utmost respect to it; at the samurai's death it was placed beside his bed, and when a child was born it found its place in the room. The idea was to prevent any evil spirit from entering into the room which might interfere with the safety and happiness of the departed spirit or of the coming spirit. Here lingers an animistic way of thinking. The idea of "sacred sword" too may be interpreted in this way.

It is noteworthy that the swordsmith invoked when making swords the aid of a guardian god. To invite him to the workshop, the smith surrounds it with consecrated ropes, thus excluding the intrusion of evil spirits, while the smith himself goes through the ceremony of absolution and dons the ceremonial dress in which he works. While striking the iron-bar and giving it fiery and watery baths the smith and his helper are in the most intensi-fied state of mind. Confident in the help of the god which will be given in their work, they exert themselves to the limits of their power, mental, physical, and spiritual. The sword thus produced is really a work of art and must reflect something of the spirit of the artist. This is probably the reason why there is something in the Japanese sword deeply appealing to the soul

力とは異なり、分離してそれ自身の通路を塞いでしまうようなことはない。うしろもわきも顧みないで前へ進む。関節を切断する「荘子」の解剖刀のごときもので、あたかも関節の方で、分離されるため刀を待っているかのようである。荘子はいつもこういったものだ。『関節が独りでに離れる。解剖刀は、長年使ったのだが、まるで研師の手から渡されたばかりのときと同じように、よく切れる。』と。「真実在の一剣」は幾多の利己心という犠牲を切った後でも、磨滅するということをけっして知らぬ。

　剣はまた、神道とも繋がりがあるが、しかし、仏教ほど高度に発展した精神的な意義に達したとは思えぬ。それはなお、自然主義的な起原をあらわしている。神道の剣は象徴ではなくて、ある精神的な力を具有した物体である。日本の封建時代には、武士階級は剣にたいしてこの種の観念を抱いた。もっとも、彼らがいかに考えていたかを的確に定義することは難しくはあるが。少くとも、彼らは剣に対して最高の敬意を払った。武士が死ぬときには剣はその床のかたわらに置かれ、子供が生れたときにも、その室にあった。離れ逝く霊や生れくる霊の安全と幸福を妨げる悪魔が、その室に入ってくるのを防ぐという観念であった。この点に万物有霊論的な考え方が残っている。「神剣」の観念もまた、この方面から解釈されるだろう。

　刀鍛冶が刀を作るときに、守り神の助けを祈るということは注目するにたる。神を鍛冶場に招くために、鍛冶匠はそこに注連縄を張りめぐらして悪魔の侵入を排し、自分は祓の式を行い、礼服を着用して、仕事をする。鉄棒を打ってそれを火に入れ水に入れる間、鍛冶匠とその助手は最も集注した心理状態に入るのである。彼らの仕事に神助が与えられることをかたく信じ、彼らは智力・体力・精神力のかぎりをつくして努める。かくして製作された刀は真に芸術品であって、作家の精神をなにかしら反映するに違いない。おそらくこういう理由で、日本刀には、人々の魂に深く喰入るものがあるのであろう。彼らはまことにそれを、破壊の武器としてではなく、霊　感の対象として見るのである。刀工正宗の作品に関する伝説

of the people. They look at it indeed not as a weapon of destruction but as an object of inspiration. Hence the legend of Masamune the swordsmith regarding his products.

Masamune flourished in the latter part of the Kamakura era, and his works are uniformly prized by all the sword connoisseurs for their high qualities. As far as the sharpness of the blade is concerned, Masamune may not exceed Muramasa, one of his ablest disciples, but the former is said to have something morally inspiring which comes from his personality. The legend goes thus: When someone was trying to test the sharpness of a Muramasa he placed it in a current of water watching how it behaved against the dead leaves flowing down from the upper part of the stream. He saw every one of the leaves which met the blade was cut in twain. He then placed a Masamune and was surprised to find that the leaves avoided the blade. The Masamune was not bent on killing, it was more than a cutting machine; but the Muramasa could not go beyond the latter quality, there was notning divinely inspiring in it. The Muramasa is terrible, but the Masamune is humane. The first is despotic and imperialistic whereas the second is superhuman if we could use this form of expression. Masamune almost never engraved his name on the hilt although this was customary with swordsmiths.

The Noh-Play "Kokaji" gives us some idea about the moral and religious significance of the sword among the Japanese. The play was probably composed in the Ashikaga era. The Emperor Ichijō (reigned 986–1011) once ordered a sword to be made by Kokaji Munechika who was one of the great swordsmiths of the day. Munechika felt greatly honoured, but he could not fill the order unless he had an able assistant equal in skill to himself. He prayed to the god of Inari who was his guardian god to send him someone fully competent for work. In the meantime he prepared his sacred platform in due accordance with the traditional rites. When all the process of purification was completed, he offered this prayer; "The work I am going to undertake is not just for my selfish glorification; it is to obey the august

もそこからでるのである。

　正宗は鎌倉時代の後半にさかえた。彼の作品はその優れた質のために刀剣の蒐集家からひとしく賞せられている。切れ味に関するかぎりでは、正宗は彼の高弟の一人なる村正にはおよばぬかも知れぬが、正宗には、正宗の人格からくる何か精神的に人を打つものがあるといわれている。伝説というのはこうだ。ある人が村正の切れ味を試めそうと思って、水流にそれをおき、上流から流れてくる枯葉にむかって、どうするかを見守った。刃に出会った枯葉は、どれも二つに切られた。彼は、今度は、正宗を立てたが、上から流れてくる木の葉はその刃に触れる事を避けて行った。これは驚くべき実験であった。正宗は人を斬るということに関心を持たなかった。それは切る道具以上のものだった。しかし村正は切るということ以外にでられなかった。村正には、心を打つような神聖なものは、なにもなかった。村正はおそろしいが、正宗は人情味（ヒューメン）がある。村正は専制的であるが、正宗は超人間的だ。もしこういう風の表現形式が用いられるとすれば、柄（つか）に銘を刻むのは刀工の習慣であったが、正宗はほとんどこれをやらなかった。

　能楽に「小鍛冶（こかじ）」がある。これは日本人間における刀の道徳的・宗教的意義について、ある示唆をあたえる。この謡曲はおそらく足利時代に作られたものであろう。一条天皇が当時の名工の一人なる小鍛冶宗近に一刀を作るように命じ給うた。宗近はいたくその光栄に感激したが、自分と技倆が伯仲する有能な助手がえられぬので、御意を果すことができなかった。彼は彼の守護神である稲荷神に、この仕事の十分できるような者を遣わされんことを祈った。それから彼は伝統的な式に正しくしたがって祭壇を設けた。浄め（祓）の順序が一切終ったとき、彼はつぎの祈りを捧げた。『私がこれからしたがおうとする仕事は、一身の栄達のためではありません。この世界全体を統べ治め給う帝の仰せを畏み奉るためです。恒河の砂ほ

order of the emperor who reigns over the entire world. I pray to all the gods numbering as many as the sands of the Ganga to come here and give their help to this humble Munechika who is now going to do his utmost to produce a sword worthy of the virtue of the august patron. Looking upwards to the sky and prostrating himself on the ground, he offers this *nusa* to the gods symbolic of his most earnest desire to accomplish the work successfully. Would the god have pity on his sincerity!" A voice is now heard from somewhere; "Pray, pray, O Munechika, in all humbleness and in all earnestness. The time is come to strike the iron. Trust the gods and the work will be done." A mysterious figure appeared before him and he was helped in striking the sword, which came out of the forge in due time with every desirable mark of perfection and auspiciousness. The emperor was pleased with the sword worthy to be treasured as sacred and merit-producing.

As something of divinity enters into the making of the sword, its owner and user ought also to respond to the inspiration. He ought to be a spiritual man, and not an agent of brutality. His mind ought to be in unison with the soul which animates the cold surface of the steel. The great swordsmen have never been tired of instilling this feeling into the minds of their pupils. When the Japanese say that the sword is the soul of the samurai, we must remember all that goes with it as I have tried to describe above, that is: loyalty, self-sacrifice, reverence, benevolence, and the cultivation of religious feelings. Here is the true samurai.

2

It was natural therefore for the samurai who carried two swords—the longer one for attack and defense and the shorter one for self-destruction when necessary—to train himself with utmost zeal in the art of swordsmanship. He could never be separated from the weapon which was really the symbol of his dignity and honour more than anything else. The training in the use of it was, besides its practical purposes, conducive to his moral and

どに数多い神々のすべてに祈る。ここにきたりて、尊貴至上の庇護者の徳にふさわしき剣を作らんと全力を尽すこの賤しき宗近に、一臂の力を与え給わんことを。天を仰ぎ地に伏して、この仕事を立派に成就せんとする、熾烈な願いを象徴するこの幣を捧げ奉る。この誠実に憐みを垂れ給わんことを。』そのとき一つの声がどこからか聞えてきた。『祈れ、宗近よ、心を空しゅうし、誠を尽くして祈れ。鉄を打つときがきた。神々を信頼せよ。仕事は成就されるであろう。』神秘的な姿が、彼の前に現れ、彼が刀を打つのを助けた。最後の仕上げのときがきたとき、刀はこの上なき完全さと、瑞兆の姿をみせて、炉のなかから現れた。帝は、神聖にして勲功めでたかるべきこの宝刀に対して、大きな満足を表せられた。

　刀剣の製作には、神徳の幾分かが加るから、持主と使い手は、当然、かかる霊感（インスピレーション）に呼応せねばならぬ。日本刀を帯するものは、精神的な人間たるべくして、獣性の代表者たるべきではない。彼の心は、鋼鉄の冷たさを表面に表わしながら、そのなかに生ける魂を蔵するものとしなければならぬ。すぐれた剣士はこの感情を弟子の心に吹込んで、倦むところを知らぬ。日本人が「刀は武士の魂だ」という時、自分が右に述べようとした一切のこと、すなわち、忠・自己犠牲・尊敬・恩愛および宗教的感情の涵養などがこれに伴うということを記憶しなければならぬ。ここに真の武士が存する。

<h1 style="text-align:center">二</h1>

　それゆえ、攻撃と防禦のための大刀（だいとう）、必要のときには自害をするための小刀（しょうとう）、この大小長短の二刀を帯びた武士にとっては、剣道の技はきわめて熱心に錬磨せらるべきものであることは当然であった。彼はなににもまして彼の威厳と名誉の象徴であるこの武器から、けっして離れることはできなかった。それを使用するための鍛錬は、実用的目的のほかに、道徳的と精神的の目的を助成した。この点に

spiritual equipments. It was here that the swordsman joined hands with Zen. Although this fact has already been demonstrated to a certain extent, I wish to give here further quotations quite illuminative of the intimate relationship between Zen and the sword.

The following is Takuan's letter to Yagyū Tajima-no-kami concerning the relationship between Zen and the art of swordsmanship. It is entitled "On Immovable Intelligence." A very concise resumé of it was given in one of my books on Zen. As it is too long to make a complete translation of the original, I have condensed it here, but all its principal ideas are preserved. It is an important document in more than one way, as it touches upon the essential teaching of Zen as well as the secrets of art generally. In Japan, perhaps as in other countries too, mere technical knowledge of an art is not enough to make a man really a master of it, he ought to have delved deeply into the spirit of it. This spirit is grasped only when his mind is in complete resonance with the principle of life itself, that is, when he attains to the mysterious state of mind known as *mushin*, "no-mind-ness." In Buddhist phraseology, it is going beyond the dualism of life and death. this is where all arts merge into Zen. Takuan in this letter to the great master of swordmanship forcibly emphasizes the importance of *mushin*, which may be regarded in a way corresponding to the conception of the Unconscious. Psychologically speaking, this state of mind is that of absolute passivity in which the mind gives itself up unreservedly to another "power;" here one becomes an automaton, so to speak, as far as the consciousness is concerned. But, as Takuan explains, it ought not to be confused with the insensibility and helpless passivity of an inorganic substance such as a piece of rock or a block of wood. "To be unconsciously conscious"—there is no other way to describe this mental state than this appalling paradox.

Takuan on "Immovable Intelligence"

Buddhism marks fifty-two stages of spiritual development, one of which

おいて剣士は禅と提携したのであった。この事実はある程度すでに説述されているが、自分はここにさらに禅と剣との間の親しい関係をよく明らかにする幾つかの引用文をあげたいと思う。

　つぎに示すのは禅と剣道との関係について柳生但馬守に送った沢庵和尚の書翰である。それは「不動智神妙録」と題されている。*これは剣道一般の秘訣を説くのみならず、禅の根本義にもふれているから、いろいろの意味で、重要な文献である。日本では、おそらくは他の国でもそうだろうが、単に芸術を技術的に知るだけでは、真にそれを熟達するには不十分である。その精神に深く入らなければいかぬ。この精神は、彼の心が生命それ自体の原則と完全に共鳴したときにのみ、すなわち、「無心」として知られる「神秘的」な心理状態に達するときにのみ、把握される。仏教の語義からいうと、それは死生の二元論を超越することである。ここに至れば一切の芸術は禅となってしまうのである。沢庵はこのすぐれた剣士にあたえた書翰のなかに無心の意義をきわめて強調している。無心はある点において、「無意識（アンコンシャス）」の概念にあたると見てよい。心理的にいえば、この心の状態は絶対受動のもので、心が惜しみなく他の「力」に身をゆだねるのである。この点で、人は意識に関するかぎりいわば自動人形になるのである。しかし、沢庵が説くように、それは木石などの非有機的な物質の無感覚性および頼りない受動性と混同してはならぬ。「無意識に意識すること」——この目もくらむばかりの逆説（パラドクス）以外に、この心的状態を叙述する道はない。

　　　沢 庵『不 動 智 神 妙 録』

　仏教の示すところによると、精神発展の段階が五十二あり、その

is known as "stopping" where one becomes attached to a point and is unable to move on freely. You have something corresponding to it in your sword-play:

When your opponent is at the point of striking you, let your mind be fixed on his sword, and you are no more free to be master of your own movements, for you are then controlled by him. This I call "stopping," because you are made to stop at one point. On the other hand, you notice the opponent's sword moving towards you, but your attention is not glued to it, you have no special discriminating design on your part as to how to deal with it, you simply follow it up to the opponent's own person, and this is said to defeat him by his own weapon. There is a statement in Zen Buddhism to the same effect: "Seize the enemy's own sword and turn it around and strike him with it." Where your attention is arrested even for a moment either by the sword in the enemy's hands, or by your own sword thinking how to use it, or by personality or weapon or time or movement, you are sure to give an opportunity to the enemy to strike. Nor do you feel concerned with the opposition between yourself and the enemy, for the latter then takes advantage of you; therefore have no thought even of yourself. To try to be on the alert, to have your attention keyed up to the highest pitch—this is all well for beginners, but it will end in your mind being carried away by the sword. When your attention is caught in one way or another, you lose your mastership. This "stopping" is to be avoided in Buddhism as well as in your art of fencing.

There is what is known as Immovable Intelligence in everyone of us. This is to be exercised. "Immovable" does not mean to remain like a rock or a tree which betrays no intelligence. Immovable Intelligence is the most movable thing in the world; it is ready to turn in every possible direction

一つを「止る」といい、それに至ると人は一点に定着して、自由に動くことができなくなる。剣道にもこれにあたるものがある。この段階を沢庵は無明住地煩悩といっている。

　　無明住地煩悩

　　無明とは、明になしと申す文字にて候。迷を申し候。その五十二位の内に、物毎に心の止る所を、住地と申し候。住は止ると申す義理にて候。止ると申すは、何事に付ても其事に心を止るを申し候。貴殿の兵法にて申し候はば、*向ふより切る太刀を一目見て、其儘にてそこにて合はんと思へば、向ふの太刀に其儘に心が止まりて、手前の働きが抜け候て、向ふの人に切られ候。是を止ると申し候。打太刀を見る事は見れども、そこに心をとめず、向ふの打つ太刀に拍子を合せて、打たうとも思はず、思案分別を残さず、振上る太刀を見るや否や、心を卒度止めず、其まま付け入て、向ふの太刀にとりつかば、我をきらんとする刀を、我が方へもぎとりて、却て向ふを切る刀となるべく候。禅宗には是を還把＿槍頭＿倒刺レ人来ると申し候。鎗はほこにて候。人の持ちたる刀を我が方へもぎとりて、還て相手を切ると申す心に候。貴殿の無力と仰せられ候事にて候。向ふから打つとも、吾から討つとも、打つ人にも打つ太刀にも、程にも拍子にも、卒度も心を止れば、手前の働は皆抜け候て、人にきられ可レ申候。敵に我心を置けば、敵に心をとられ候間、我身にも心を置くべからず。我身に心を引しめて置くも、初心の間、習入り候時の事なるべし。太刀に心をとられ候。拍子合に心を置けば、拍子合に心をとられ候。我太刀に心を置けば、我太刀に心をとられ候。これ皆心のとまりて、手前抜殻になり申し候。貴殿御覚之可レ有候。仏法と引当て申すにて候。仏法には、此止る心を迷と申し候。故に無明住地煩悩と申すことにて候。

　　諸 仏 不 動 智

と申す事。不動とは、うごかずといふ文字にて候。智は智慧の智にて候。不動と申し候ても、石か木かのやうに、無性なる義理にてはなく候。向ふへも、左へも、右へも、十方八方へ、心は動き

and yet it has no "stopping" points. Fudō, the God of Immovable Intelligence (*Acalavidyārāja*), holds a sword in his right hand and a rope in his left; and his teeth are rigidly set, his eyes are glaring with anger; he threatens such evil spirits as attempt to do harm to Buddhism. He symbolises Immovable Intelligence, he is no real existence having a fixed abode somewhere on earth, he assumes this form in order to be a protector of Buddhism against all its enemies. Ordinary people fail to understand the significance of this figure, while those aspiring for enlightenment realise it and endeavour to dispel their ignorance and confusion in order to feel its presence in their own persons. Fudō stands for Immovable Intelligence which is our own mind remaining forever tranquil and yet mobile all the time. "Immovable" means not to be upset, not to fix one's attention at one point and make it "stop" there, which prevents it from moving on to points that rapidly follow one after another. As soon as an object appears before you, you naturally perceive it, but you are not to "stop" with it; for if you do, all sorts of discrimination crowd into your mind, each contending for supremacy. When you try to quiet them down, the mind will all the more be put to confusion.

When you find yourself surrounded by opponents each one of whom is trying to strike you with his sword, you just parry it and move on from one sword to another without "stopping" at any one particular sword which is directed at you. You then are able to meet them on an equal footing. If, on the contrary, your attention is arrested by one and refuses to be transferred to another, you thereby give yourself up to the mercy of your opponents. You must keep your mind completely free from being caught by one particular object so that it can retain its natural motility.

In the case of Kwannon Bosatsu provided with one thousand arms you may think how he can make use of so many of them. That is true if his mind "stops," for instance, with the bow he has in one of his hands, for then the mind is incapacitated to work with the remaining nine hundred and ninety-nine arms. But because of its not being made to "stop" at any one of the objects he carries, he is successful with everyone of them. When Immovable Intelligence

度きやうに動きながら、卒度も止らぬ心を、不動智と申し候。不動明王と申して、右の手に剣を握り、左の手に縄を取りて、歯を喰出し、目を怒らし、仏法を妨げん悪魔を、降伏せんとて突立て居られ候姿も、あの様なるが、何国の世界にもかくれて居られ候にてはなし。容をば、仏法守護の形につくり、体をば、この不動智を体として、衆生に見せたるにて候。一向の凡夫は、怖れをなして仏法に仇をなさじと思ひ、悟に近き人は、不動智を表したる所を悟りて、一切の迷を晴らし、即ち不動智を明めて、此身則ち不動明王程に、此心法をよく執行したる人は、悪魔もいやまさぬぞと、知らせん為めの不動明王にて候。然れば不動明王と申すも、人の一心の動かぬ所を申し候。又身を動転せぬことにて候。動転せぬとは、物毎に留まらぬ事にて候。物一目見て、其心を止めぬを不動と申し候。なぜなれば、物に心が止り候へば、いろいろの分別が胸に候間、胸のうちにいろいろ動き候。止れば止る心は、動きても動かぬにて候。

　譬へば、十人して一太刀づつ我へ太刀を入るるも、一太刀を受流して、跡に心を止めず、跡を捨て跡を拾ひ候はば、十人ながらへ働を欠かさぬにて候。十人十度心は働けども、一人にても心を止めずば、次第に取合ひて、働は欠け申す間敷候。若し又一人の前に心が止り候はば、一人の打太刀をば受流すべけれども、二人めの時は、手前の働き抜け可レ申候。

　千手観音とて手が千御入り候はば、弓を取る手に心が止らば、九百九十九の手は皆用に立ち申す間敷、一所に心を止めぬにより、手が皆、用に立つなり。観音とて身一つに千の手が何れに可レ有候。不動智が開け候へば、身に手が千有りても、皆、用に立つと云ふ事を、人に示さんが為めに、作りたる容にて候。

is awakened in you, you can work such miracles. Kwannon really has no use for so many arms, the idea is to show that when Immovable Intelligence is awakened in us we can use any number of arms each to its best advantage.

Here is a tree with so many branches and leaves, and if one's mind is stopped by one of the leaves, it cannot see all the rest. Instead of this, let us stand before the tree without any preconception or fixation of attention, and we can take cognisance of every one of its leaves. Therefore, have no "stopping" at any single point which is cut out of the whole stretch of being. Those who do not perceive this truth bow before Kwannon imagining him to be a wonderful deity with one thousand arms or one thousand eyes. Those who claim their little knowledge declare that there are no such beings as Kwannon with so many arms, that it is all fiction. But the truth is that the wise know much better than blind worshippers as well as iconoclasts. The former in some respects are better than the latter; the thing is that we ought to realise the truth hidden in all these ideas. When they are analysed to the last degree, they are seen to be issuing from one ultimate experience.

When you have your Immovable Intelligence awakened, you come back in a sense to the point where you first started. Enlightenment is after all something like Ignorance itself. Here you regain your original naivité. In your art of swordsmanship the beginner knows nothing about how to hold the sword, how to fortify himself, and so on. Therefore, he is quite free from the "stopping "attitude of mind; when the opponent tries to strike him, he simply parries. But as soon as he begins to be taught it the art and to know many things about it, he loses as it were his former confidence, his mind is made to "stop "at various points, and he is altogether uneasy. He is training for many years, he masters the art, he is no more concerned with its particulars, all is natural with him, he is now himself again as he was before. It is like counting numbers. When you have finished counting up to ten you begin again with one; one and ten are neighbours now.

† This reminds us of the story of the centipede. When it was asked how it could move so many legs all at once and all in coordination, the question made it "stop"

仮令、一本の木に向うて、其中の赤き葉一つを見て居れば、残りの葉は見えぬなり。葉一つに眼をかけずして、一本の木に何心もなく打ち向ひ候へば、数多の葉残らず目に見え候。葉一つに心をとられ候はば、残りの葉は見えず、一つに心を止めねば、百千の葉みな見え申し候。是を得心したる人は、即ち千手千眼の観音にて候。然るを一向の凡夫は、唯一筋に、身一つに千の手千の眼が御座して　難レ有と信じ候。又なまものじりなる人は、身一つに千の眼が、何しにあるらん、虚言よ。と破り譏る也。今少し能く知れば、凡夫の信ずるにても破るにてもなく、道理の上にて尊信し、仏法はよく一物にして其理を顕はす事にて候。諸道ともに斯様のものにて候。神道は別して其道と見及び候。有のままにて思ふも凡夫、又打破ればなほ悪し。其内に道理ある事にて候。この道、かの道さまざまに候へども、極所は落着き候。

　さて初心の地より修行して不動智の位に至れば、立帰て、住地の初心の位へ落つべき仔細御入り候。貴殿の兵法にて可レ申候。初心は身に持つ太刀の構へも何も知らぬものなれば、身に心の止る事もなし。人が打ち候へば、つひ取合ふばかりにて、何の心もなし。然る処にさまざまの事を習ひ、身に持つ太刀の取様、心の置所、いろいろの事を教へぬれば、色々の処に心が止り、　人を打たんとすれば、兎や角して、殊の外不自由なる事、日を重ね年月をかさね、稽古をするに従ひ、後は身の構へも太刀の取様も、みな心のなくなりて、唯最初の、何もしらず習はぬ時の、心の様になる也。是れ初と終と同じやうになる心持にて、一から十までかぞへまはせば、一と十と隣になり申し候。……

（原註）この事は私に百足の話を思い出させる。百足が、どうしてそんなにたくさんの脚を、一時に揃えて動かすことができるのか、と尋ねられた時、

and think about it. This stopping and thinking caused great disconcert among the legs, each trying to move in its own way. The centipede then lost its life. Chwang-tsu's story of Chaos (*hun-lun*) will also be found quite interesting in this connection.

It is the same with Buddhist discipline. When you reach the highest stage of it you may be likened to a simple-minded child who knows nothing of the Buddha, nothing of the Dharma. You are free from self-conceit, from hypocrisy. You can then say that Immovable Intelligence is after all Ignorance—they are not two but one, for here there is no discriminating intellect which makes a man hesitate in the choice of one point against another and therefore no "stopping" anywhere which is so harmful to the mastery of the state of mind known as "no-thought" (*mushin* or *munen*). The ignorant have not yet awakened their Intelligence and therefore they retain their naïvité. The wise have gone to the end of their intellection, and therefore they no more resort to it. The two are in a way good neighbours. Only those of "half knowledge" have their heads filled with discriminations.

There are two kinds of discipline, the first one in Ultimate Reason and the other in technique. The first is as aforesaid to reach the ultimate reason of things where there are no scheduled regulations directing your action; there is just One Mind which goes on its own way. But the mastery of technical details is also necessary; when you have no knowledge of them, you are therefore to know, in your case, how to handle the sword, how to make a thrust, what positions to take in actual engagements, and so on. Both forms of discipline are needed, they are like two wheels of a cart.

There is a phrase we frequently use, "Not a hair allowed between," which means immediacy of response. When the hands are clapped a sound issues from the impact with not a minute's delay; there is not a hair's breadth between the two events. The sound makes no cogitation as to whether it will come out or not when the hands are clapped, it immediately follows the clapping. When the opponent's sword falls on you, if your mind "stops" at it, there is an interval which is instantly turned into the opponent's own advan-

その間が百足を「止め」て、それについて考えさせた。この「止る」ことと考えることが、脚の間に大混乱を起して、めいめい勝手に動こうとした。百足はそれで命を失った。荘子の渾沌の話＊も、これに関連して、はなはだ興味があろう。

仏教徒の修業も同じことである。その最高の段階に到達すれば、仏陀のことも、法のことも、なにも知らぬ無邪気な子供と同じようになれよう。自己欺瞞からも、偽善からも、自由になる。しかるときは、不動智は、結局、無智であり——両者は二ならず、一である、ということができる。ここには、ある点に対して、ある点を選択する際に、人を躊躇させるところの、分別智というものがなく、したがって、無念無想という心境の熟達にとって有害な、「止まる」ということが、どこにも存しないからである。無智の人は、智力をいまだ目ざまさぬから、素朴のままにある。賢い人は智力のかぎりを尽くしているから、もはや、それに頼らない。両者は睦まじい隣り同志である。「生ま知り」の人にかぎって、頭を分別でいっぱいにする。

二種の修業がある。一は究竟理性に関し、一は技術に関するものである。(訳註、沢庵はこの二つを理の修業、事の修業と称している)前者は、前にいったように、行動を図表にした規定で律することなどないところの、究竟理性に到達するためである。ここにはただ自ら進んでゆく「唯一心」があるだけである。しかし、技術約な細かい事の熟達も必要である。その知識が少しもないと、目前の仕事に関していかに歩を進むべきかを見ることができない。それゆえ、剣道の場合でいえば、太刀の持ちかた、突きの入れかた、実際の仕合の場合の姿などを知るべきである。この二形式の鍛錬が要る。それは一つの車の両輪のごときものである。

　　　間不レ容レ髪

と申す事の候。貴殿の兵法にたとへて可レ申候。間とは、物を二つかさね合ふたる間へは、髪筋も入らぬと申す義に候。たとへば、手をはたと打つに、其儘はつしと声が出で候。打つ手の間へ、髪筋の入る程の間もなく声が出で候。手を打つて後に、声が思案し

tage. When, however, no interval even of a hair's breadth is left between the opponent's attack and your counter-attack, his sword will be your own. In Zen this "stopping" interval is very much disliked and called *Bonnō* (*klesa*), a "disturbing passion," you must keep your mind flowing all the time like a ball in the running stream.

This leaving no interval for response is also likened to the flying of sparks when the flint is struck. There is no idle moment between the two operations—striking and sparking take place almost simultaneously. Here no special reference is made to the quickness of sequence, but the "no-stopping" of mind anywhere in its activity is suggested. If you want to be quick just for the sake of being quick, your mind "stops" at this thought and you are no longer master of yourself. When Saigyo asked a courtesan of Eguchi for a night's lodging, she answered in verse thus:

"As I see you to be a man fleeing from the world,
My only prayer is that you 'stop' not
At the thought of a worldly habitation."

The important point of this verse is the "not stopping" of mind, here alluded to as a worldly habitation.

When a monk asks, "What is the Buddha?" the master may raise his fist; when he is asked "What is ultimate idea of Buddhism?" he may exclaim even before the questioner finishes his sentence, "A blossoming branch of the plum," or "The cypress-tree in the court-yard." The point is that the answering mind does not "stop" anywhere but responds straightway without giving any thought to the felicity of an answer. This "not-stopping" mind remains immovable as it is never carried away by the things of relativity. It is the "substance" of things, it is God, it is the Buddha, the "Essence" of Zen, the "ultimate secret," etc. If your answer comes out after a deliberation, it belongs to the category of "disturbing passion," however fine from the literary point of view. The response ought to be with the rapidity of lightning.

て間を置いて出で申すにては無く候。打つと其儘、音が出で候。人の打ち申したる太刀に心が止り候へば、間が出来候。其間に手前の働が抜け候。向ふの打つ太刀と、我働との間へは、髪筋も入らず候程ならば、人の太刀は我太刀たるべく候。禅の問答には、此心ある事にて候。仏法にては、此止りて物に心の残ることを、嫌ひ申し候。故に止るを煩悩と申し候。たてきつたる早川へも、玉を流すやうに乗つて、どつと流れて、少しも止る心なきを尊び候。

　　石　火　之　機

と申す事の候。是も前の心持にて候。石をハタと打つや否や、光が出で、打つと其まま出る火なれば、間も透間もなき事にて候。是も心の止るべき間のなき事を申し候。早き事とばかり心得候へば、悪しく候。心を物に止めまじと云ふが詮にて候。早きにも心の止らぬ所を詮に申し候。心が止れば、我心を人にとられ申し候。早くせんと思ひ設けて早くせば、思ひ設ける心に、又心を奪はれ候。西行の歌集に、

「世をいとふ人とし聞けばかりの宿に　心止むなと思ふばかりぞ」

と申す歌は、江口の遊女のよみし歌なり。

「心止むなと思ふばかりぞ」と云ふ下句の引合せは、兵法の至極に当り可〻申候。心をとどめぬが肝要にて候。

　禅宗にて、「如何か是れ仏」と問ひ候はば、拳をさしあぐべし。「如何か仏法の極意」と問はば、其声未だ絶たざるに、一枝の梅花なりとも、庭前の柏樹子となりとも答ふべし。其答話の善悪を撰ぶにてはなし。止まらぬ心を尊ぶなり。止まらぬ心は、色にも香にも移らぬ也。此移らぬ心の体を神とも祝ひ、仏とも尊び、禅心とも、極意とも、申し候へども、思案して後に云ひ出し候へば、金言妙句にても、住地煩悩にて候。石火の機と申すも、ぴかりとする電光の早きを申し候。

When you are spoken to, you at once say, "Yes"—which is Immovable Intelligence. If you deliberate when you are spoken to, wondering what business there could be, etc., this is the "stopping" of your mind—which is Confusion and Ignorance, indicating that you are still a man of ordinary intelligence. That which makes an instant response to the call is Buddha-wisdom, which is universally shared by all beings including gods and men, the wise and the ignorant. When you act as dictated by this Wisdom, you are a Buddha or god. However various are the teaching of Shintoism, of poetical culture, of Confucianism, they all ultimately point to the realisation of One Mind. [One Mind, Buddha-wisdom, and Immovable Intelligence are names of one and the same thing.] Words are insufficient to explain the Mind; when we do, the Mind is divided, and there are "I" and "not-I," and [because of this dualism] we commit ourselves to all kinds of deeds good and bad, and become the playthings of Karma. Karma indeed starts from Mind, and what is most needed here is for us to have an insight into the Mind itself. Few have this insight, and most of us are altogether ignorant of its workings.

Mere insight however is not enough, we ought to make this insight function in our practical life. What is the use of talking about water all the time when we are really thirsty? However much we may argue about fire, we all never become warm. Both Buddhism and Confucianism elucidate what the Mind is, but unless it is made to shine in our daily living, we cannot be said to have a real insight into its truth. The main point is to think about the matter constantly, trying to realise it in yourself.

Where should the mind be placed [while engaged in sword fighting]? If it is placed on the bodily movements of the opponent, it stops with them; if it is placed on the sword of the opponent, it stops with it; if it is placed on the thought of striking him down, it stops with the thought; if it is placed on my own sword, it stops with it; if it is placed on the thought of not being killed by the opponent, it stops with this thought; if it is placed on the postures

たとえば、人から話しかけられたときには、ただちに、『諾』と答える。——それが不動智である。話しかけられたとき、いかなる用があるのかと、不審がったりして、熟考するならば、それは、心の『止る』のであり —— すなわち、混乱と無智（訳註、沢庵のいう住地煩悩）とであり、いまだ尋常の智の人であることを示すのである。問に対して即座に応ずるところのものは、「仏陀の智慧」であり、それは、神々と賢愚の別なく人間を含めたいっさいのものに、あまねく分ち与えられているものである。この「智慧」に命ぜられて行動するときは、人は仏か神である。神道・歌道・儒教の教えはさまざまであるが、みな究竟において、「唯一心」の実現を目指している。（唯一心・仏陀の智慧・不動智は同一物の名称である。）この「心」を説明するために、言葉は不十分である。説明すれば、心は分割されてそこに「我」と「非我」が生じ、（この二元性のゆえに）われわれは善悪のいっさいの行為をとげることとなり、「業」のもてあそびものとなるよりほかない。「業」もじつは「心」から発する。ゆえに最も肝要なことは、「心」そのものを洞徹することである。この洞徹力を持つ人は少なく、われわれの多くはまったくその働きに関して無知である。

　しかし、たんなる洞徹では不十分である。この洞徹力を実生活の機能となさねばならぬ。実際に喉が乾いているとき、終始、水のことを語って、なんの役に立とう。火についていかに多く議論をしても、けっして温かくはならぬ。仏教も儒教も「心」のなんたるかを明らかにするが、「心」が日常生活に輝くようにされなければ、その真理をほんとうに洞徹しているとはいわれない。主要な点は、絶えず事物について考えて、これを自己の内に実現せんとするにある。

　　　心 の 置 所

　心を何処に置かうぞ。敵の身の働に心を置けば、敵の身の働に心を取らるるなり。敵の太刀に心を置けば、敵の太刀に心を取らるるなり。敵を切らんと思ふ所に心を置けば、敵を切らんと思ふ所に心を取らるるなり。我太刀に心を置けば、我太刀に心を取らるるなり。われ切られじと思ふ所に心を置けば、切られじと思ふ

assumed by the opponent, it stops with them. Where should the mind be placed if one desires its free, unobstructed functioning?

Someone asks; When the mind is placed on those several points, it stops and the opponent never fails to take up with it; is it not better to have it in the abdominal region? Thereby one can follow the movement of the opponent and act accordingly. I would answer, this is excellent. But viewed from the stage of Buddhist discipline this practice is far from perfect, it is still the stage of apprenticeship, and corresponds to "reverence-attitude" of Confucianism, and also to Mencius teaching about "seeking your run-away mind." This is not yet the culmination. For when you are intent on having your mind securely in your abdominal region, this very thought of yours to keep it there arrests the free functioning of the mind, and you will be very much inconvenienced in your activity.

Question: In this case where else should the mind be placed if not in our abdominal region?

Answer: When it is placed on your right hand, it stops in the right hand, and hampers the movements of the other part of the body. When it is placed on the eyes, it stops with them and interferes with the working of the entire body. So with any other points of the body. You cannot have the mind fixed at one single spot, for this will surely cause inconveniences in all the rest. Where should the mind be placed in order to secure a maximum of mental and bodily efficiency? My answer is: Have no thought at all as where to place the mind, for then the mind will fill the entire body even to the tips of the fingers and toes. If the hands are to be moved, they obey the mind at once; if the eyes are to look about, they instantly follow the order of the mind. This is true with every part of the body, which you can most effectively make to work.

The mind is therefore not to be left with any one part of the body, if it is to function to its fullest capacity in all the parts of the body. The thought of doing something turns the mind to that one side and all the other sides are neglected. Have no thought, no deliberation, no discrimination, and the

所に心を取らるるなり。人の構えに心を置けば、人の構えに心を取らるるなり。兎角、心の置所はないと言ふ。

　或人問ふ。我心を兎角、余所へやれば、心の行く所に志を取止めて、敵に負けるほどに、我心を臍の下に押込めて余所にやらずして、敵の働によりて転化せよと云ふ。尤も左もあるべき事なり。然れども、仏法の向上の段より見れば、臍の下に押込めて余所へやらぬと云ふは、段が卑しく、向上にあらず。修業稽古の時の位なり。（儒教の）「敬」の字の位なり。又は孟子の「放心を求めよ」と云ひたる位なり。上りたる向上の段にてはなし。敬の字の心持なり。放心の事は、別書に記し進じあるべく、御覧候。臍の下に押込んで、余所へやるまじきとすれば、やるまじと思ふ心に、心を取られて、先の用欠け、殊の外、不自由になるなり。

　或人問ふて云ふは、心を臍の下に押込んで働かぬも、不自由にして用が欠けば、我身の内にして何処にか心を置くべきぞや。答へて曰く、右の手に置けば、右の手に取られて身の用欠くなり。心を眼に置けば、眼に取られて、身の用欠け申し候。右の足に心を置けば、右の足に心を取られて、身の用欠けるなり。何処なりとも、一所に心を置けば、余の方の用は皆欠けるなり。然らば、則ち心を何処に置くべきぞ。我答へて曰く、何処にも置かねば、我身一ぱいに行きわたりて、全体に延びひろごりてある程に、手の入る時は、手の用を叶へ、足の入る時は、足の用を叶へ、目の入る時は目の用を叶へ、其入る所々に行きわたりてある程に、其入る所々の用を叶ふるなり。万一、もし一所に定めて心を置くならば、一所に取られて用は欠くべきなり。思案すれば思案に取らるる程に、思案をも分別をも残さず、心をば総身に捨て置き、所々に止めずして、其所々に在て用をば外さず叶ふべし。

　それゆえに、心を身体のいかなる一部分にも残しておくべきでない。身体のあらゆる部分に心を充せて思ふままに働かせなければならぬ。なにかなすという考えは、心をその一方面に向け、他のすべての方面が等閑にされる。考えるな、思い煩うな、分別を持つな、

mind will be present everywhere, working itself to its fullest capacity and accomplishing the business then at hand. In all things one-sidedness is to be avoided. When the mind is once arrested somewhere at one part of the body, it will have to be taken out of that particular point and made to function anew where it is required. This transference is really no easy task, the mind generally wants to stay where it once made a "stop." It takes time even when the transference is readily made. You must not keep your mind tied to the post like a cat wishing her to stay with you. In order to make it work at all the ten points, let it not stay with anyone of them; when made to stay anywhere, it ends in the neglect of the other nine. This however requires a great deal of training.

The distinction is to be made between "original" mind (*honshin*) and "superficial" mind (*mōshin*). Original mind is one filling the whole body; when it is made to "stop" at one point and be fixed there, it loses its fluidity and becomes superficial mind. As original mind is no more there, the body meets many obstructions. Original mind is like water, it flows all the time, while superficial mind is ice, you cannot even wash your face with it. To be of any use, it is to be melted so that it can stream through the body and all its parts.

Another distinction we make between *ushin*, "mind present" and *mushin*, "no-mind." By "mind present" is meant the mind which becomes one-sided and fixed, corresponding to superficial mind. It "stops" and deliberates and discriminates. It is always "present" and this presence clogs the flow of original mind. The mind of *mushin* is original mind, which knows no fixation, no "stopping," no deliberation, no discrimination; it, however, pervades the entire being and is very much alive; it is not like a piece of stone or a block of wood; it never "stops" at any one point, for the "stopping" means the presence of something, i.e., an obstruction [and if there is something that obstructs, this is not *mushin*]. *Mushin* means not to have any "mind" and just because of this "no-mind-ness," the mind moves from one thing to another.

そうすれば心は到るところに行きわたってその全力が働き、つぎつ
ぎと手近の仕事を成就するであろう。いっさいの事において一面的
ということを避けるべきだ。心が一度、どこか身体の一部分に捕え
られていると新たに働くときは、その特定の場処から取出して、いま
ま要するところに持ってこなければならぬ、この転換はじつに容易
ならぬ仕事である。心は一般に「止」まらせられたところに、停滞
することを欲する。転換が楽になされるときですら、時間はかかる。
自分のところになつかさせたいと思って猫をつないでおくように、
心を、その場処場処に括りつけておいてはならぬ。十の地点のすべ
てにおいて、心を働かすためには、どの地点にも、心をとどめるな。
いかなる一定の地点にでも、一たび踏みとどまると、結局、他の九
地点を等閑にする。これはしかし非常に鍛錬を要する事である。

　　本 心 妄 心

と申す事の候。本心と申すは、一所に留らず、全身全体に延びひろ
ごりたる心にて候。妄心は何ぞ。思ひつめて、一所に固まり候
心にて、本心が一所に固り集りて、妄心と申すものに成り申し候。
本心の失せ候はば、所々の用が欠ける程に、失はぬ様にするが専
一なり。たとへば、本心は水の如く一所に留まらず、妄心は氷の
如くにて、手も頭も洗はれ不申候。氷を解かして水となし、何
処へも流れるやうにして、手足をも何をも洗ふべし。心一所に固
り一事に留り候へば、氷固りて自由に使はれ申さず、氷にて手足
の洗はれぬ如くにて候。心を溶かして総身へ水の延びるやうに用
ゐ、其所に遣りたきままに遣りて使ひ候。是を本心と申し候。

　　　有心之心、無心之心

と申す事の候。有心の心と申すは、妄心と同じ事にて、有心とは
あるこころと読む文字にて、何事にても一方へ思ひ詰る所なり。
心に思ふ事ありて、分別思案が生ずる程に、有心の心と申し候。
無心の心と申すは、右の本心と同事にて、固り定りたる事なく、
分別も思案も何も無き時の心、総身にのびひろごりて、全体に行
き渡る心を無心と申す也。どつこにも置かぬ心なり。石か木かの
やうにてはなし。留る所なきを無心と申す也。留れば心に物があ

This may sound strange, but the fact is that this "no-mind" is like water filling a pond which is always ready to flow out wherever it is needed. It is again like a wheel moving around the axle which is neither too tight nor too loose. When the wheel is fitted to the axle too tightly at any point, it refuses to revolve, and it does not perform its intended function. When the mind is fixed on one thing, it fails to receive things coming from other quarters. When you are prepossessed of certain thoughts, your mind is to that extent closed to other thoughts. When you are preoccupied, you can neither hear nor see; you keep your mind empty or open and you can take in all that comes to you—this is called *mushin*. If you however cherish the thought of keeping the mind empty, this very state of mind will not make you realise *mushin* or original mind. This is where the difficulty lies in the realisation of "no-mind-ness." But when your discipline matures it comes upon you by itself. You cannot precipitate this state of *mushin*. We have this in an ancient poem: "To try not to think is still thinking; O how I wish to do away with both thinking and not-thinking!"

When an empty gourd is pressed on water, it will dance up down with each touch, and you can never make it stay in one place. When the mind is not arrested by anything, it is just as lively as the gourd.

"Keep your mind awakened without having it abide anywhere"—this is quoted from the *Prajñā-pāramitā Sūtra*, which means to keep the mind perfectly unobstructed by anything. When it moves to do something, it "stops" there and does not go any further. All kinds of attachment come out of this "stopping," and also transmigration takes place here. The mind so "stopped" is the cause of birth and death. With the wise who have mastered the secrets of any art it is different; they move about to do things just as much as anybody, but their mind never "stops," it retains its original motility. They look

り、留る所なければ心に何もなし。心に何もなきを無心の心と申し、又は無心無念とも申し候。此無心の心に能くなりぬれば、一事に止まらず、一事に欠けず、常に水の湛へたるやうにして、此身に在りて、用の向ふ時出て叶ふなり。一所に定り留りたる心は、自由に働かぬなり。車の輪も堅からぬにより廻るなり。一所につまりたれは廻るまじきなり。心も一時に定れば働かぬものなり。心中に何ぞ思ふ事あれば、人の云ふ事をも聞きながら聞かざるなり。思ふ事に心が止るゆゑなり。心が其思ふ事に在りて、一方へかたより、一方へかたよれば、物を聞けども聞えず、見れども見えざるなり。是れ心に物ある故なり。あるとは、思ふ事があるなり。此有る物を去りぬれば、心無心にして、唯用の時ばかり働きて、其用に当る。此心にある物を去らんとする心が、又、心中に有る物になる。思はざれば、独り去りて自ら無心となるなり。常に心にかくすれば、何時となく、後は独り其位へ行くなり。急にやらんとすれば、行かぬものなり。古歌に「思はじと思ふも物を思ふなり、思はじとだに思はじやきみ」

　水上打_胡蘆子_
　胡蘆子（瓢単）を捺着するとは、手を以て押すなり。瓢を水へ投げて押せば、ひよつと脇へ退き、何としても一所に止まらぬものなり。至りたる人の心は、卒度も物に止らぬ事なり。水の上の瓢を押すが如くなり。

　応無_所_住、而生_其心_
　この文字を訓に読み候へば、「応に往する所なくして、而も其の心を生ず。」と読み候。よろづの業をするに、しようと思ふ心が生ずれば、そのすることに心が止まるなり。然る間、止まる所なくして、心を生ずべしとなり。心を生ずる所に生ぜられば、手も行かず、行けば、そこに止まる心を生じて、その事をしながら止ることなきを、諸道の名人と申すなり。この止る心から執着の心起り、輪廻もこれより起り、この止まる心、生死のきづなとな

at the flowers and admire their beauty, they do not "stop" there. The flowers bloom in accordance with their nature, they are in a state of *mushin*, "no-mind-ness." But the onlookers are attached to them, and because of this attachment, their minds are said to be stained. The Confucian teaching of reverence-attitude is meant for apprentices in the Tao, whose consummation must be found in the Buddhist doctrine of "no-mind-ness." The reverence-attitude attempts to keep mind from going loose and wild; when this is perfected after many years of training, every check put on the mind will naturally fall off, and can safely be let alone. It is then that the stage of awakening the mind without "stopping" anywhere will be realised. As long as it is closely watched every minute of the hour, it is like a newly-adopted cat kept on a string all the time*, there is no freedom for it, and without freedom it dose not function to its full capacity. The ultimate objective is to have the cat wander about freely inside and outside the house and not to do any harm even to the birds kept with her.

To apply this to the mastering of swordsmanship, the utmost degree of perfection is gained when your mind is no more troubled with how to strike the opponent and yet knows how to use the sword in the most effective way when you stand before him. You just strike him down, forgetting that you have a sword in your hand and that somebody is standing against you. No idea of personality is here—all is empty; the opponent, yourself, the striking sword, the sword-holding arms; not only that, even the idea of emptiness is also done away with. From this absolute emptiness there is the most wonderful display of activities.

When Bukko Kokushi, of Engakuji, while still in China was threatened for his life by the Mongolian invaders, he referred to "the cutting in twain the spring breeze in a flash of lightning." The sword lifted by the murderous soldier of Yuan to kill him appeared as if it were no more than a flash of lightning; there was in the act of killing nothing concerning him any more than the spring breeze softly blowing about him. To him the sword threatening his life was a nothing, the person about to strike him down was a noth-

り申し候。花紅葉を見て、花紅葉を見る心は生じながら、そこに止まらぬを詮と致し候。慈円の歌に、「柴の戸に匂はん花もさもあらばあれ、ながめにけりな恨めしの世や。」とあり。花は無心に匂ひぬるを、我は心を花に止めて眺めけるよと、身のこれに染みたる心が恨めしとなり。* 見るとも、聞くとも、一所に心を止めぬを至極とする事にて候。敬の字をば主一無適と註を致し候て、心を一所に止めぬを至極とする事にて候。……然れども、仏法にては、敬の字の心は至極の所にてはなく候。我が心をとられて乱さぬやうにして習ひ入る修行稽古の法にて候。この稽古年月日積りぬれば、心を何方へ追放しやりても自由なる位に行くことにて候。右の応無┛所┛住の住は句上至極の位にて候。敬の字の心は、心の余所へ行くを引とめて、やるまい、やれば乱ると思ひて、そつとも油断なく心を引きつめて置く位にて候。これは当座心を散らさぬ一旦のことなり。常に是の如くありては、不自由の義なり。譬へば、雀の子を捕へられ候て、猫の縄を常に引きつめておいて放さぬ位にて、我が心を猫をつれたるやうにして、不自由にしては、用が心のままになるまじく候。猫によく躾をして置いて、縄を追ひ放して行きたき方へやり候て、雀と一つにゐても捕へぬやうにするが、応無┛所┛住、而生┛其心┛の文の心にて候。我が心を放し捨て、猫のやうに打捨て行きたき方へ行きても、心のとまらぬやうに心を用ひ候。

　貴殿の兵法に当て申し候はば、太刀を打つ手に心を止めず、一切打つ手を忘れて打つて人を切れ、人に心を置くな。人も空、我も空、打つ手も打つ太刀も空と心得、空に心を取られまいぞ。

　鎌倉の無学禅師、大唐の乱に捕へられて、切らるる時に、電光影裏斬┛春風┛といふ偈を作りたれば、太刀をば捨てて走りたると也。無学の心は、太刀をひらりと振上げたるは稲妻の如く電光のぴかりとする間、何の心も、何の念も、ないぞ。打つ刀も心はなし。切る人も心はなし。切らるる我も心はなし。切る人も空、太刀も空、打たるる我も空なれば、打つ人も人にあらず。打つ太刀も太刀にあらず。打たるる我も、稲妻のぴかりとする内に、春

ing, the self so called who was about to break down was also a nothing; in this play of Emptiness, there was no mind to be arrested, there were no points at which the mind was made to stop. The lightning flashed, the breeze blew, the sword moved, the man fell, and Emptiness remains as ever before.

The same can be said of the art of dancing. You just take up the fan in your hand and stamp your feet as you move about. But as soon as the thought possesses you as to how to move your arms and legs effectively, and so on, your mind is arrested and your dance is spoiled. Perfect abandon means perfect forgetting of personality and all that belongs to it.*

To supplement Takuan, the following story is given as illustrating the mind of "no-mind-ness":

A wood-cutter was busily engaged in cutting down trees in the remote mountain. An animal called Satori appeared. It was a very strange-looking creature, not usually found in the villages. The woodcutter wanted to catch it alive. The animal read his mind: "You are now wishing to catch me alive, are you not?" Completely taken aback, he did not know what to say, whereupon the animal remarked, "You are evidently astonished at my telephathic faculty." Ever more surprised, he conceived the idea of striking it with one blow of his ax, when Satori exclaimed, "Now you want to kill me." The woodman felt entirely disconcerted, and fully realising his impotency to do anything with this mysterious animal, he thought of resuming his business. Satori was not charitably disposed, for he pursued him, saying; "So at last you have abandoned me."

The woodman did not know what to do with the animal as well as with himself; altogether resigned to the situation he took up his ax and paying no attention whatever to the presence of Satori, he vigorously and single-heart-edly began the cutting of the trees again. While so engaged, the head of the ax flew off its handle and struck the animal dead, who with all its mind-reading sagacity failed to read the mind of "no-mind-ness."

の空を吹く風の如くなり。一切止らぬ心なり。風を切つたのは、太刀に覚えもあるまいぞ。かやうに心を忘れ切つて、万の事をするが、上手の位なり。

　舞を舞へば、手に扇を取り、足を踏む。其手足をよくせむ、舞を能く舞はむと思ひて、忘れきらねば、上手とは申されず候。未だ手足に心止らば、業は皆面白かるまじ。悉皆、心を捨てきらずして、する所作は皆悪敷候。

沢庵和尚の書翰はなお続くが多少、専門技術的になるからここでは略する。*
　禅師の意を補うために、つぎの話によって「無心」というものを説明しよう。
　一人の樵夫が奥山でせっせと樹を切っていた。さとりという動物が現れた。平素は里に見当らぬたいへん珍らしい生きものだった。樵夫は生捕りにしようと思った。動物は彼の心を読んだ。『お前は己を生捕りにしようと思っているね。』度胆を抜かれて、樵夫は言葉もでないでいると、動物がいった。『そら、お前は己の読心力にびっくりしている。』ますますおどろいて、樵夫は斧の一撃によって彼を打ち倒しくれんという考を抱いた。すると、さとりは叫んだ。『やア、お前は己を殺そうと思っているな。』樵夫はまったくどぎまぎして、この不思議な動物を片附けることの不可能を覚ったので、自分の仕事のほうを続けようと思った。さとりは寛大な気配を見せなかった。なおも追求していった。『そら、とうとう、お前は己をあきらめてしまったナ。』
　樵夫は、自分をどうしてよいか、わからなかった、おなじくこの動物をどう扱っていいか判らなかった。とうとう、この事態にまったく諦めをつけて、斧を取り上げた。さとりのいることなぞ気に掛けないで、勇気をだして一心に、ふたたび樹を切り始めた。そうやっているうち、偶然に斧の頭が柄から飛んでその動物を打ち殺した。いくら読心の智慧を持っていたこの動物でも「無心」の心まで読む

At the last stage of swordsmanship there is a secret teaching which is not imparted to any but fully-qualified masters. Mere technical training is enough, proficiency in this does not go beyond apprenticeship. The secret teaching is known among the masters as "The Moon in Water." According to a writer, it is explained as follows, which is in truth no more than tne teaching of Zen, the doctrine of *mushin*:

"What is meant by 'the moon in water'?

"This is explained variously in the various schools of swordsmanship, but the main idea is to grasp the way the moon reflects itself wherever there is a body of water, which is done in a state of *mushin* ('no-mind-ness'). One of the Imperial poems composed by the pond of Hirosawa reads:

"'The moon has no intent to cast its shadow anywhere,

Nor does the pond design to the moon;

How serene the water of Hirosawa!'

From this poem one must get an insight into the secrets of *mushin*, where there are no traces of artificial contrivance, everything being left to Nature itself.

"Again, it is like one moon reflecting itself in hundreds of streams; the moonlight is not divided into so many shadows, but the water is there to reflect them; the moonlight remains ever the same even where there are no waters to hold its reflection. Again, it is all the same with the moonlight whether there are so many bodies of water, or there is just one little puddle. By this analogy the mysteries of mind are made easier to understand. But the moon and water are tangible matter, while mind has no form and its working is difficult to trace. The symbols are not thus the whole truth, only suggestive."

3

The Atlantic Monthly, February, 1937, contains an article by a Spanish bull-fighter called Juan Belmonte telling of his own experience in the art. Bull-

わけにはゆかなかったのだ。

　剣道の最後の段階には、十分資格のある師範だけにしか与えられ
ぬ奥義がある。腕の鍛錬だけでは不十分である。腕の熟達だけでは
まだ弟子気分を超えない。この秘伝（奥義）は、「水月」といって
師範の間に知られている。ある著者によると、つぎのように説明さ
れている。しかし、それは、じつのところ、禅の教えである「無心
論」に過ぎない。

　『水中の月とはどういう意味であるか。』

　『剣道の各流儀では、いろいろに説明されているが、要するに、
　水のあるところ、いかなるところにも、月が「無心」の状態で映
　る、その映りかたを会得することである。嵯峨の広沢ノ池の畔で
　詠まれた御製の一つに、

　　　　うつるとも月もおもはず

　　　　うつすとも水もおもはぬ

　　　　広沢の池』

この歌から、人は無心の秘訣を洞徹するに違いない。そこには、人
の手による工夫の痕は一つもない、あらゆるものが大自然に任される。

　『さらにそれは幾百の流れに映る一つの月の如きである。月光が
　幾百の影に分れるのではなくて、影を映す水があるのである。月
　光はそれを映す水がない所でも、依然同じことである。さらに又、
　多くの水のある所でもささやかの水溜りの所でも、月の光に変り
　はない。是から類推すれば心の神秘は理解しやすい。しかし、月
　と水とは触れうる物質である。心には形なく、その働きは跡づけ
　難い。象徴はかくして全ての真理ではなくして、暗示にすぎぬ。』

（原文は佚斎樗山子）

三

　1937年の *The Atlantic Monthly* 2月号に、Juan Belmonte（フア
ン・ベルモンテ）というスペインの闘牛士の、その技に関する自己

fighting is evidently very much like the Japanese art of fencing. His story is full of interesting suggestions, and I quote part of the translator's note and Juan Belmonte's own account of the fight for which he earned great reputation as the foremost fighter of the day. In this fighting he realised the state of mind referred to in Takuan's letter to Yagyū Tajima-no-kami; if the Spanish hero had the Buddhist training, he would surely have had an insight into Immovable Intelligence.

The translator's note in part runs:
"Bullfighting is not a sport, and you can't compare it with one. Bullfighting, whether you like it or not, whether you approve of it or not, is an art, like painting or music, and you can only judge it as an art; its emotion is spiritual, and it touches depths which can only be compared with the depths that are touched in a man who knows and understands and loves music by a symphony orchestra under a great conductor."

Juan Belmonte describes his psychology at the intensest moment of his fight in the following terms:
"As soon as my bull came out I went up to it, and at third pass I heard the howl of the multitude rising to their feet. What had I done? All at once I forgot the public, the other bull-fighters, myself, and even the bull; I began to fight as I had fought so often by myself at night in the corrals and pastures, as precisely as if I had been drawing a design on a black-board.

"They say that my passes with the cape and my work with the muleta that afternoon were a revelation of the art of bullfighting. I don't know, and I'm not competent to judge. I simply fought as I believed one ought to fight, without a thought outside my own faith in what I was doing. With the last bull I succeeded for the first time in my life in delivering myself body and soul to the pure joy of fighting without being consciously aware of an audience. When I was playing bulls alone in the country I used to talk to them;

の経験を語る一文がのっている。闘牛の技はあきらかに日本の撃剣に酷似する。彼の話は興味ある示唆に富んでいるから、翻訳者のノートと、この一流の闘牛士として多大の名声をえている彼の闘い振りに関するフアン・ベルモンテ自身の説明の一部を引用してみよう。この闘争において、彼は柳生但馬守にあたえた沢庵の書翰中に述べてある、あの心境を自覚しているといってよい。このスペインの闘牛士が仏教的鍛錬を持っていたなら、たしかに「不動智」に徹底したに違いない。

　翻訳者のノートの一部に曰く、

　『闘牛はスポーツではない。それと比較するわけにはゆかない。闘牛は、諸君が好むと好まざるにかかわらず、認めると認めざるにかかわらず、絵画や音楽と同じく一つの芸術である。諸君はそれを芸術としてのみ判断することができる。その情 感は精神的である。それが心の深奥にふれる点では、偉大な指揮者のもとで行われる交響管弦楽を知り、理解し、愛する人の心に比すべきものがある。』

　フアン・ベルモンテは、彼が闘牛の真只中で最も精神力の強調した瞬間における自分の心理を、つぎのような言葉で述べている。

　『相手の猛牛がでてくるや否や、私はそっちへ向って行った。三度目の「あしらい」で観衆が起ち上ってウッと叫ぶのが聞えた。私はなにをしたのか。私は不意に、公衆も、他の闘牛士も、私自身も、そして相手の牛のことさえも忘れた。私は以前、囲地や牧場で夜独りでしばしば牛と闘ったように、闘い始めた。まるで黒板に図案を描いているような、精確さで闘った。

　ケープする私のパーセと、ムレータ（訳註、赤い布をつけた棒で、これで牛を怒らせたり、パーセをする）でする私の働きは、その日の午後、見物にきた人々にとって、闘牛術における一種の天啓であったということだ。私は知らない。私には判断する力はない。私はこう闘うべきであると、信じた通りに闘ったに過ぎない。やっていることに信念を持つ以外になんらの考をも持たなかった。最後の闘牛をやったときにも、私は観衆のあるなしには意識を持たずに、ただ闘うと

and that afternoon I held a long conversation with the bull, all the time that my muleta was tracing the arabesques of the faena. When I didn't know what else to do with the bull I knelt down under its horns and brought my face close to its muzzle.

'Come on, little bull,' I whispered. 'Catch me!'

"I stood up again, spread the muleta under its nose, and went on with my monologue, encouraging it to keep on charging.—

"'This way, little bull. Charge me nicely. Nothing's going to happen to you. . . Here you are. Here you are. . . Do you see me, little bull?. . . What? You're getting tired?. . . Come on! Catch me! Don't be a coward . . . Catch me!'

"I was executing the ideal faena, the faena that I had seen so often and in so much detail in my dreams that every line of it was drawn in my brain with mathematical exactness. The faena of my dreams always ended disastrously, because when I went in for the kill the bull invariably caught me in the leg. It must have been some subconscious acknowledgment of my lack of skill in killing that always dictated this tragic conclusion. Nevertheless, I went on realising my ideal faena, placing myself right between the horns of the bull and hearing the acclamation of the crowd only as a distant murmur; until at last, exactly as I had dreamed it, the bull did catch me and wounded me in the thigh. I was so intoxicated, so outside myself, that I scarcely noticed it. I went in for the kill, and the bull fell at my feet."

I may add that before Belmonte had his final encounter with the bull his mind was in a most distracted condition; rivalry, desire for success, a sense of inferiority, and feeling for the public ready to make fun of him. So he confessed:

"I was overcome with despair. Where had I got the idea that I was a bull-

いうことの純粋なよろこびに自分の身も魂も任せ切ることに、初めて成功したのだ。私は国でただ独り牛をあしらっている時、よく彼らに話しかけたものだった。その午後も私は牛と長い会話をつづけた、私のムレータがわ ざ（訳註、闘牛師の苦労心労のこと、元来は仕事の意）の渦紋を描きつづけている間、絶えずやった。外にどうしてよいか判らなかったときは、私は牛の角の下に膝まずいて、その鼻先に自分の顔を持って行った。

「さあ、チビ公」、私はささやいた。「つかまえて御覧」

　私はまた起ち上って、牛の鼻の下にムレータをひろげ、独白をつづけ、牛をはげまして突撃をつづけさせるようにした。

「こっちだ、チビ公。しっかりと進んでこい。どうもありゃしない……ソラおいでなすった。……ソラおいでなすった。……己が見えるか、チビ公。どうした？　疲れてきたのか。さあこい。己を捕えろ。卑性になるな。己を捕えろ」

　私は理想的なわざを作成しつつあった、夢でたびたびしかも詳細に見ているので、その一本の線も数学的精確さで脳中に描かれていた。私の夢のわざはいつも不幸に終っていた。なぜかというに、とどめにかかったとき、牛は誤またず私の片脚を捕えるからだった。かく悲劇的結末をいつも示したというのは、なにか潜在意識的にとどめをさす際の腕前に僥倖を認めようとしたからに違いなかった。にもかかわらず、私は理想的なわざの実現をつづけ、牛の両角の間に身を置き、群集の叫喚をただ遠くのつぶやきと聞いた。そしてついに、夢で見たように的確に、牛は私を捕え、私の腿を傷けた。私は陶酔しており、夢中だったので、それには気づかなかった。私はとどめにかかり、牛は私の足下にたおれた。』

　ここに一言を附け加える。

　ベルモンテが牛と最後の格闘に入る前、彼の心理状態ははなはだ錯乱していた。競争心・成功熱・劣等感・公衆の嘲笑を買いはせぬかという心配、こういう感じが、彼の心を掻き乱していた。これについて彼はこう告白している。

　『私は絶望状態に陥った。「自分は闘牛士だなどという考えをどこ

fighter? 'You have been fooling yourself,' I thought. 'Because you had some luck in a couple of novilladas without picadors, you can do anything.'"

Out of this feeling of despair, however, Belmonte discovered something else in him lying hitherto altogether unsuspected, when he saw his bull coming out and confronting him.

This something sometimes came out in his dreams, that is, it was sleeping deeply in his Unconscious, but it never came out in the broad daylight. The feeling of despair pushed him to the very edge of his mental precipice, from which he finally leaped; and the result was, "I was so intoxicated, so outside myself, that I had hardly noticed it"—not only it (that he was wounded) but in fact everything. "Immovable Intelligence" was his guide, he left himself entirely to its guidance. Sings a noted Zen master of the Kamakura era:

"The bow is broken,
Arrows are all gone—
This critical moment:
No fainting heart cherish,
Shoot, with might and main."

When a shaftless arrow is shot from a stringless bow, it will surely penetrate the rock as it once happened in the history of the Far-Eastern people.

In all departments of art as well as in Zen Buddhism, this passing of the crisis is considered very important in order to reach the source of all creative works. I wish to discuss this more specifically from the religio-psychological point of view in a separate work on Zen.

でえたのか。馬鹿な、自惚れにもほどがある。」と思った。「お前はピカドール（訳註、闘牛の初めに槍をもって牛を怒らせる騎士）も使わずに一度や二度ノビリャーダス（訳註、犢を相手にする闘牛、但し、殺さない）に僥倖をえたというだけのことで、なんの取柄があるのだ。」』

しかし、彼はこの絶望感から覚醒した。彼はいま、荒狂う牛の面前に立っている。彼は忽然として、これまでまったく気もつかなかったものが、その心の奥底からでてくるのに目ざめた。

このあるものはしばしば彼の夢にでてきた。すなわち、それは彼の無意識のなかに深く眠っていて、白昼はけっしてでてこなかったものである。いまや絶望感に押し詰められて心理的絶壁の頂に突立った彼は、心身を捨ててそこから跳び下りた。その結果、『私は陶酔状態でなにがなにやら夢中だった。「それ」には気づかずにいた。』事実は「それ」（彼が傷いたこと）のみならず、いっさいの環境に気づかずにいたのだ。「不動智」のみが彼の案内者だった。彼は自己をまったくその案内者に任せたのだ。鎌倉時代の有名な禅匠＊は歌う。

　　弓も折れ
　　矢も尽きはつる
　　ところにて
　　さしもゆるさで
　　強く射てみよ。

箭幹なき矢を弦なき弓より射れば、そはかならず、かつて極東の人々の歴史に起ったように岩をも貫き通すであろう。

禅宗と同様に、芸術のすべての部門において、この危機の通過ということは、あらゆる創造的作品の根源に到達するためにきわめて肝要だと考えられている。自分は禅に関する別著で、この事を広い意味の宗教心理学、あるいは宗教哲学ともいうべき立場からさらに専門的に論じたいと思っている。

The Shinkage-ryū used to be one of the most popular schools of fencing in the feudal days of Japan. It started in the Ashikaga era with Kami-idzumi Isenokami as its founder, who flourished in the second half of sixteenth century, while its first originator claimed that he learned the secrets of his art directly from the god of Kashima. It no doubt went through stages of development since then, and the so-called secrets must have increased in volume, for we have at present a variety of documents which were given by the master to his most proficient pupils considered worthy of them. Among such documents we find phrases and epigrams in verse highly flavouring of Zen which have superficially no connection whatever with the use of the sword.

The final certificate, for instance, which is given to one qualified to be a master of this school contains nothing but a circle. This is supposed to represent a mirror bright and altogether free from film and dust, and its meaning is no doubt the allusion to the Buddhist philosophy of "great-perfect-mirror-wisdom," which is "Immovable Intelligence" of Takuan as quoted before. The fencer's mind must be kept entirely free from selfish passions and intellectual calculations so that "original intuition" is ready to work at its best—which is a state of no-mind-ness. Mere technical skill in the use of the sword does not necessarily give one full qualification as a swordsmaster; he must once realise the final stage of spiritual discipline which is to attain no-mind-ness symbolised as a circle empty of contents.

There is a phrase, among other highly technical terms, in the secret documents of the Shinkage-ryū school of fencing, which has apparently no connection with the art as far as its literal meaning is concerned. As all these secrets are to be orally transmitted and as I am an absolute stranger to them, it is beyond my conjecture to find out how this particular phrase obtains its organic signification in the actual wielding of the sword. But as far as I can judge the phrase is derived from Zen literature outside which it cannot mean anything. It reads; "Waters of the West River." A commentator who

　神陰流<ruby>神陰流<rt>しんかげりゅう</rt></ruby>は日本封建時代における最もポピュラーな流儀の一つとなっていた。足利時代に始まったが、その創設者の上泉伊勢守*は、十六世紀の後半にさかえた。この創始者は彼の剣技の秘伝を鹿島の神から直接さずかったと主張している。爾来、それは幾多の発展段階を通って、いわゆる秘伝は増えて巻を成したにちがいない。現在、いろいろな古文書があるが、これは師から授けるに値すると考えられた最も優秀な弟子達に与えられたものである。かかる文書のなかには、表面的には剣の使用とはなんら連絡のない、はなはだ禅臭い文句や詩の形をした警句を見る。

　たとえば、この流儀の師範となる資格ある者に与える最後の証書（免許・皆伝書）には一円相のほかなにも書かれなかった。これは照りかがやいて一点の曇りなき鏡を表わすものと想われる。その意味はもちろん仏教の大円鏡智の哲学、すなわち、前に引用した沢庵の「不動智」にたとえたものである。剣士の心は、つねに利己的な感情と智的な策略とをまったく去って、「本来の直覚」がいつでもまったく至上に働きうる——すなわち、無心の状態にあらねばならぬ。単に太刀の使いかたが技術的に巧みだという事は、かならずしも、剣匠として十分な資格にならない。精神約鍛錬の最後の段階を自覚しなければならぬ。それは円空によって象徴される無心境に到達することである。

　神陰流の免許皆伝の目録のなかには、他の高遠な専門語と混じって、一見字義からいえば剣技となんら無関係と思われる句がある。これらの秘伝はすべて口伝<ruby>口伝<rt>くでん</rt></ruby>であるし、自分はそれにはまったく門外漢であるから、この特殊の句がじっさいの剣法の上で、どれほど根本的意義を持つかを知ることは、自分の臆測を超えている。自分の判断するところでは、この句は禅文学からでているのであって、それを外にしては意味の取りようのないものである。それは「西江の水」というのであるが、註釈者は明らかにその真の趣意を知らぬ

evidently does not know the real purport of it interprets it as indicating a bold venturous dare-devil attitude of mind which does not recoil from swallowing up the whole river. This is ridiculous to say the least. It refers to a Zen *mondo* which took place between Baso (Ma-tsu, –788), of the T'ang dynasty, and his lay-disciple Hō Koji (P'ang Chüchih).

Hō asked:

"What kind of man is he who does not keep company with anything [or anybody]?"

"I will tell you," said Baso," when you have swallowed up in one draught all the waters of the West River."

This is said to have opened the mind of Hō to a state of enlightenment.

When we have this incident in mind, we can understand why the phrase," Waters of the West River," has found its way into the secret documents of the fencing school. Hō's question is a very important one, and so is Baso's answer. In Zen discipline this *mondo* is frequently made use of, and there is no doubt that among the fencers of the feudal days there were many swordsmen who gave their lives to the study of Zen in order to attain a state of absolute no-mind-ness in connection with their art. As has been mentioned elsewhere, the thought of death proves the greatest stumbling block to a victorious conclusion when engaged in a life-and-death combat.

The secret documents also contain a number of *waka*, versified epigrams, in regard to the mastery of swordsmanship, some of which decidedly reflect the spirit of Zen:

"Upon a soul absolutely free from thoughts and emotions,
Even the tiger finds no room to insert its fierce claws."

"One and the same breeze passes,
Over the pines on the mountain and the oak-trees in the valley;
And why do they give different notes!"

とみえ、これを大河を飲み干すことをも辞せぬという勇猛心を指すと解している。これは可笑しいというより外ない。この句は唐代の馬祖（西紀788歿）と弟子の龐居士との問答からでたのである。

龐が尋ねた。

『万法と侶たらざる者これ何人ぞ』（いかなる事《またはいかなる人》とも伴侶となれぬ者とは、どんな人間ですか。）

『儞が一口に西江の水を吸尽せんを待つて、即ち汝に向て道はん』（お前が西江の水を一息に飲み干したら答えてやろう。）と馬祖はいった。これによって龐の心は悟りを開いたというのである。

（碧巌集）

　この冪件を念頭に置いてあれば、「西江の水」の一句が剣道流儀の秘伝書に入っている所以を理解できるのである。龐の問はすこぶる重大であり、馬祖の答もまたそうである。禅の鍛錬はこの公案がしばしば利用せられた。封建時代の剣士たちの間にも、剣技と関係する絶対無心の心境に到達するために、禅の修学に一身を捧げた剣士が多かったことはいうまでもない。他の場所ですでに述べたごとく、生死の争闘にしたがう場合、生死の考に捉えられていては、最後の結果に対する大きな障礙物となる。

　免許皆伝の目録にはまた剣道の極意に関し、詩的警句としてつぎのような意味の歌が載っているが、その数首はたしかに禅の精神を反映している。

　　思想と感情から全く自由である魂には
　　虎もその爪を挿しいれる余地がない。

　　風は一様に吹きまわる
　　山上の松と谷間の樫の上を
　　何ぞ、その音色の相同じからざる。

"Some think that striking is to strike:
But striking is not to strike, nor is killing to kill."

"No thinking, no reflecting,
Perfect emptiness:
Yet therein something moveth,
Following its own course."

"The eye sees it,
But no hands can take hold of it—
The moon in the stream:
This is the secret of my school."

"Clouds and mists—
They are mid-air transformations:
Above them eternally shineth the sun, and the moon."*

"Victory is due to the one,
Even before the combat,
Who has no thought of himself,
Abiding in the no-mindness of Great Origin."

† Emerson on "Brahma":
  "If the red slayer think he slays,
      Or if the slain think he is slain,
  They know not well the subtle ways
      I keep, and pass, and turn again.
  "Far or forgot to me is near;
      Shadow and sunlight are the same;
  The vanished gods to me appear;
      And one to me are shame and fame."

打つことは打つためと考えるものあり
されど打つは打つに非ず
斬るは斬るに非ず。(原註)

無念無想
かけたることなき大空
されどそこに、何やら動くものあり
進むべき道を進み行く。

眼には見れども
手には取りえず
流れの月——
これ我流派の秘訣。

雲と霧——
宙にかかりて幾たびか変るも
その上に、永えに輝く日と月。

勝利は帰す
闘いの始まるに先立って
太源の無心境に住し
自己を思わざるものに。

(原註) エマーソンの「梵天(ブラーマ)」
　　殺す者は殺すと思い、
　　殺さるる者又殺さると思う、
　　彼等は共に己が妙法を知らず
　　護持異滅、又、是れ吾力なり。
　　遠き昔、忘れられしものは吾にありては近し、
　　影も光も同じきなり、
　　消えし神々吾に現れ、
　　恥も誉も吾には一なり。

This apparently corresponds to the principle of "emptiness" as taught by Miyamoto Musashi as the ultimate secret of swordsmanship, which is attainable only after long and arduous training in the art. This insistence on the spiritual discipline entitles the art to be called creative. Musashi was great not only as a swordsman but as a *sumi-ye* painter.

5

A recent writer on "the Way of the Sword" and its history* remarks to the following effect as regards the principle of the art: In the *Kendō* ("the way of the sword") what is most essential to attain besides its technique is the spiritual element controlling the art throughout. It is a state of mind known as *munen* or *musō*, "no-reflection" or "no-thought." This does not mean just to be without thoughts, ideas, feelings, etc., when you stand with the sword before the opponent. It means to let your natural faculties act in a consciousness free from thoughts, reflections, or affections of any kind. This state of mind is also known as egolessness (*muga*) in which you cherish no egoistic thoughts, no consciousness of your own attainments. The so-called idea of *sabi-shiwori* controlling the art of Saigyō or Bashō also must have come from a spiritual state of egolessness. This is comparable to the lunar reflection in water. Neither the moon nor water has any preconceived idea to produce the incident designated by us as "the moon in water." Water is in a state of "no-mind-ness" as much as the moon. But when there is a sheet of water the moon is seen in it. The moon is just one, but its reflections are seen wherever there is water. When this is understood your art is perfect. Finally, Zen and the Sword's Way are one in this that both ultimately aim at transcending the duality of birth and death. Since of old this has been recognised by masters of the sword, and the great ones have invariably knocked at the gate of Zen as is instanced in the case of Yagyū Tajimanokami and Takuan, and of Miyamoto Musashi and Shunzan.

The writer of the aforementioned book further gives interesting infor-

これは一見、宮本武蔵が剣道の極意として教えた「空」の原理に
相当し、斯道における多年の錬磨によって、始めて達せられるもの
である。精神的鍛錬に関するかくのごとき主張のゆえに、その技は
創造的(クリエチヴ)と称しうるのである。武蔵は剣聖として偉大なりしのみなら
ず、水墨画家としてもまた偉大であった。

五

「剣道及剣道史」の著者高野弘正氏はつぎのごとく述べている。剣
道においてその技術以外に最も大事なことは、その技を自由に駆使
する精神的要素である。それは「無念」または「無想」という心境
である。これは、太刀を取って相手の前に立った時に、思想・観念・
感情などを持たない、という意味ではない。思想・反省あるいは、
すべての愛着を断った意識によって、生来の能力を働かせる意味で
ある。この心境をまた「無我」といい、利己的思想を抱かず、自分
の所得を意識せぬ状態である。西行や芭蕉の芸術を支配するいわゆ
るさび・しおりの観念も無我の心境からきたに違いない。これは水
に映る月影に比較することができる。月も水も「水月」と呼ばれる
事象を作りだそうという考を、前もって有していたわけではない。
水は月と同じく「無心」の状にある。が、一帯の水あれば、そこに
月がうつる。月はただ一個だが、水あるところどこにもその影をう
つす。これが理解されるとき、その技は完全になる。結局、禅と剣
道とは、両者が究竟において生死二元を超越することを目的とする
点で一である。古来このことは剣匠の認むるところで、偉大な剣士
は例外なく禅門をたたいたことは、柳生但馬守と沢庵、宮本武蔵と
春山の場合の例証通りである。

　前記の著者はさらに興味ある知識を与えるが、それによると、日

mation that in the feudal days of Japan a master of the sword or the spear was often called an "Oshō" (*upādhyāna*, in Sanskrit), which is the title of a Buddhist monk or priest. The origin of this custom is traceable to the fact that there was once a great monk in the Kōfukuji Temple of Nara. The monk belonged to one of the minor temples called Jizō-in under the jurisdiction of the Kōfukuji. He was an expert of the spear, and all the Jizō-in monks after him learned the art from him. He was naturally an Oshō to all his disciples, and the title came to be transferred upon all the masters both of the spear and the sword, irrespective of their Buddhist qualifications.

The hall in which swordsmanship is practised is called *Dojō*. *Dojō* is the name of a place devoted to religious exercises, and its original Sanskrit meaning, *bodhimandala*, is the place of enlightenment. There is no doubt the name was borrowed from Zen Buddhism.

There is another thing the swordsmen inherited from the Zen monk. In olden days they used to travel all over Japan in order to perfect themselves in their art by experiencing every form of hardship which befell them and also by undergoing all kinds of training under all kinds of mastership. The example was furnished by the Zen monk who did the same thing before they attained to final enlightenment. This practice is known as *angya*, "traveling on foot" among the monks whereas the swordsmen call it *musha-shu-gyō*, "practising warriorship."

I do not know how early this practice started among the swordsmen, but we read about the founder of the Shinkage-ryū travelling all over the country. One incident connects him with a Zen monk both of whom were engaged in a similar form of training. One day when Kami-idzumi Isenokami was passing through a small village in a remote mountain district, he found the people in extreme excitement; for a desperate outlaw took refuge in a deserted house snatching away a little village-boy with him, and threatened to kill the victim if the villagers attempted to arrest or do harm to the criminal himself. Isenokami realised the grave situation. Seeing a monk pass by who was no doubt a wandering Zen monk, the swordsman asked

本の封建時代には、剣や槍の師範はしばしば「和尚」と称せられていた。この習慣の起りは、奈良興福寺に偉い坊さんがかつていた事実に跡づけることができる。僧は興福寺管轄下の宝蔵院という小さい寺に属していた。彼は槍術の名手で、宝蔵院の僧たちはみな、彼についてその技をまなんだ。彼は当然、弟子たちには「和尚」であった。そしてその称号は仏徒であろうが、なかろうが、刀槍両道の師範のすべての人の上に移されることとなった。

　剣道を錬磨する広間を道場といっている。道場は宗教的練習に使われる場所の名である。その梵語 bodhimandala の原意は「悟りの場所」である。

　剣士が禅僧から受継いだものがいま一つある。往昔、彼らは日本国中を旅して、その技を完成するためにあらゆる種類の艱難辛苦をなめ、あらゆる師の許にあらゆる鍛錬をへたものであった。その範例は、最後の悟りに達するために同じ事を行なった禅僧が示したのであった。この錬磨を、僧の間では「行脚」といい、剣士の間では「武者修業」と呼んでいる。

　この習慣が剣士の間にいつの頃から起ったかは判らぬが、神陰流の建設者は日本全国を旅行したという。ある因縁で、彼は雲水の僧にでくわした。ある日、上泉伊勢守が、山間の僻村を通りかかった時、村人の騒いでいるのを見た。自暴自棄になった咎人が村の子供を引っさらって一軒家に逃込んだ。村人が彼を捕えるかまたは害を加えんとするならば、彼はその犠牲を殺そうと脅していた。伊勢守は事の由々しさを悟った。一人の出家の通りかかるのを見れば、疑いもなく旅の禅僧なので、ちょっとその衣を拝借したいと頼んだ。真個の僧に見えるように自分の頭を剃って貰った。彼は弁当を二つ持って一軒家の方へ近づいて、その咎人に、子供の親がわが子の餓

him to lend him his monkish robe for a while. He had his head shaved so as to appear as a genuine monk. He approached the house with two lunch boxes, and told the outlaw that the child's parents did not wish to see it die of starvation and commissioned him to give it something to eat. So saying he threw out one of the boxes before the man. Isenokami then continued; "As you yourself may be hungry, I had another box prepared for you." When the desperado stretched his arm to receive it, the monk-swordsman lost no time to seize him by the arm and forcibly throwing him down on the ground made him a complete prisoner. The monkish robe was returned to its original owner who praised him highly, saying, "You are truly a 'man of the sword,'" and gave him the *kara*, a symbol of monkhood, which is generally carried by a Zen monk over his chest hanging from the neck—a kind of abridged *kesa* (*kāshāya* in Sanskrit). It is said that Isenokami never parted with it. The wandering Zen monk could not have been a mere novice in Zen, he must have been one of some understanding. "A man of the sword" is a phrase much used in Zen denoting a seasoned Zen monk who has really gone beyond the line of life and death. Isenokami must have indeed had good reason for treasuring the *kara* as a gift from the monk "travelling on foot."

死するのを見るに忍びないので、食べ物を与えるようにと自分に頼んだと言った。かくいって、彼は男の前に弁当箱の一つを差出した。伊勢守は続けて『お前も空腹であろうから、いま一つ弁当を用意させてきた。』兇漢がそれを受取ろうと片腕を差延したとき、僧形の剣士はときを失わず彼の利腕を捕えて、力任せに地に投げつけ、見事に彼を生捕りにしてしまった。衣を元の持主に返すと、出家はいたく彼を賞揚して、『貴殿こそ真に「剣刃上の一句を悟った人」だ』といって、禅僧の象徴である掛絡(訳註、普通、禅僧が首から胸に掛ける小さい方形の略式袈裟のこと)を贈った。伊勢守は、けっして、それを手放さなかったという。この旅の僧も、禅の方では、ただ者ではなかったのだろう。相当の悟者だったに違いない。「剣刃上の一句」というのは、禅の方でよく用いる言葉で、生死の線を真に超えた、風霜をへた禅僧をさす。なるほど、伊勢守が、行脚僧からの贈物——掛絡を大事にしたという事も、十分の理由はあったわけだ。

A portrait of the Emperor Godaigo.

後醍醐天皇肖像。

Zen and the Study of Confucianism

禅と儒教

Paradoxical or rather ironical thought it may seem, Zen whose teaching is against all learning and literary reconstruction was really the agency in Japan for encouraging the study of Confucianism and also for promoting the art of printing—and this consisted in printing not only Buddhist books but Confucian and Shinto literature. The Kamakura and the Ashikaga period (1192–1333–1573) are generally considered the dark ages of Japanese history, but the fact is that they are far from being so, because the Zen monks were busy in bringing Chinese culture into this country and preparing the way for its assimilation later on, and because what can be regarded as particularly Japanese has been in the process of hatching during these periods. The beginning of *haiku*, *nogaku*, theatre, landscape gardening, flower arrangement, tea-cult, etc., is to be sought in them. Here I wish to confine myself to the development of Confucian study in Japan as influenced by Zen monks. To do this, it is advisable to say a word about the "Sung philosophy" in China.

Politically, the Sung (960–1278) was a troubled age, the existence of the "Middle Kingdom" was constantly menaced from the North until it had to cross the Wei Southward and finally submit to the domination of the Northern tribes in 1127. The Southern Sung too, however, vanished, being absorbed by the Mongolian invaders in 1278, and the Yuan came to power

逆説的あるいはむしろ反語的に見えるかも知れぬが、いっさいの学問と文字的再構成に反対する禅が、じつは日本において、儒教の研究を奨励し、印刷術を促進する作因となった。禅徒は仏教の書籍のみならず、儒教や神道の文学類をも印刷したのである。鎌倉・室町時代（1192-1333-1573）は一般に日本歴史の暗黒時代と考えられているが、事実はそうでない。禅僧が中国文化を日本にもたらし、後日同化の道を開いたのはこの時代である。また、とくに日本的と見做しうるものが、この時期を通じて孵化の過程にあった。俳句・能楽・芝居・造園・生花・茶の湯などの始まりがこの時期に求められる。ここでは禅僧によって影響された日本における儒教の発達について記述したい。これがためには、中国宋学のことを一言いうのが順序である。

　政治上からいうと、宋（960-1278）は多難な時代であった。「中華」の存在はたえず北方から脅され、ついに淮河を渡って南方に移り、結局、1127年北方種族の支配に屈しなければならなかった。しかし、南宋もまた1278年に蒙古人の侵略によって奪われて消滅し、元が中国全土に勢力を振うこととなった。しかし、思想と一般文化

all over China. But in the world of thought and general culture the Sung, Northern and especially Southern, left brilliant records; philosophy achieved a phenomenal development in the South. It seemed as if the original speculative impulses pent up during the Han and the succeeding dynasties and kept more or less suppressed by the powerful Indian thought, burst out and asserted themselves in this period even under the pressure of an alien power. The result was the rise of a philosophy to be properly called "Chinese" in which all the trends of thought imported from abroad as well as those primarily native to China were syncretised and formulated on the basis of the Chinese mentality, and, therefore, more readily acceptable to it. The Sung philosophy is the flower of the Chinese mind.

One powerful factor at least which helped to give such a fruit-bearing stimulus to Chinese speculation was the teaching of Zen. Zen is always stimulating and thought-provoking because it directly goes to the root of things regardless of superstructures. When Confucianism turned into mere study of rituals, the practice of earthly morals, a matter of textual criticism, and an opportunity for schools of commentators, we can say that it was on the verge of collapse and final death as the fountain of creative speculations. It required a new force to be resuscitated. Taoism, the rival school of Chinese thought, was deeply buried under its own more popular and superstitious frame. There was in it nothing intellectually vigorous to instill fresh blood into Confucianism. If Zen failed to stir the depths of Chinese psychology during the T'ang, the people of the Sung would probably never have taken up their own philosophy with a new interest for its reconstruction and further unfoldment. Almost all the thinkers of the Sung at least once in their lives betook themselves to the Zen monasteries, and with whatever insight or no-insight they carried out of the institution, they re-examined their philosophy born of their own soil. The Sung philosophy is the outcome of their spiritual adventures. While denouncing Buddhism and the Buddhist way of thinking, they drank from the Indian fountain presented to them in the more digestible form of Zen.

の世界においては南北の宋、ことに南宋は輝やかしい記録を残した。哲学は南方において稀有の発展をとげた。それは漢代とそれにつづく王朝の間、閉じこめられて、かつ、強力な印度思想によって多少抑えられていた中国本来の思索的衝動が、この期に至って夷狄の政治的勢力の圧迫下にもかかわらず、爆発して現れた観がある。その結果は正しく「シナ的」と呼ぶべき哲学の勃興であり、いっさいの思想傾向は元来の中国土着のものはもとより、外来のものをもことごとく綜合され、中国人の心的傾向を基礎として公式化されたのであった。宋学は中国心理の精華である。

　中国人の思索にかかる結実的な刺激を与える助けとなったところの、少なくとも一つの強力な要因は、禅の教えであった。禅がいかにしてつねに刺激を与え思想を湧かせる原因となったかというに、それは思想上の上層建築物を無視して、直接に事実の根元に突き進むことを教えるからである。儒教が単なる典礼の学、世俗的道徳の実践、原典批判の問題、各派の注釈をうながす機会を与えるようになった時、儒教は創造的思索の源泉でなくなった。崩壊と最後の死滅とに瀕したときだといえる。新しい力を蘇らせることが必要であった。一面、儒教に対抗してきた道教は世俗的・迷信的な機構のしたに深く埋れていたので、儒教にたいして新鮮な血液を注ぎこむべき知性的活気は少しもなかった。もし禅が唐代をつうじて中国人心理の深処を、攪拌しえなかったなら、宋代人はおそらく新しい興味をもって、自分たちの哲学を取上げ、これを改造し展開するようなことはけっしてしなかったろう。ほとんどすべての宋代思想家は、少くともその生涯に一度は禅林にこもった。しかしこの僧院から、彼らがどんな洞察どんな不洞察を獲得してきたかは、いま問わぬにしても、自分たちが生れた土壌に培われてできあがった哲学は、これを再検討しなければならぬようになった。宋学は彼らの精神的冒険の成果である。仏教と仏教徒の考えかたを批議しつつあった間に、彼らは禅というより消化しやすい形で贈られたインドの泉から十分飲んだのである。

The Zen monks, on the other hand, were also students of Confucianism as well. As Chinese, they could not be anything else; the only difference between Confucian scholars and Zen masters was that the Confucians based their philosophy on the native system, while the Confucian vocabulary, indeed quite frequently expressed themselves in terms of Confucianism. The difference between the two classes of mind can be said to be in the placing of emphasis.

The Zen monks interpreted the Confucian texts in the Indian fashion, so to speak, that is, more or less idealistically and were naturally not averse to commentating on their Buddhist literature from the Confucian point of view.

When they came to Japan, they brought both Zen and Confucianism. The Japanese monks who went over to China to study to Zen did the same, that is, together with their own Zen books they filled their luggage cases with books on Confucianism and Taoism. While in China, they sat at the feet of the Zen-Confucian masters from whom they learned much of Confucianism as well as Zen. And there were many such Chinese masters in Sung, especially in Southern Sung.

I will not enter into too much detail in regard to the interrelationship of Zen and Confucianism and of Zen and Taoism in China. Suffice it just to state this here that Zen is in fact the Chinese way of responding to Indian thought as represented by Buddhism and that this being so, Zen, as it developed in the T'ang and later flourished in the Sung, could not be anything else but a reflection of Chinese mentality—by which I mean its being eminently practical and ethical. In this latter respect, there was every probability of Zen's taking the Confucian colouring. But in the beginning of Zen's history its philosophy was Indian, that is, Buddhistic, for there was nothing corresponding to it in the traditional teaching of Confucianism. And this was the element the later Confucian thinkers consciously or unconsciously wished to incorporate in their own system. In other words, Zen acquired its practicalness from Confucianism whereas Confucianism absorbed through the teaching of Zen, thought in some respects indirectly, the Indian habit of

一方禅僧もまた同様の儒教の学徒であった。中国人としての彼らはもとよりそうなるより外なかったのである。儒教学者と禅匠との唯一の相違は、禅教徒はその哲学の基礎を自国の思想体系においたが、仏教徒は仏教的のシステムを固守して、その語彙は儒教から採用することにした。じっさい、禅徒は儒教の用語を使って自家の体験を表現したのである。これら両系統の相違は力点のおきどころに存するといえる。

　いわば禅僧は儒教諸原典をインド式に解釈した。すなわち、多少理想主義的なところがあった。それから儒教的観点で自分たちの仏典に註釈を加えることも嫌わなかった。

　彼らが日本にきたときは、禅と儒を二つながらもたらした、禅をまなぶため中国に渡った日本の僧も同じだった。すなわち、自分の禅書とともに旅嚢には儒・道の書物をみたしたのである。中国にいたときは、彼らは禅・儒兼学の師匠の膝下にあって、禅はもちろん儒教をも多分にまなんだ。宋、ことに南宋にはかかる中国人の学匠が多かったのである。

　中国における禅と儒教、禅と道教との相互関係に関してはあまり詳細にわたりたくない。ここでは禅は事実、仏教によって代表されたインド思想に対して中国的に順応したのであり、これがために禅は唐代に発達して宋代に栄えたように、中国人の心理傾向を反映するものに他ならないと、これだけを述べておく。その意味は禅はインド思想の型をはなれて、きわめて実践的で倫理的であるということである。この点からいえば、禅が儒教的色彩を帯びるということには十分の理由があったが、禅宗史の初めには、その哲学はインド的であった、すなわち仏教的であった。儒教の伝統的教義にはこれに相当するようなものはなにも無かったからである。しかもこの要素こそ、後になって儒者が意識的にか、無意識的にか、自己の思想体系のなかに体現せんと欲したところのものなのであった。換言すれば、禅はその実践性を儒教から得、儒教は禅の教えを通して、ある点間接にだが、インド的な抽象的思索癖を吸収し、結局、孔子一

abstract speculation, and finally succeeded in giving a metaphysical foundation to the teaching of Confucius and his followers. To do this, the Sung philosophers emphasised the utmost importance of the "Four Books"* in the study of Confucianism. They found in them some statements which could be elaborated for the establishment of their system. This naturally paved the way to a rapprochement between Zen and Confucianism.

It was thus natural for the Zen monks to become propagators of Confucianism besides being Buddhists. Strictly speaking, Zen has no philosophy of its own. Its teaching is concentrated on an intuitive experience and the intellectual content of this experience can be supplied by a system of thought not necessarily Buddhistic.

If the masters find it more expedient for some reason, they may build up their own philosophical structure not always in accordance with the traditional interpretation. Zen Buddhists are sometimes Confucians, sometimes Taoists, or sometimes even Shintoists; Zen experience can also be explained by Western philosophy.

In the fourteenth and the fifteenth century the "Five Mountains," that is, the Zen monasteries in Kyoto were the publishing headquarters of the Confucian texts, not to say anything about the Zen books. Some of these earlier texts including those of the thirteenth century, both Buddhist and Confucian, are still obtainable and, among the most highly prized wood-cut prints in the Far East.

Not only did the Zen monks edit and print the text-books of Buddhism and Confucianism, but they compiled books for popular education, using them in their monasteries where those crowded who were desirous of improving their knowledge and culture. The term "*terakoya*" thus came in vogue. *Tera* means a "Buddhist temple," *ko* "children," and *ya* "a house." The *Terakoya* system was the only popular educational institution during the feudal ages of Japan until it was replaced by the modern one after the Restoration in 1868.

派の教えに形而上学的な基礎を与えることに成功した。これがために宋代哲学者は儒教研究における四書のこのうえなく重要なることを力説した。彼らは四書のなかに見いだした所説を念いりに仕上げて自分たちの思想体系を樹立しえた。これは自然に禅と儒教との間の和 解への道をひらいた。

　かくして、禅僧が仏教徒たる以外に儒教の宣伝者となったのは当然だった。厳格にいえば、禅には自己の哲学というようなものは無い。その教えは直覚的経験に焦点をおき、この経験の知的内容はかならずしも仏教哲学にかぎられるというわけではない。いかなる思想体系からでも供給されうるともいいえられる。

　禅匠は、ある理窟づけに対して、その方が都合がいいと思えば、かならずしも伝統的の解釈にしたがわずに、それによって、自分自身の哲学的構造を打樹てていいのだ。禅徒はときとすると儒教徒、ときとすると道教徒、また、ときとすると神道家とさえなりうるのである。禅的経験は、また、西洋哲学によっても説明することができる。

　十四世紀、十五世紀において京都の五山が、禅書はもちろんだが、儒書の発行所でもあった。これら初期の儒・仏諸書のなかには、それ以前の十三世紀のものとともに、いまなおえられるが、極東における木活版としてきわめて高く評価される一つである。

　禅僧は儒仏原典を編修印刷したのみならず、普及版を編纂して知徳をみがくために禅寺に参集するものの用にした。「寺子屋」という用語はかくして流行してきた。寺子屋制度は封建時代の唯一の普通教育の機関であったが、ついに1868年の維新以後には現代ふうの教育機関によっておきかえられるようになった。

The activities of the Zen monks were not confined to the central parts of Japan, they were invited out by the provincial lords to look after the education of their vassals and retainers. They were Buddhist-Confucians. As one of the most notable examples we mention a Zen monk Kei-an (1427–1508), who went to Satsuma, the southwestern province in Kyushu. His special study was the "Four Books" which he explained according to Shushi's (Chu Hsi in Chinese) commentaries. But being a Zen monk he did not forget to emphasise his own teaching in connection with the Confucian philosophy. The study of Mind was the guiding spirit of his discipline. He also lectured on the *Shu Ching*, one of the "Five Canons,"* which contains the ethical edicts of the ancient rulers of China. He left in Sastuma an enduring spiritual influence. Among his distant disciples the name of Shimadzu Nisshinsai (1492–1568) stands most prominent. Although he was not taught by Keian himself, his mother and his teachers were personally acquainted with Keian, and all their families were great admirers of the monk-scholar. Nisshinsai was born of the Shimadzu family and his eldest son was later adopted by the main family and came to rule the three provinces of Satsuma, Ōsumi, and Hyūga in the southwestern part of Japan. Nisshinsai's moral influence spread through his son all over the feudal estate under his jurisdiction. Until the Restoration of 1868, he was rightly honoured by the people as one of the greatest figures among them.

Of the Zen masters of the "Five Mountains," mention may be made of Muso the National teacher (1275–1351), Gen-ye (1269–1352), Kokwan Shiren (1278–1346), Chyūgen Yengetu (1300–1375), Gidō Shūshin (1321–1388), and others, all of whom furthered the study of the Confucian classics in accordance with the spirit of Zen Buddhism. The emperors and the Shōguns also followed the example of the Zen masters. They were earnest students of Zen and at the same time attended their lectures on Confucianism. The Emperor Hanazono (reigned 1308–1317), whose residence was given to his Zen teacher, Kwanzan (1277–1360), which became the foundation of the present Myōshinji, the most powerful branch of Rinzai Zen, in the west-

禅僧の活動は日本の中央部にかぎられたわけのものではなく、地方大名に招聘されてその家臣たちの教育を世話した。彼らは儒仏兼学の徒であった。その最も著しい例の一つとしては薩摩藩に招聘せられた禅僧桂庵（1452–1508）をあげうる。彼の専門は四書を朱子の註釈にしたがって説明するにあった。が、禅僧であるから儒教と関連させて、禅宗の教義をも力説することを忘れなかった。心性の研究が彼の鍛錬の指導精神であった。彼はまた、五経の一つの「春秋」すなわち中国古代支配者の倫理的布令を内容としたものを講義した。桂庵は薩摩にながく精神的影響をのこした。その遠い弟子のなかに島津日新斎の名が卓越している。桂庵が親しく教えたのではないが、彼の母と彼の師たちは親しく桂庵と知り、一族ことごとくこの学僧を深く尊崇した。日新斎は島津家の一族でその長子は後に宗家の嗣となり、薩摩・大隅・日向の三国を支配するようになった。日新斎の道徳的影響は彼の子を通してその支配下の封建領土の上におよんだ。明治維新まで、彼は当然その領民から最大人物の一人として尊敬された。

　五山の禅匠たちのうち、夢窓国師（1275–1351）、玄慧（げんえ）（1269–1350）、虎関師錬（こかんしれん）（1278–1346）、中巌円月（ちゅうがんえんげつ）（1300–1375）、義堂周信（ぎどうしゅうしん）（1321–1388）およびその他の禅匠たちはみな禅宗精神にしたがって儒教の研究を進めた。皇室と将軍も禅匠たちの例にならった。いずれも熱心に禅に参究すると同時に儒書の講義を聴いた。花園天皇（1308–1317、御在位）はその行宮を関山国師（1277–1360）に賜ったが、国師は洛西花園における臨済禅の有力な一派なる妙心寺の開山となった人である。天皇は宋学を真摯にまなび、また、禅にも熱心に参し、その点においてはジレッタンチズムの域をはるかに超えていた。その皇儲に賜わった遺誡は著名なものであり、天皇の聡明さをかたる

ern part of Kyoto, was a sincere scholar of the Sung school of Chinese philosophy, and an earnest follower of Zen in which he really went far beyond mere dilettantism. The admonition he left for his successor is a remarkable document of royal wisdom. His statue in the attire of a Zen monk and sitting cross-legged in serene dignity is still preserved in his own room at Myoshinji, where he used to sit in meditation. His "Journal" is an important historical source-material.

I may add here that even in the early days of the Tokugawa Shogunate, that is, at beginning of the seventeenth century, the Confucian scholars used to shave their heads like Buddhist priests. From this fact we naturally gather that the study of Confucianism was kept up among the Buddhists, especially the Zen monks, and even when the study came to be pursued independently among the intellectuals, its professors simply followed the old custom.

In connection with this chapter, the writer wishes to add a few remarks about the part played by Zen in the cultivation of the nationalistic spirit during the Kamakura and the Ashikaga period. Theoretically speaking, Zen has nothing to do with nationalism. As long as it is a religion, its mission has universal validity and its field of applicability is not limited to one specified nationality. But from the point of view of history it is subject to accidents and particularisation. When Zen first came to Japan it found itself connected with persons steeped with Confucianism and patriotic spirit, and Zen naturally took their colour on itself, that is to say, Zen was not received in Japan in its pure form divorced from all its accidents. Not only that, the Japanese followers themselves were willing to take Zen with everything that came along with it, until later the accidentals were separated from the body to which they were attached and came to establish themselves independently even in defiance to their original associates. To describe this process in the history of Japanese thought does not belong here, but I wish to refer to it more less tentatively tracing it back to the Chinese thought-movement.

As I said elsewhere, the culmination of Chinese intellectuality is found in the philosophy of Shushi or Chu Hsi (1130–1200) who flourished mainly

文書である。禅僧の装いをして、端然として結跏趺坐した天皇の像が、いまなお妙心寺に、在世の当時、瞑想静坐を常とせられた一室に保存されている。天皇の「御日記」は重要な史料である。

　江戸時代の初期、すなわち、十七世紀の初めにおいてさえ、儒者は僧侶のごとく剃髪するのがつねであったことをここでつけ加えておこう。この事実から当然推測できるのは、儒教の研究が僧侶の間に、とくに禅僧の間に持続されたこと、および、その研究が独立して知識人の間に行われるようになった時でも、その教授者たちは単に旧習にしたがったということだ。

　本章に関連して、著者は鎌倉・室町の時代を通して国民精神涵養に禅が演じた役割について一言つけ加えておきたいと思う。理論的にいえば、禅は国家主義とは何にも関わりがない。宗教であるかぎり、その使命は普遍妥当性を有し、その適用の範囲はとくに国民性にかぎられはせね。が、歴史的見地から見れば、偶発事件と特殊化との影響をこうむる。禅が日本に始めてはいったとき、それは儒教と愛国精神にみがかれた人々と結びつき、当然そういう色彩を帯びた、すなわち、日本においてはあらゆる事件から離れた純粋の形では受容されなかった。そればかりか、日本の参禅者は禅が伴ってきたいっさいのものをもよろこんで受けとったが、後にはそれに附帯する偶発的なものが、本体から離れて独立に存在するようになった。そして、両者従来の親密な関係は敵性をもってさえ見られるにいたった。日本思想史におけるこの経過を述べることは本書の領域外であるが、試みにその跡をたどれば中国の思想運動にまでさかのぼるものであることを指摘したいと思う。

　他のところでいったように、中国民族の知性的発展は、主として南宋に栄えた朱子（朱熹）（1130–1200）の学にいたってその極に達

in the Southern Sung. He was probably the greatest Chinese thinker who tried to systematise Chinese thought along the line of the psychology of his own people. There were greater philosophers prior to him among his countrymen, but their thought moved along the Indian line of speculation somewhat against their native trends. For this reason their philosophy did not influence the people so directly as did that of the Southern Sung. It is no doubt true that the latter could not have its existence without its Buddhist predecessors. We must now see how the so-called "Science of the Tao" developed in Sung, for this will help us to understand Zen's specific influence on the thought and feeling of the Japanese people.

There are two original currents of Chinese thought, Confucianism and pure Taoism, i.e. the one not wedded to popular beliefs and superstitions. Confucianism represents the practicalness or positivism of the Chinese mentality whereas Taoism represents its mystic and speculative trends. When Buddhism was brought to China in the early Latter Han Dynasty (64 A.D.), it found a real associate in the thought of Lao-tzu and Chuang-tzu. In the beginning, Buddhism was not very active in the Chinese world of thought, it occupied itself mostly with translating its texts into the Chinese, and the people did not know exactly how to take it into their system of thoughts and beliefs. But through the translations they must have realised the fact the there was something very deep and aspiring in the philosophy of Buddhism. Since the second century when the *Prajñāpāramitā Sutras* began to be rendered into Chinese, thinkers who were deeply impressed by them took up their study in all seriousness. While they could not clearly grasp the idea of *Sūnyatā*, "Emptiness," they found it somewhat akin to the Laotzuan idea of *Wu*, "Nothingness."

During the Six Dynasties (386–587) when the study of Taoism carried the day to the extent that the Confucian texts themselves were interpreted in the light of Taoism, Kumārajā came from a western kingdom to China in 401 and translated a number of the Mahayana sutras. He was not only a brilliant translator but a great original thinker who gave much light on

した。朱子は自国民本来の心理的傾向線にそって、中国思想を体系づけようとした最大の中国思想家であった。彼の国人のなかにも彼にまさる偉大な哲学者はいたが、その思想は自国本来の傾向にやや反してインド人の思索方向にそって動いた。かかる理由でその哲学は南宋の哲学のように、直接国民に影響を与えなかった。が、南宋の哲学は仏教徒の先蹤なくしては存在しえなかったということは疑いを容れぬ事実である。われわれはいわゆる「理学」がいかにして宋に発達したかを知らねばならぬ。これによって日本人の思想、感情におよぼした禅の特別の影響を理解することができるからだ。

中国思想には二つの源流、儒教と純粋の道教（すなわち民衆的信仰、迷信に囚われぬもの）がある。儒教は中国人心理の実践と積極主義を代表するが、道教はその神秘的にして思索的な傾向を代表する。仏教が後漢時代（西紀64）の初めに中国に入った時、老荘の思想に大いに似通うものがあることを認めた。が、その当初、仏教は中国思想界においてあまり活動的ではなかった。その原典を中国語に翻訳することに多くの力を費した。中国の人々は、仏教をとり入れて、これを自国の思想信仰体系のなかにこなす道を的確に知らなかった。が、翻訳された仏典を通して彼らは仏教哲学にきわめて深遠高大なもののある事実を悟ったにちがいない。第二世紀に般若波羅密経が訳され始めてから、それに深い感銘をうけた思想家たちは、きわめて真摯にその研究にしたがった。彼らは「空」の観念を明確に把握することはまだできなかったが、老子の「無」の観念に多少近いものと知った。

六朝時代（386-587）に道教の研究が興隆してきて、儒教の原典まで道教の見地から解釈されるまでになったころ、鳩摩羅什が401年に西域から中国にきて大乗仏教の諸経を訳した。彼は立派な翻訳者であったのみならず、偉大な独創的思想家でもあったから、大乗仏教の理解に多大の光を投じ、中国における彼の弟子たちはその民族

the understanding of the Mahayana, and his Chinese disciples busied themselves in developing his ideas in the way most adapted to the mentality of their people.

The San-lun (Sanron in Japanese) Shool of Buddhism thus came to be established in China by Chi-tsang (549–623), who based his philosophy on the teaching of Nāgārjuna. It was a wonderful thought-system rising for the first time in the land of Confucius and Lao-tzu. But we can say that the author of the School was still under the influence of Indian thought. He thought as Indians did and not necessarily in the Chinese fashion. He was no doubt a Chinese Buddhist, but a Buddhist scholar; if this were possible he thought as a Buddhist and not as a Chinese.

The san-lun School was followed by the T'ien-tai (Tendai), the Wei-shih (Yuisiki), and the Hua-yen (Kegon) in the Sui and the T'ang Dynasty. The T'ien-tai is based on the *Saddharma-pundarīka*, the Wei-shih on the idealistic teaching of Asanga and Vasubandhu, and the Hua-yen on the *Avatamsaka*. This last was the culmination of Chinese Buddhist thought. It demonstrates the height of religious speculations reached by Chinese Buddhist minds. It is the most remarkable thought-system ever elaborated by oriental people. The *Avatamsaka Sutra*, including the *Dasabhūmika* and the *Gandavyūha*, is no doubt the climax of Indian creative imagination which is utterly foreign to Chinese thinking and feeling, and it is really an intellectual feat of the Chinese Buddhists that this so completely strange imagination of the Indians could be intelligently and systematically digested. The philosophy of the Hua-yen School proves the depths of the Chinese religious consciousness which revealed itself after centuries of Buddhist education and reflection. And this was really what stirred up the Chinese mind from its long slumber and gave it the strongest possible stimulus to bloom forth as the Sung philosophy.

While the Hua-yen School represented the intellectuality, so to speak, of

心理性に最も適応した方法で孜々として彼らの思想発展に努めた。

　三論派がかくして吉蔵（嘉祥大師、549–623）によって中国に樹立されるにいたったが、吉蔵の哲学は竜樹の教義にもとづいたのである。これこそ孔子と老子の国に初めて擡頭したすばらしい思想体系であった。この派の著述はなおインド思想の影響の下にあったといいうる。彼はインド思想と同じように考えたので、かならずしも中国ふうに考えたのではなかった。彼は中国の仏教徒であったことは疑いないが仏学者であった。こんな事がいえるとしたなら、彼は仏教徒として考えたので、中国人としてではなかった。その意味は、彼の考にはまだインド的なものがくっついていて、まだ十分に中国人化しなかったということなのである。
　三論派を継承したものは、隋・唐両朝の天台・華厳・唯識であった。天台は法華経に、華厳は華厳経に、唯識は無着と天親の唯心主義的教説にもとづいた。華厳哲学は中国における仏教思想の極致であったといいうる。それは中国の仏教精神が到達した宗教的思索の最高度を示したものである。それはこれまで東洋人の労作したなかで最も注目すべき思想体系である。華厳教は、十地経および入法界品をも含んでいるが、このなかに盛られている思想・感情は、中国人心理にとってはまったく異邦的なものであるが、これはじつにインド人の創造的想像力の最高峯を示すものである事は疑いないのである。しかしながら、このインド的なるもの、自分らのとまったく異なった想像力から生れたものを自分に取りいれ、これを知的に体系的に咀嚼しえた杜順・智儼のごときはじつに中国仏教徒の知力的放れ業である。華厳の哲学は、幾世紀にわたって、仏教的教育と反省をへて、始めて実現した中国的宗教意識というべきものの深さを証するものである。そして、これこそじつに中国の思索精神をその長い眠りからよび醒まし、これにできるだけ強い刺激を与えて、宋学として開華せしめたところのものであった。
　華厳哲学が中国仏教徒の、いわば、知力を代表したとき、それと

the Chinese Buddhists, there was another school rising to power along with it and taking a stronger hold oh their minds—which is Zen (*Ch'an* in Chinese). Zen appealed partly to the empirical proclivity of Chinese mentality and partly to its craving for mysticism. Zen despised learning as it upheld the intuitive mode of understanding which its followers were convinced was the most direct and effective instrument to grasp ultimate reality. In fact, empiricism and mysticism and positivism can walk hand in hand quite readily. They all look for the facts of experience and are shy of building up an intellectual frame-work around them.

But as a social being man cannot remain contented with mere experience, he wants to communicate it his fellow-being—which means that intuition is to have its contents, its intellectual reconstruction. Zen did its best to remain on its intuitive plane of understanding, and made the best use of imageries, symbols, and poetic tricks although the latter in not a very dignified term.

When it, however, had to have recourse to intellection, it was a good friend of the Hua-yen philosophy. The amalgamation of Zen and Hua-yen (Kegon) philosophy, though by no means deliberately carried out, became most noticeable with Ch'êng-kuan 澄観 (738–838) and Tsung-mi 宗密 (780–841), both of whom were great scholars of the Hua-yen School and at the same time followers of Zen. It was through this approach that Zen came to influence the Confucian thought of the Sung scholars.

The T'ang dynasty thus prepared the way to the rise of the Sung "Science of the Tao" (*tao-hsiao*), which as I consider is the most precious native product from the Chinese mental crucible into which the Hua-yen, Zen, Confucianism, and Laotzuanism have thrown together.

Chu Hsi 朱熹 (Shushi) had his predecessors: Chou Tun-i 周敦頤 (Shu Ton-i, 1017–1073), Chang Hêng-chü 張橫渠 (Cho Wo-kyo, 1077–1135), and the Cheng 程 (Tei) Brothers, Ming-Tao 明道 (Mei-do, 1085–1139), and I-ch'uan 伊川 (I-sen, 1107–1182). They all tried to establish philosophy on a purely Chinese basis, as they found it chiefly in the "Four Books"—the *Lun-yü*, the *Meng-tzu*, the *Ta-hsiao*, and the *Chung-yung*, and also in the *Yi-ching*,

ならんで勢力をえて中国人の心をよりつよく把握した別派があった。——それが禅である。禅は一部分は中国人心理の実証的性癖に、また一部分はその神秘的思念に訴えたものである。禅は文字の知識を軽蔑し、究極の実在を直接に把握するためには最も有効な手段だと修禅者たちが確信する直観的理解を唱道した。事実、経験主義・<ruby>経験主義<rt>エンピリシズム</rt></ruby>・神秘主義・および実証主義はきわめて容易に手をたずさえて歩くことができるのだ。この三者はいずれも、経験事実そのものを求め、その事実のまわりに知識的構造を築きあげることを嫌う。

　しかし、社会的存在たる人間は、単なる経験をもって満足しておられぬ。彼はそれを仲間に伝える事を欲する。すなわち、直観は直観に止まらず、かならず、他の一面にその観念、その知的再構成というものを持つのである。禅はその直観的理解の面に踏み止まるため、最善の方法をつくす。そして、念象・表象・および詩的表現というべきものを自由に使役する。

　しかしこういえる、禅が知的作用に訴えねばならなかったとき、それは華厳哲学の好伴侶となったと。禅と華厳哲学の合金作用はけっして故意に意図的に行われたのではないが、この関係は、華厳宗の大学者で、同時に禅の参究者である澄観（738-838）と宗密（780-841）などによって、最も注目すべきものとなった。この接近によって禅は宋学者の儒教的思想に影響をおよぼすこととなったのである。

　唐代はかくして、「理学」勃興の道を用意した。理学は、思うに、華厳・禅・孔子・老子の諸説がいっせいに投げ込まれた中国民族心理の大坩堝からでた最も貴重な中国土着の産物である。

　朱熹には先蹤があった。周敦頤（1017-1073）、張横渠（1077-1135）、程明道（1085-1139）、程伊川（1107-1182）——彼らはいずれもみな純粋に中国的心理の基礎のうえに哲学を樹立せんとし、そしてこの基礎を主として「四書」——論語・孟子・大学・中庸——および易経のなかに見いだした。彼らはみな禅を研究して、それによって自分たちの学説の形成につとめた。彼らが禅に負うところがあっ

Book of Changes. That they all studied Zen and were indebted to it in the formulation of their doctrine, is seen from the fact that they place so much significance on the experience of a sudden illumination that will come on them when they have sufficiently applied themselves to the study of the classics or meditated on their meaning. In their cosmogony or ontology, they set up as primordial substance *Wu-chi*, or *Ta-chi*, or *Ta-hsu*;* these are the ideas derived from the *Yi-ching* and Lao-tzu, but one may suspect that *Ta-hsu* here has a Buddhist ring. When this principle is translated in terms of ethics, it is sincerity, and the ideal of man's life consists in cultivating the virtue of sincerity; for it is by this that the world is what it is, and that the male principle and the female principle which have their origin in the "Great Limit" interact and make possible the orderly growth of all things. Sincerity is also called *Li* (Reason) or *T'ien-li* (Heavenly Reason).

The Sung philosophers have *Ch'i* (氣) opposed to *Li* (理), and this antithesis is unified in *Ta-chi*, which is *Wu-chi*. *Li* is the Reason running through all things and impartially possessed by everyone of them; without *Li* nothing is possible, existences lose their being, and are reduced to non-entity. *Ch'i* is a differentiating agency, whereby one Reason multiplicates itself and produces a world of pluralities. *Li* and *Ch'i* are thus interpenetrating and complementary.

The relation of *Ta-chi* to *Li* and *Ch'i* is not very clear, except that it is the synthesis of the two principles and that the Sung philosophy did not apparently wish to remain dualistic, which is probably due to the influence of the Hua-yen School of Buddhism. As to *Ta-chi* itself, it is an ambiguous idea—it appears to be primordial matter which is *Wu-chi*, the Limitless. When it is said that Great Limit is the Limitless, the one is something "above matter" and the other is something "below matter," and how can that which is above become that which is below and *vice versa*? The same dilemma may be encountered in the case of *Li* and *Ch'i*, but the Sung philosophers were decidedly Chinese and had no inclination in this respect to follow the Buddhists who did not hesitate to deny the materiality of the

たという事実は、つぎのごとくである。すなわち、彼らが古典の研究に没頭して、その意味を了解せんとつとめたとき、彼らの脳裡に不意にひらめきでるものがあった、この経験にたいして彼らは相当意義あるものと信じたのである。その宇宙発生論や本体論のなかに、彼らは元始的素質として、「無極」・「太極」・「太虚」などを説いた。これらは易や老子から発した観念ではあるが、ここでいう「太虚」には仏教的なひびきがある。この原理を倫理学の用語で訳せば誠実であり、人生の理想は誠実の徳を涵養するにあると彼らは信じた。なぜかというに、これによって世界は如実に存し、太極に源を発する陰陽の二原理が相交感して、万物の運行を可能ならしめるからである。彼らは誠実を「理」あるいは「天理」とも呼ぶ。

　宋学には「理」に対して「気」が存する。この対立は「太極」すなわち「無極」によりて綜合される。「理」は万物を貫き、あまねく個々のものに分有せられる。「理」なければ何ものも不可能で、存在はその理を失い、非実在に帰する。「気」は分化的作用をなし、それによって一つの理性が多様化し特殊の世界を生ずる。理と気とはかくして相互滲透しあい補足しあっている。

　太極と理・気との関係はあまり明らかでない。ただ太極は二原理の綜合であるとみられるが、宋学では二元論に止まることを欲せぬらしい。これはおそらく華厳哲学の影響のせいであろう。太極そのものは曖昧な観念である。元始的物質のようにみえる、そしてこれが無極だというのである。かく太極は無極なりというときには、一は「物質以上」のあるもの、一は「物質以下」のあるものであるやに解せられる。すると「以上のもの」がどうして「以下のもの」になりうるかという疑問がでる。またその反対の疑問も可能である。同じジレンマは理と気の場合にも起りうる。が、宋の哲学者は、断然、中国人であり、この点において、世界の具象性を躊躇なく否定し、世俗と、そこにあるいっさいは、等しくこれ「空」なりとした

world and declare it with all things in it to be equally "empty" (*sūnya*). The Chinese mind always upheld a world of particular realities. Even when it closely approaches the Hua-yen it stops short at materiality.

What is significant in the Sung philosophy of Chu Hsi and made it wield a great influence in China and Japan in the most practical way is its view of history. It is the development of the idea dominating the *Spring and Autumn* (*Ch'un-Cch'in*), one of the great classical works compiled by Confucius. The work was written by the Master with the view morally to weigh the claims of the different states of his day which is known as "Kingdoms at War." China was then divided into several kingdoms each trying to gain the upper hand of others; usurpers claimed to be transmitting the orthodox line of kingship; politics lost their compass drifting along as the fancy of the rulers moved. Confucius's idea of compiling annals of his time was to establish a universal ethical standard for all the future statesmen of his country. The *Spring and Autumn* therefore embodies the practical codes of ethics as illustrated by the events of history.

Chu Hsi followed the example of Confucius by compiling an abridged history of China from Ssŭ-ma Kang's larger work. In this he enunciated the great principal of propriety known as "Names and Parts" (*ming-fên* 名分) which he thought ought to be made the governing principle of politics for all ages. The universe is governed by the laws of Heaven, so are human affairs; and these laws require of each of us to observe what is proper to him. He has a "name," he performs a certain "part" as he occupies a definite position in society, he is assigned to a place where he is asked to render his service as a member of the groups to which he belongs. This network of social relationships is not to be ignored if the peace and happiness of its component parts are to be preserved and enhanced. The ruler has his proper duties to perform and his subjects theirs, the parents and their children have also their well defined obligations to each other, and so on. There ought not to be any disturbance or usurpation of names, titles, and parts.

Chu Hsi was quite emphatic about what he called "names and parts"

仏教徒にしたがう気はでなかった。中国精神はつねに特殊存在の世界を主張した。華厳哲学に最も接近するときですら、彼らは世界の具象性を超えて進むことを敢えてしなかった。

　朱氏の宋学において意義あり、かつ最も実際的な方法で、中国と日本に大きな影響を与えた点は、その歴史観である。それは孔子の編せる偉大な古典の一つである「春秋」を支配する観念の発展したものである。この書は戦国時代として知られる当時の中国諸侯伯の主張を道徳的秤で量らんため、孔子の書いたものである。中国は当時数個の王国に分れ、それぞれが他を負かそうとしていた。僭取者は正統な王位を伝えつつありと主張した。政策は支配者の気まぐれなるままに動揺して指針盤を失っていた。孔子が彼の時代の年代記を編纂するという考は、自国の将来の政治家すべてにとって普遍的な倫理上の標準を樹立するにあった。「春秋」はそれゆえ、歴史上の事象によって説明された実際的な倫理法典であるといえる。

　朱子は孔子の例にならい、自ら司馬光の大著を簡約して一部の中国史を編纂した。この書において、彼は「名分」という礼節の大原則を宣言し、それをもってあらゆる時代に通ずる政策の指導原理となすべきものと考えた。宇宙は天地の諸法則によって支配され、人事もまたそうである。これらの諸法則はわれわれのすべてに本来自らそなわるところのものを遵守することを要求する。人は「名」を有し、社会において一定の地位を占めるがゆえに、ある「分」を果すべきである。人はその割当てられた場所において、その属している集団の一員として、自分の務めをつくすように要請せられる。この社会関係網はその合成分子の平和と幸福を保持し、たかめるためには、これを無視するわけにはゆかない。支配者には果すべき本分あり、臣下には臣下の分あり、親と子もまた互いに定まった義務を有する。かくして名・位・分の上には、なんらの障礙も僭冒もあってはならぬ。

　朱子が彼のいわゆる「名分」論をきわめて強く主張したのは、北

seeing that the northern invaders were beating hard against the suzerainty of the Sung and that the government dignitaries were wavering as to how to deal with these encroaching enemies, and that some of the former were even negotiating with the latter to carry out a policy of compromise. All these scenes going on before his eyes stirred his patriotic and nationalistic spirit, and he upheld his teaching strongly even at the risk of his life, against some of the politicians who were trying to induce the government to yield to the pressure of the northern races. Although his philosophy was not able to save the Southern Sung from the invasion of the overwhelming Mongolian armies, it enjoyed popular support ever since not only in China but particularly in Japan during her feudal days.

One of the principal reasons why the philosophy of Chu Hsi appealed so forcibly to Chinese psychology and came to be an officially sanctioned thought-system under the successive dynasties, was that it comprehended in its frame-work all the representative orthodox thoughts that had played any part in the advancement of Chinese culture and that this was accomplished by him even to the fulfilment of all conditions required by the Chinese way of thinking and feeling. Another reason was that it was the philosophy of order dear to the Chinese heart and earnestly sought by the people generally. The Chinese are just as patriotic and full of nationalistic pride as any other nations, no doubt; but they are more practical I imagine than sentimental, more given up to positivism than to idealism. Their feet are glued to the earth, they may occasionally gaze at the stars as they are very beautiful to look at; but they never forget that they cannot live even for a day separated from mother-earth. They are, therefore, attracted more to Chu His's philosophy of social order and utility than to his idealism and emotionalism. In this respect the Chinese differ from the Japanese.

The following statement by Ch'êng Hao (Tei Meido) fitly describes the Chinese mentality:

"The reason why the Tao is not made more manifest is due to the harmful interference of heathenism. This harm was more obvious in ancient

方からの侵入者が宋の主権に対抗しており、政府の大官たちが、い
かにしてこの侵入する敵軍を処理すべきかの問題で動揺しており、
大官中には敵と談判して妥協策を施さんとさえしているのを見たか
らであった。かく目前に行われている光景のすべてが、彼の愛国的・
国民的精神を刺激したので、彼は生命を賭してまで自分の教義を主
張して、政府を北方民族の圧迫にゆだねようとする一部政治家に反
対した。彼の哲学は南宋を圧倒的な蒙古の勢力から救うことはでき
なかったが、爾来、中国のみならず、とくに日本の封建時代を通し
て、一般的の支持をうけた。

　朱子学が、かく中国人の心理に強く訴えて、各王朝の下で、官許
の思想体系となるに至った主なる理由の一つは、その骨組のなかに
中国文化促進に関して、なんらか代表的な正統的思想をことごとく
含んでおる点に在る。また、それが朱子によって成就され、中国風
の考えかたや感じかたに必要な一切の条件を充してさえいるという
点にある。いま一つの理由は、それが中国人心理に最もなつかしい
「秩序の哲学」であったからである。これは疑いもなく一般の人々
によって、熱心に求められた。もちろん、中国人は他の国民と同様、
愛国的で国民的自負心に充ちているが、察するに彼らは感傷的であ
るよりは比較的に実際的であり、理想主義よりは実証主義に終始す
る。彼うの足は地に着いている。星は美しいものゆえ、彼らも星を
見ることはあろう。しかし、彼らは母なる大地を離れては一日も生
活できぬということを忘れてはいない。それゆえに、彼らは朱子の
理想主義と主情主義よりは、朱子の社会秩序論と功利哲学によけい
心を惹かれたのである。この点において、中国人は日本人と違って
いる。
　つぎに示す程明道の声明は中国人の心性を的確に述べている。
　『道の明らかならぬは、異端がそれを害するからである。古はそ
　の害たるや、近うして知り易かったが、今日の害は深くして弁
　じ難いのである。昔は人の愚闇に乗じて之を惑わしたが、今日は

times and easily detected, but in these days it goes deeper and hard to discern. Of old they [i.e. followers of heathenism] took advantage of our ignorance and put us into a state of intellectual perplexity; but nowadays they appeal to our intelligence, saying that they have fathomed the mysteries of existence and know the reason of transformation. But their speculation falls short of exploring particular things and perfoming social duties. They claim for the universal applicability of their teaching, but in reality they go against the moral order of our ordinary life. They state that there is nothing in their system whose depths and subtleties have not been thoroughly examined, but they are unable to follow up the path of the wise men of ancient days such as Yao and Shun."

By "heathenism" here is no doubt meant Buddhist thought whose soaring flight however high is not suited, those Sung philosophers think, for the consumption of their practical and socially-minded countrymen. This practicalness of the Sung philosophy came over to Japan on the same boat with Zen and also its nationalism as instilled into it by the militaristic spirit of Chu Hsi.

In those latter days of the Southern Sung there were many patriotic soldiers and statesmen and even Zen monks who volunteered as fighters against the aggressors. The spirit of nationalism penetrated into all the intellectual layers of society, and the Japanese Zen monks who visited China at the time came back also saturated with the spirit and its philosophy as formulated by Chu Hsi and his school. Not only Japanese visitors to China but the Chinese monks who came mostly from the Southern Sung to settle in Japan brought along with their Zen the message of the Sung philosophers. Their combined efforts to propagate the philosophy of nationalism in Japan met success in various quarters. The most notable one appeared in the epoch-making decision on the part of the Emperor Godaigo and his court to restore to their own hands the power of government which had hitherto been entrusted to the Kamakura Bakufu. This imperial movement is said to have started from the inspiration which the Emperor and his ministry felt by the study of Chu Hsi's *History of China*, and this study was carried on

人の高明をたどって、そこから入りこんでくる。即ち彼らは自ら以為らく、神を窮め而して他を知ると。しかしその実彼らは、物を開き務めを成ずるに足らぬのである。道に通じて周徧ならざるところなしと自ら云ってはいるが、その実は倫理に背いている、理を究め、微を極めたと自分では云っているが、しかも堯舜の道には入ることが出来ないのである。』　　　　　　　　　（鳴道集説）

　ここにいう異端とはもちろん仏教思想を意味するのであるが、宋学者の考によれば、仏教はたかく飛翔するが、実践的で現実的な国民の力では消化されぬものである。この宋学の実践性が禅と同じ船で日本に渡ってきたのであり、朱子の軍国精神によって滲み込んだ宋学のナショナリズムもまた渡ってきたのであった。
　南宋後期には多くの愛国的軍人・政治家・禅僧が率先して外敵にあたって闘った。ナショナリズムの精神が社会の全インテリ層に滲透して、当時渡宋した日本の禅僧も朱子派によって定められたその精神と哲学を吸収して帰った。中国に渡った日本人のみならず南宋から多く来って日本に居を卜した中国人もまた禅とともに宋学者のメッセイジをたずさえてきた。日本においてナショナリズムの哲学を宣伝しようという団結的な努力はいろいろの方面で成功した。そのもっとも著しい成功は、後醍醐天皇の朝廷が従来鎌倉幕府に委ねていた政権を、その手に恢復せんとする劃期的な決断をしたときに現れた。この運動は天皇とその廷臣が朱子の中国史を研究して、ふかく感銘した結果、出発したといわれている。しかも、この研究は禅僧指導のもとに行われた。史家の説くところによれば、北畠親房の「神皇正統記」も、また、朱子学研究の結果の一つである。親房は後醍醐天皇をめぐるすぐれた文臣の一人であり、禅の参究者でもあった。

under the guidance of the Zen monks. It is also stated by the historians that Kitabatake Chikafusa's monumental work on the "Succession of the Imperial Rulers in Japan" (*Jinnō Shōtō Ki*) was one of the results of his pursuit of Chu Hsi. Chikafusa was one of the great literary men who surrounded the Emperor Godaigo, and like his august master also a student of Zen.

Unfortunately, the Emperor Godaigo and his court failed to restore the imperial government to their own power. The political abnormality that followed, however, did not mean the weakening of the Confucian learning among the intellectual elements of Japan; for it went on as vigorously as ever assisted by the Zen monks of the Five Mountains and also those in the provinces. During the Ashikaga period, the position of the Chu Hsi philosophy as upholding the orthodox doctrine of Confucianism was generally recognised and the Zen monks began to pursue its study with more than a zeal for sheer leaning. They knew where their Zen was most needed and where the Sung philosophy proved its most practical usefulness. They thus became its real official propagators, and their influence radiated from Kyoto as centre out into the remoter parts of the country.

This tendency on the part of the Zen scholars to differentiate Zen from the Sung philosophy as systematised by Chu Hsi and his school helped to define sharply the division of labour or sphere of influence between Buddhism and Confucianism in Japan under the regime of the Tokugawa Shogunate. The practical spirit animating the Chinese way of thinking and feeling, as is to be especially recognisable in Chu Hsi, strongly appealed to the founders of the Tokugawa; for they were now most anxious to see peace and order quickly restored all over the country after so many years of wars, and for this purpose the Chinese teaching was found by them to be most eminently suited. The first official exponents of the Sung philosophy with Chu Hsi's commentaries were Fujiyama Seikwa and his disciple Hayashi Razan. Seikwa was originaly a Buddhist monk, but took more to the study of the Confucian texts so much so that he finally cast off his Buddhist robe, although he retained his shaven head for some time. After him and Razan,

不幸にして後醍醐天皇とその朝廷は政権恢復の挙に敗れた。しかし、その後の政治的変動は、日本の知的分子の間における儒学の衰退を意味することにはならなかった。五山および地方の禅僧の助けによって依然活発に続いたからである。室町時代には儒教の正統派理論をとるものとして朱子学は一般に認められ、禅僧も単なる学識に対する以上の熱心をもってその研究を遂行しはじめた。彼らは禅がどの点で最も必要とされているか、また、宋学がどの点で最も実際的な効果を示すかをよく知っていた。かくして彼らは宋哲学の官許的宣伝者となり、その影響は中央の京都から発して遠く僻陬におよんだ。

　朱子によって体系づけられた宋学と、禅とを区別して考えた禅僧側のこの傾向は、徳川時代になって、日本の仏教と儒教との間に、おのおのその勢力範囲を劃然と定めるのにあずかって力があった。中国風の考えかた・感じかたを鼓吹する実践的精神は、朱子のばあいにもとくに認められたところであるが、徳川幕府の創設者たちは、とくに、この点をつよく感じたのである。彼らは多年の戦乱の後、全国一般に平和と秩序を恢復せんことを熱望し、この目的のために中国の教えが最も適当だと知ったからだ。朱子訓註による宋学の祖述をした最初の御用学者は藤原惺窩と林羅山とであった。惺窩はがんらい禅僧であったが、儒書の研究を好みついに僧衣を捨てた。もっともしばらくは円頂のままでいたが。彼と羅山の後、儒教の研究はつづいたが、禅僧はもっぱら自己の教義を顕現することに甘んじていた。しかし、忘れてならぬことは、中国と同様、日本においても、宋学の紹介されて以来たえず儒教・仏教・神道三教の協調主義が唱

the study of Confucianism found its own followers, and the Zen monks were quite satisfied to confine themselves at least officially to the exposition of their own doctrine. However, we must not forget to notice that as in China there has been constant attempt in Japan ever since the introduction of the Sung philosophy to effect a syncretism of the three teachings, Confucianism, Buddhism, and Shintoism. One remarkable fact deserving notice here in the history of Japanese thought is that Shintoism which is regarded as the official embodiment of the national spirit of Japan did not assert itself as doctrinally independent of either Confucianism or Buddhism. The most probable reason for this is that Shintoism has no philosophy to stand on by itself and is awakened to its own consciousness and existence only when it comes in contact with either, and thereby learns how to express itself. It is true that Motoori Norinaga (1730–1801) and his disciples started a vigorous attack on Confucianism and Buddhism as doctrines imported from abroad and not quite congenial to the Japanese ways of living and feeling. Their patriotic conservatism, however, was instigated more by political motives than by any philosophical reasons. They no doubt helped a great deal to usherm in the new Meiji regime known as the Restoration of 1868. But from the purely philosophical point of view, it is highly problematical if their religio-nationalistic dialectic had much of universal element.

道されたことである。日本思想史上この点で注目に値する著しき事実は、日本の国民精神の体現として政治的に認められている神道が、教義上からみてべつに儒教や仏教から独立したものを肯定しなかった点である。これが主な理由は、おそらくは神道が自分で本来に独立するにたる哲学を持たず、儒仏いずれかと接触したときに始めて自己存在の意識に目ざめ、それによって自己を表現することをまなんだからだろうと思う。なるほど、本居宣長（1730–1801）とその門弟たちは、儒教をもって外来の説とし、日本人の生活方法や感じかたにまったく合わないものとして、猛烈に攻撃した事実はある。しかし、その愛国的保守主義は哲学的理由よりもむしろ政治的動機によって刺激された。彼らは疑いもなく明治維新促進に多大の力をつくしたが、純粋の哲学的見地からみれば、彼らの宗教的・国民主義的弁証法には、どれほどの普遍的要素があったかは、はなはだ問題となるところである。

A portrait of Sen no Rikyū.

千ノ利休肖像。

卍

Zen and the Tea-cult
禅と茶道

卍

1

What is common to Zen and the tea-cult is their constant attempt at simplification. The elimination of unnecessaries is achieved by Zen in its intuitive grasp of final reality and by the tea-cult in the art of living which is typified by serving tea in the tea-room. The tea-cult is the estheticism of primitive simplicity. Its ideal to come close to Nature is realised by sheltering oneself under a thatched roof and sitting in a room which is hardly ten feet square, but which must be artistically constructed and furnished. Zen also aims at stripping off all the artificial wrappings humanity has devised supposedly for its own solemnisation. Zen first of all combats the intellect, for in spite of its practical usefulness the intellect goes against our attempt to delve into the depths of our being. Philosophy may propose all kinds of questions for their intellectual solution, but it is never meant to give us spiritual satisfaction, which must be accessible to every one of us, however intellectually undeveloped he is. Philosophy is open only to those who are specifically endowed along its own line, showing that it cannot be a subject of universal appreciation. Zen, or, more broadly speaking, religion is to cast off all one thinks he possesses, even life, and to get back to the last state of being, the "Original Abode," or to one's own Father or Mother. This can be done by every one of

卍

一

　禅の茶道に通うところは、いつも物事を単純化せんとするところ
に在る。この不必要なものを除き去ることを、禅は究極実在の直覚
的把握によって成しとげ、茶は茶室内の喫茶によって典型化せられ
たものを生活上のものの上に移すことによって成しとげる。茶は原
始的単純性の洗煉美化である。自然に親しむというその理想を実現
するために、茅の屋根の下に身を寄せ、わずか四畳半ではあるが構
造と調度に技巧を凝した小室に坐るのである。禅の狙うところも、
人類が己を勿体づけるために工夫したと思われるような、いっさ
いの人為的な覆いものをはぎとる点にある。禅がまず知性と闘うの
は、知性というものが実用には役立つであろうが、われわれが自分
の存在をふかく掘り下げようとするのを妨げるからである。哲学は
あらゆる問題を提供して知的解決を要求しようとするが、われわれ
の精神的満足はそれによって、かならずしも与えられぬ。しかし、
何人も知識的にはあまり発達していなくても、精神上の安心はえな
ければならぬ。哲学の途はその傾向を具えている特殊の人々にのみ
開かれ、一般鑑賞の題目とはなりえない。禅、さらに広くいって宗
教は、人がその持っていると考える一切物を、生命をさえ、かき捨
てて、最後の存在状態・「本住地」、または「父母未生前本来ノ面目」

us, for we are what we are because of it, or him, or her, and without the latter we are nothing. This is to be called the last stage of simplification, since things cannot be reduced to any simpler state. The tea-cult symbolises it in a solitary hut erected under an old pine-tree. The form once thus symbolised, allows itself to be artistically treated. It goes without saying that the principle of treatment is to be in perfect conformity with the original idea which prompted it, that is, of elimination of unnecessaries.

Tea was known in Japan even before the Kamakura era, but its first wider propagation is generally ascribed to Eisai (1131–1215), the Zen teacher, who brought tea-seeds from China and cultivated them in his monastery grounds. It is said that his book on tea together with the tea prepared from his plants was presented to Minamoto Sanetomo (1172–1219), the Shōgun of the time, who happened to be ill. Eisai thus came to be known as the Father of tea-cultivation in Japan. He thought that tea had some medicinal qualities, and was good for a variety of diseases. Apparently, he did not teach how to conduct the tea-ceremony which he must have observed while at the Zen monasteries in China. The tea-ceremony is a way of entertaining visitors to the monastery or sometimes of entertaining its own occupants among themselves. The Zen monk who brought it to Japan was Dai-ō the National Teacher* (1236–1308), about half a century later than Eisai. After Dai-ō came several monks who became masters of the tea-ceremony, and finally Ikkyū (1394–1481), the noted abbot of Daitokuji, taught the technique to one of his disciples, Shukō (1422–1502), whose artistic genius developed it and succeeded in adapting it to Japanese taste. Shukō thus became the originator of the tea-cult and taught it to Ashikaga Yoshimasa (1435–1490), Shōgun of the time, who was a great patron of the arts. Later, Shō-ō (1503–1555), and especially Rikyū further improved it and gave a finishing touch to what is now known as *Cha-no-yu*, translated generally "tea-ceremony" or "tea-cult." The original tea-ceremony as practised at Zen monasteries is carried

に帰ることである。これはわれわれの誰でもなしうることである。われわれはそういうものによって、現在身をえているのであって、そういうものがなければわれわれは 無 (ナッシング) である。これを最後の単純化と称していいのは、物事をこれ以上単純な状態にかえすことはできないからである。茶はそれを老松の蔭に建てられた一茅屋によって象徴する。その形態はかように象徴化された以上は、技巧的に扱われてもかまわはないのであるが、いうまでもなく、これを扱う指導原理 (プリンシプル) は、それを起した独創的な観念、すなわち不要物の除去ということとまったく一致しているという点にある。

　茶は日本では鎌倉以前すでに知られていたが、これをひろく一般に伝えたのは、その種子を中国から持ち帰って、禅院の庭に栽培した栄西禅師 (えいさい) (1131-1215) といわれる。禅師は自分の栽培した茶に関する書（「喫茶養生記」）を添えて、たまたま病に在った、ときの将軍源実朝 (1172-1219) に献上したという。栄西は、かくして、日本における茶の栽培の祖として知らるるに至った。彼は茶に薬効あり、種々の病に利くと考えた。彼は中国の禅院にいるあいだに、茶の湯の作法をみてきたに違いないのだろうが、別段それを教えなかったようである。茶の作法は、禅院に人を饗応したり、ときとして、己が寺中の者たちを饗応したりするときの作法である。日本にそれをもたらした禅僧は、栄西より半世紀ほど後の大応国師 (1236-1308) であった。大応の後、数人の禅僧が来朝して茶の湯の師となったが、ついに有名な大徳寺の一休和尚 (1394-1481) がその法を弟子の一人の珠光 (1422-1502) に教え、珠光の芸術的天才はこれを発展させて、日本的趣味に取りいれることに成功した。珠光は、かくして、茶道の創始者となり、芸術の大きな庇護者であった、ときの将軍足利義政 (1435-1490) にそれを教えた。後に、紹鷗 (1503-1555) と利休、とくに利休がそれを改良して、最後の仕上げを施して、いまの茶の湯、英訳して一般に "tea-ceremony" または "tea-cult" と知られるものにした。禅院で実施される本来の茶の湯は、いま、巷間に流行している作法とは独立して行われる。

on independently of the cult in vogue now among the general public.

I have often thought of the tea-cult in connection with the Buddhist life which seems to partake so much of the characteristic of tea. Tea keeps the mind fresh and vigilant, but it does not intoxicate. It has qualities naturally to be appreciated by scholars and monks. It is in the nature of things that tea came to be extensively used in the Buddhist monasteries and that its first introduction to Japan came through the monks. If tea symbolises Buddhism, can we not say that wine stands for Christianity? Wine is used extensively by the Christians. It is served in the church as symbolising Christ's blood, which, according to the Christian doctors, was shed for sinful humanity, and probably for this reason the medieval monks kept wineries in their monasteries. They look jovial and happy surrounding the cask and holding up the wine cups. Wine first excites and then inebriates. In many ways it contrasts with tea, and this contrast is also that between Buddhism and Christianity.

We can see now that the tea-cult is most intimately connected with Zen not only in its practical development but principally in the observance of the spirit which runs through the ceremony itself. The spirit in terms of feeling consists of "harmony" (和), "reverence" (敬), "purity" (清), and "tranquillity" (寂). These four elements are needed to conduct the cult to a successful end, they are all the essential constituents of a brotherly and orderly life, which is no other than the life of the Zen monastery. That the monks behaved in perfect orderliness can be inferred from the remark made by Ch'êng Ming-tao (程明道), a Confucian scholar of the Sung, who once visited a monastery called Ting-1in Ssǔ (定林寺): "Here, indeed, we witness the classical form of ritualism as it was practised in the ancient three dynasties." The ancient three dynasties are the ideal days dreamed of by every Chinese scholar-statesman, when a most desirable state of things prevailed and people enjoyed all the happiness that could be expected of a good government. Even now the Zen monks are well trained individually and collectively in conducting cer-

自分は、茶の特色を多分に含むと思われる仏教生活に関連して、茶の湯のことをしばしば考えてきた。茶は心神を爽快にさせるが、陶酔はさせない。学者や僧侶が賞味するような性質を元来持っている。茶がひろく仏教寺院に用いられるようになったことも、これが日本に初めての紹介が禅僧によったということも、きわめて当り前のことである。茶が仏教を象徴するならば、葡萄酒はキリスト教を代表する、といえぬだろうか。葡萄酒はひろくキリスト教徒に用いられる。教会ではキリストの血を象徴するものとしているが、その血なるものはキリスト教学者にしたがえば、罪業深き人類のために救世主によりて流されたものである。こういう理由からか、中世の修道院では酒窖を持っていた。肥えふとった修道僧たちが樽をかこみ酒盃をとって、陽気に楽しげにみえる画はわれわれのときどき見るところである。葡萄酒は初めはその飲手をうきうきさせ、やがては彼を酩酊させる。多くの点で、茶といい対照をなすが、このコントラストはやがてまた仏教とキリスト教とのあいだのそれでもある。

　茶の湯はその実際的な発展の上ばかりでなく、おもにその作法を通して流れる精神をたっとぶ上で、禅と密接な関連があることをわれわれは知るのである。この精神は、感情上の用語でいえば、「和・敬・清・寂」からなる。これら四要素は、茶の湯の首尾をまっとうするために必要であり、いずれもみな、同胞相親しむ、秩序的な生活の本質をなす成分であるが、この生活とは禅寺の生活に他ならない。禅僧の進退挙措がまったく秩序正しいということは、かつて定林寺という禅刹を訪れた宋代儒者程明道の言葉から推せられる。曰く、『なるほど、ここでは、三代の古に行われたと同じき、昔ながらの形の儀礼が、目のあたり見られる。』古の三代とは、中国の政治家たちが夢想する理想的な時代で、世情きわめて申分なく人民は泰平至上の恵みを享けたのであった。現今でさえ、禅僧は、個人的にも、集団的にも、諸儀礼をふむ鍛錬を十分に積んでいる。小笠原流の礼儀作法は「百丈清規」という禅院の諸規定に源を発すると考えられる。（註、百丈は唐代の偉い禅匠、720-814）禅の教義は、形態を超越し

emonies. The Ogasawara school of etiquette is thought to have its origin in the "Monastery Regulations" of Pai-chang* ("Hyakujō Shingi" 百丈清規). While Zen teaching is to transcend form and to grasp the spirit, it never forgets to remind us of the fact that the world in which we live is a world of particular forms, and that the spirit expresses itself only by means of form. Zen is, therefore, at once an antinomian and a disciplinarian.

The character for "harmony" also reads "gentleness of spirit," and to my mind this "gentleness of spirit" seems to describe better the spirit governing the whole procedure of the tea-cult. Harmony refers more to form while gentleness is suggestive of an inward feeling. The general atmosphere of the tea-room is to create this kind of gentleness all around—gentleness of touch, gentleness of odour, gentleness of light, and gentleness of sound. You take up a tea-cup, hand-made and irregularly shaped, the glaze is probably not uniformly overlaid, but in spite of this primitiveness the little utensil has a peculiar charm of gentleness, quietness, and unobtrusiveness. The incense burning is never strong and stimulating, but gentle and pervading. The windows and screens are another source of a gentle charm prevailing here. The light permitted into the room is always soft and restful and conducive to a meditative mood. The breeze passes through needles of the old pine-tree sheltering the tea-house, which harmoniously blends with the sizzling iron-kettle over tile fire. The entire environment thus reflects the personality of the one who has created it.

"What is most valuable is gentleness of spirit; what is most essential is not to contradict others."

These are the first words with which the so-called "Constitution of Seventeen Articles" starts. The Constitution was compiled by Prince Shotoku in 604. It is a kind of moral and spiritual admonition given by the Prince-Regent to his subject. But it is significant that such an admonition, whatever its political bearings are, should begin with an unusual emphasis placed on gentleness of spirit. In fact, this is the first utterance given to the Japanese consciousness to which the people have been awakened after centuries

て精神を把握することなのであるが、それは、われわれに自分たちの住む世界は特殊諸形態の世界である事実、精神は形を媒介としてのみ表現される事実を想起させることをけっして忘れぬ。禅は、それゆえ、律法背反主義者<ruby>律法背反主義者<rt>アンチノミアン</rt></ruby>であると同時に鍛錬主義者<ruby>鍛錬主義者<rt>デシプリネーリアン</rt></ruby>である。

　調和（harmony）の和は和悦（gentleness of spirit）の和とも読める。思うに、この意味の和こそ茶の湯の行程全体を支配する精神をさらによく表しているようだ。調和は形の方を意味するが、和悦は内的感情を示唆する。総じて茶室の雰囲気はむしろこの種の和を周囲につくりだすことである。——触感の和、香気の和、光線の和、音響の和を。まず茶碗を取りあげれば、手づくりで歪んでいる。釉<ruby>釉<rt>くすり</rt></ruby>の掛けかたも一様になっていないらしい。かく原始的ではあるが、このささやかな器は和・静・慎、特有の美<ruby>美<rt>チャーム</rt></ruby>を持っている。香をたいてもけっして強くなく刺激もせぬ、やわらかく漂いわたる。窓と襖も茶室に漂いわたる和らぎの美の源である。室に許される光線はいつも柔かくやすらかで、瞑想的な気分に誘いこむ。風は茶室をかばう老松の葉に通い、炉にたぎり鳴る釜の音と相和す。この環境のすべては、かようにして、それをつくりだした人の人格を反映するのである。

「和をもつて貴しとなす。忤らふことなきを宗となす」
　これは憲法十七箇条の初めの言葉である。この憲法は、604年に聖徳太子がつくったものである。太子から臣下にたまわった一種の道徳的・精神的な訓誡である。かかる訓誡が、政治関係はともかくとして、その初めにまず、精神の和ということになみなみならず重きがおかれたことは意義深い。事実、これは最初に吐露された日本意識で、人々は幾世紀の文明を経てこれに目ざめてきたのである。日本は近来好戦国として知られてきたが——全然誤りである——自己の性格について持つ意識は、自分たちは、全体としては、穏和

of civilisation. Although Japan has lately come to be known as a warlike nation—quite erroneously—the consciousness they have of their own character is that they are on the whole a gentle-natured people. And they have good reason to presume it, for the physical atmosphere enveloping the whole island of Japan is characterised with general mildness, not only climatically but meteorologically. This is mostly due to the presence of vapour in the air. The mountains, villages, woods, etc., enwrapped in vapour give a soft appearance; and flowers are not as a rule too richly coloured but somewhat subdued and delicate; while the spring foliage is vividly fresh. Sensitive minds brought up in an environment like this cannot fail to imbibe much of it, which is gentleness of spirit. We are, however, apt to deviate from this basic virtue of Japanese character as we come in contact with various difficulties social, political, economic, and racial. We have to guard ourselves against contaminations and Zen has come to help us in this.

When Dōgen (1200–1253) came back from China after some years' study of Zen there, he was asked what he learned there. He said, "Not much except soft-heartedness." "Soft-heartedness" is "tender-mindedness," in this case means "gentleness of spirit." Generally we are too egotistic and full of hard resisting spirits. We are too individualistic and are unable to accept things as they are or as they come to us. Resistance means friction, friction is the source of all trouble. When there is no self, the heart is soft and offers no resistance to outside influences. This does not necessarily mean to be devoid of all sensibilities. But from the spiritual point of view, Christians and Buddhists alike know how to follow Dōgen to appreciate the significance of selflessness or "sort-heartedness." In the tea-cult they speak of "gentleness of spirit" in the same form as enjoined by Prince Shōtoku. Indeed, "gentleness of spirit" or "soft-heartedness" is the foundation of our life on earth. If the tea-cult purports to establish a Buddha-land in its small group, it has to start with gentleness of spirit. To further illustrate this point, Takuan (1573–1645) the Zen master is quoted below.

な性質の国民だということである。そう考えるのも道理である、日本全島をとりまく自然科学的雰囲気は気候上のみならず気象学上からも、総体的に温和という特色を持っている。これは多く空気中の水蒸気の存在にもとづく。山嶽・村落・森林などは水蒸気につつまれて柔かな外貌を呈する。花は概して色がけばけばしくなく、やや和らぎを帯びてたおやかである。そして、春の葉ぶりは目にもさわやかである。このような環境に育てあげられた感じやすい心は、誤りなくそこから多くのものを吸収するが、それが心の和となる。しかし、われわれは社会的・政治的・経済的・民族的種々の難題に接触するにつれ、この日本的性格の基礎的な美徳からそれやすい。われわれは汚染に対して自分をまもらねばならぬ。禅がこのときに際してわれわれを助けにくる。

　道元（1200-1253）が中国で数年間禅をまなんで帰ってきたとき、彼地でまなんだことを尋ねられた。彼は言った『柔軟心のほかにはまなばなかった』と。「柔軟心」とは優き心であり、この場合精神の和を意味する。一般に人は利己的にすぎてかたくなな反抗心に充ちている。個人主義的にすぎて物事をありのままに受取ることができぬ。反抗は摩擦を意味し、摩擦はあらゆる面倒事の源である。我がなければ心は柔であり、外面の力に反抗を示さぬ。これはかならずしもあらゆる感受性の欠けていることを意味せぬ。しかし、精神的見地からみれば、キリスト教徒と仏教徒はひとしく道元にしたがって滅我や柔軟心の意義を味うべきを知っている。茶の湯にいうところの和は聖徳太子の訓えたものとおなじ形である。まことに和や柔軟心はこの世の生活の基礎である。茶の湯がそのささやかな集団に浄土を建立する目的ならば、和から出発せねばならぬ。この点をさらに説くために、沢庵（1573-1645）の言葉を次に引用しよう。

TAKUAN ON THE TEA-CULT

"The principle of *cha-no-yu* is the spirit of harmonious blending of Heaven and Earth and provides the means for establishing universal peace. People of the present time have turned it into a mere occasion for meeting friends, talking of worldly affairs, and indulging in palatable food and drink; besides, they are proud of their elegantly furnished tea-rooms, where, surrounded with rare objects of art, they would serve tea in a most accomplished manner, and deride those who are not so skilful as themselves. This is, however, far from being the original intention of *cha-no-yu*.

"Let us the construct a small room in a bamboo-grove or under trees, arrange steams and rocks and plant trees and bushes, while [inside the room] let us pile up charcoal, set a kettle, arrange flowers, and allot in order the necessary tea-utensils. And let all this be carried out in accordance with the idea that in this room we can enjoy the steams and rocks as we do the rivers and mountains in Nature, and appreciate the various moods and sentiments suggested by the snow, the moon, and the trees and flowers as they go through the transformation of seasons, appearing and disappearing, blooming and withering. When visitors are greeted here with due reverence, we listen quietly to the boiling water in the kettle which sounds like a breeze passing through the pine-needles, and become oblivious of all the worldly woes and worries; we then pour out a dipperful of water from the kettle reminding us of the murmuring waters of the mountain steam, and thereby our mental dust is wiped off. This is truly a world of recluses, saints on earth.

"The principle of propriety is reverence which in practical life functions as harmonious relationship. This is the statement made by Confucius when he defines the use of propriety, and is also the mental attitude one should cultivate at *cha-no-yu*. For instance, when a man is associated with persons of high social ranks his conduct is simple and natural, and there is no cringing self-deprecation on his part. When he sits in the company of people socially below he retains a respectful attitude towards them, being entirely free from

沢庵の茶亭之記

『茶の湯は天地中和の気を本として、治世安穏の風俗となれり。今の人は、偏に朋友を招きて会談の媒とし、飲食を快とし、口腹の貹とす。且茶室に美を尽し、珍器の品を揃へ、手の巧みなるを誇り、他人のつたなきを嘲る。みな茶の湯の本意にあらず。

　されば竹陰樹下に小室をかまへ、水石を貯へ、草木を植ゑ、炭を置き、釜を掛け、花を生け、茶具を飾る。皆是山川自然の水石を、一室の中に移して、四序雪月花の風景を翫び、草木栄落の時を感じ、客をむかへて礼敬をなす。松風の颯々たるを釜の中に聞て、世上の念慮を忘れ、渭水の涓々たるを一杓より流して、心中の塵埃を洗ふ。真に人間の仙境なるべし。

　礼の本は敬にして、其用は和を貴しとす。是孔子の礼の用をいへる詞にして、則茶の湯の心法なり。たとへば公子貴人の来坐にても、其交り淡泊にして、しかも謟ふ事なく、又我より下輩の会席にも、敬をいたして、しかも不慢。是空中に物ありて、和して流れず、久うして猶敬す。迦葉の微笑、曾子の一唯、真如玄妙の意味不可説の理なり。

the feeling of self-importance. This is due to the presence of something pervading the entire tea-room, which results in the harmonious relationship of all who come here. However long the association, there is always the persisting sense of reverence. The spirit of the smiling Kashyapa and the nodding Tseng-Tzu must be said to be moving here; this spirit, in other words, is the mysterious reason of Suchness which is beyond all comprehension.

"For this reason, the principle animating the tea-room, from its first construction down to the choice of the tea-utensils, the technique of service, the cooking of food, wearing apparel, etc., is to be sought in the avoidance of complicated ritualism and mere ostentatiousness. The implements may be old but the mind can be invigorated therewith so that it is ever fresh and ready to respond to the changing seasons and the varying views resulting therefrom, it never curries favour, it is never covetous, never inclined to extravagance, but always watchful and considerate for others. The owner of such a mind is naturally gentle-mannered and always sincere—this is *cha-no-yu*."

"The way of *cha-no-yu*, therefore, is to appreciate the spirit of naturally harmonious bending of Heaven and Earth, to see the pervading presence of the five elements by one's fire-side where the mountains, rivers, rocks, and trees as they are in Nature are found transported, to draw the refreshing water from the well of Nature, to taste with one's own mouth the flavour supplied by Nature. How grand this enjoyment of the harmonious blending of Heaven and Earth!

Had the tea-cult and Zen something to contribute to the presence of a certain democratic spirit in the social life of Japan? In spite of the strict social hierarchy established during her feudal days, the idea of equality and fraternity persists among the people. In the tea-room, ten feet square, guests of various social grades are entertained with no discrimination; for once therein all such worldly considerations are cast to the winds: the commoner's knees touch those of the nobleman, and they talk with due reverence to each other on subjects in which they both are interested. In Zen of course

されば茶室を構へるより茶具の備へ、手前・会席・衣類等に至るまで、わづらはしからず、美麗を好まず、古き道具を以て心を新らたにして、四時の風景を忘れず、詔はず、貪らず、奢らず、謹みて疎かならず、すなほにして真実なるを茶の湯といふなるべし。

　是則天地自然の和気を翫び、山川木石を炉辺に移して、五行備る。天地の流れを汲て、風味を口に味ふ。大なる哉。天地中和の気をたのしむは、茶の湯の道なるべし。』

（「結縄集」・「古今茶話」）

　茶の湯と禅は日本の社会生活におけるあるデモクラチックな精神の現存になにか貢献したろうか。封建時代には厳格な階級制が設けられたが、平等博愛の観念も人々の間に存した。四畳半の茶室のなかに種々雑多の階級の客が無差別に饗応される。ここではかかる世俗的な考慮はいっさい風に流す。平民が貴人と膝を交えて、ともに興に入ったことを慇懃に語りあう。禅にはもちろん世俗的な区別は許されぬ。禅僧は社会のあらゆる階級に自由に近づき、誰とでも打ちとける。社会がわれわれの上に人為的においた羈絆を棄てて、た

no earthly distinctions are allowed, and its monks have free approach to all classes of society and are at home with them all. It is indeed deeply ingrained in human nature to wish to throw off the restraints society has artificially put on us, and once in a while to have free and natural and heart-to-heart intercourse with fellow-beings, including the animals, plants, and inanimate objects so called. We, therefore, always welcome every opportunity for this kind of liberation. No doubt this is what Takuan means when he refers to "the harmonious blending of heaven and earth," where all angels join in the chorus.

"Reverence" is fundamentally and originally a religious feeling—feeling for a being higher than ourselves who are poor human mortals. The feeling is later transferred to social relationships, and then degenerates into mere formalism. In modern days of democracy, though this is suspected very much lately in some parts of the world, everybody is just as good as everybody else at least from the social point of view, and there is nobody specially deserving reverence. But when the feeling is analysed back to its original sense, it is a reflection on one's own unworthiness, that is, the realisation of one's limitations, physical and intellectual, moral and spiritual. This realisation evokes in us the desire for transcending ourselves and also for coming in touch with a being who stands to us in every possible form of opposition. The desire directs our spiritual movements towards an object outside us; but when it is diverted towards ourselves, it becomes self-abnegation, humility, and a feeling of sin. These are all negative virtues, while positively they lead us to reverence, the feeling not to slight others. We are beings full of contradictions: in one respect we feel that we are just as good as anybody else, but at the same time we have an innate suspicion that everybody else is better than ourselves—a kind of inferiority—complex. There is a Bodhisattva in Mahayana Buddhism, who is known as Sadaparibhuta (常不輕菩薩) "one who never slights others." Perhaps when we are quite sincere with ourselves, that is, when we are all alone with ourselves in the innermost chamber of our being, there is a feeling there which makes us move towards

まには、自由自然に心を向けあって、同類──それは動物・植物・無生物などをも含めた同類とかたらいたいという望みは、人性に深く染みこんでいるのである。人は、それゆえ、いつもこの種解放の好機をよろこび迎える。沢庵の「天地自然の和気を翫び」といったのもこの意味に違いない。そこでは天使たちがことごとく相和して合唱するのである。

「敬」とは元来宗教的感情──憐れむべき死に身たるわれわれ以上の存在物に対する感情である。この感情が後に社会関係に移され、たんなる形式論に堕した。現代においては、これは世間の一部には疑惑視されているが、少くとも社会的見地からみれば、人は誰でも同様であってとくに尊敬に値するものはないわけであるが、この感情をその本来の意味にさかのぼって分析すると、自己の無価値への反省、すなわち、肉体的にも知力的にも、道徳的にも精神的にも、その有限性の自覚となる。この自覚が自己を超越したいという念、できるだけ反対の形をとってわれわれに対立するところの存在と接触したいという念を心中にひき起す。この熱望はわれわれの精神的の動きをわれわれの外なるものの方にむかわせるが、それがそれて自己に向うと自己否定、慚愧、謙譲、罪悪感となる。これらはみな消極的の徳であるが、積極的には敬、他人を蔑ろにせぬ感情となる。人間は矛盾に充ちた存在である。ある点自分が他人とまったく同じであると感じるが、同時に、他のものは誰も自分より立派だという疑い──一種の複雑な劣等感を内心に抱く。大乗仏教には他人をけっして軽視せぬという常不軽菩薩というのがある。人が自分の存在の一番奥の間にひとり閉じこもるときには、謙譲の念をもって己を他人の方に動かせる感情が生ずる。これはどんなものにせよ、「敬」のなかに深い宗教的の傾向が存するのである。禅は寒夜温まるために寺中の仏像をことごとく焼きうる。禅は外眼には妖かしに見える表面の虚飾一切を切捨てた真理として、その存在を救うために貴重

others with a sense of humiliation. Whatever this may be, there is a deep religious attitude of mind in reverence. Zen may burn all the holy statues in the temple to warm itself on a cold wintry night; Zen may destroy all the literature containing its precious legacies in order to save its very existence as the truth shorn of all its external trappings however glamorous they appear to outsiders; but it never forgets to worship a storm-broken and mud-soiled humble blade of grass; it never neglects to offer all the wild flowers of the field just as they are, to all the Buddhas in the three thousand chiliocosms. Zen knows how to revere because it knows how to slight. What is needed in Zen as well as in anything else is sincerity of heart, and not mere conceptualism or physical imitation of it.

Toyotomi Hideyoshi was the great patron of the tea-cult in his day and an admirer of Sen-no-Rikyū (1521–1591), who was virtually the founder of the modern tea-cult. Although he was always after something sensational, grandiose, and ostentatious, he seems to have understood finally somewhat of the spirit of the tea-cult as advocated by Rikyū and his followers, when he gave this verse to Rikyū at one of the latter's "tea parties":

"When tea is made with water drawn from the depths of Mind
Whose bottom is beyond measure,
We really have *cha-no-yu* so called."

Hideyoshi was a crude and cruel despot in many ways, but in his liking for the tea-cult we are inclined to find something genuine in him besides just "using" the cult for his political purposes. His verse touches the spirit of reverence when he can make reference to the water deeply drawn from the mind-well.

Rikyū teaches that "the art of *cha-no-yu* consists in nothing else but in boiling water, making tea, and sipping it."

This is simple enough as far as it goes. Human life, we call say, consists in being born, eating and drinking, working and sleeping, marrying and giving

な遺産を含む文献一切を破却しうる。しかし、禅は嵐に裂れ泥にまみれた、つまらぬ草の葉を崇めることをけっして忘れぬ。あるがままなる野の花を三千世界の仏陀に捧げることをけっして怠らぬ。禅は軽視することを知るがゆえにまた敬うことを知る。他のいかなるものともおなじく、禅に必要なのは心の誠実であり、そのたんなる概念化や物理的摸倣ではない。

　豊臣秀吉は当時の茶の湯の大きな庇護者であり、現代の茶の湯の実質上の創始者である千ノ利休（1521–1591）の尊崇者であった。彼はつねになにかしら人気の立つ、大掛りで、派手なことを求めたが、結局、利休一派の唱えた茶の湯の精神を多少理解していたらしい。利休の茶会の一つで彼はつぎの歌を利休に示した。

　　　　底ひなき心の内を汲みてこそ
　　　　　　お茶の湯なりとはしられたりけり

　秀吉は多くの点で粗野にして残虐な圧制家であったが、茶の湯を好む点では茶をたんに政略に使ったという以外に、どこか純粋なところもあったと考えたい。心の泉ふかく水を汲むといいうるところに彼の歌は「敬」の精神に触れている。

　利休は教えている。
　　　　茶の湯とは只湯をわかし茶をたてて
　　　　　　呑むばかりなるものと知るべし
　これはどこまでも簡単である。人生とは要するに生れて、食い、

birth to children, and finally in passing away to nowhere anyone knows. Nothing seems to be simpler than living this life, when it is so stated. But how many of us are there who can live this kind of matter-of-fact or rather God-intoxicated life, cherishing no desires, leaving no regrets but absolutely trustful of God? While living we think of death; while dying we long for life; while one thing is being accomplished, so many other things not necessarily always cognate, but in most cases altogether irrelevant, crowd into our brains, and divert and dissipate the energy which is to be concentrated on the matter in hand. When water is poured into the bowl, it is not the water alone that is poured into it—varieties of things go into it, good and bad, pure and impure, things about which one has to blush, things which can never be poured out anywhere except into one's own deep Unconscious. The tea-water when analysed contains all the filth disturbing and contaminating the stream of our consciousness. Art is perfected only when it ceases to be art, this is when there is the perfection of artlessness, when the innermost sincerity of our being asserts itself, and this is the meaning of reverence in the tea-cult. Reverence is, therefore, sincerity or simplicity of heart.

"Purity" estimated as constituting the spirit of the tea-cult may be said to be the contribution of Japanese mentality. Purity is cleanliness or sometimes orderliness, which is observable in everything and everywhere in connection with the cult. Fresh water is liberally used in the garden called *roji*; in case natural running water is not available, there is a stone basin as one approaches; the tea-room itself is spotless—this goes without saying.

Purity in the tea-cult may remind us of the Taoistic teaching of Purity. There is something common to both, for the object of discipline in both is to free one's mind from the defilements of the senses. A tea-master says:

"The spirit of *cha-no-yu* is to cleanse the six senses from contamination. By seeing the *kakemono* in the *tokonoma* (alcove) and the flower in the vase, one's sight is cleansed; by smelling the burning incense one's sense of odour is cleansed: by listening to the boiling of water in the iron kettle and to the dripping of water from the bamboo pipe, one's ears are cleansed; by tasting

飲み、働き、眠り、結婚し、子供を生み、ついに誰も知らないところに逝ってしまうことだ。そう考えるとこの人生を送るくらい簡単なことはないようである。が、この種の、神を絶対に信頼する以外に望みを抱かず悔いを残さず、ありのままの、というよりむしろ神に心酔せる生活を、送りうる者がはたして幾人かありえようか。人は生きている時は死を考え、死なんとする時は生を望む、一つの事が成らんとする時、かならずしもこれと同様とはかぎらぬ。多くの場合、見当ちがいの他の多くの事が頭に群がり、手ぢかの問題に集中するはずの精力を逸し散らしてしまう。水を鉢に注げば注入するのは水だけではない——善悪、純不純の種々雑多のものが、拭わねばならぬもの、自分の深い無意識のなか以外どこにも注ぎだすことのできぬものが、入ってくる。茶を点てる水を分析すれば意識の流れをみだし汚す穢物いっさいを含んでいる。技術の完成されるのはそれが技術たることを止めるときのみである。この時に無技巧の完成が存し、人間の奥底の誠実がおのずから現れるが、これが茶の湯における「敬」の意味である。敬は、それゆえ、心の誠実か、単純さである。

　茶の湯の精神を作る一つと考えられている「清」は日本的心理の寄与であるといってよい。清は清潔であり、ときとして整頓であり、茶の湯と関係するいかなる事、いかなる場所にもこれを窺うことができる。露地と称する茶庭では清水を自由に使用するが、自然の流水を利用できぬ場合には手ぢかに石の手洗鉢（訳註、つくばい）がある。茶室に一塵も止めぬはいうまでもないことである。

　茶の湯の「清」は道教の「清」を想起させる。両者に相通うところがあるのは、鍛錬の目的が五官の汚れから心を自由にすることにあるからであろう。ある茶人がつぎのようにいっている。

　　『茶の湯の本意は、六根を清くする為なり。眼に掛物・生花を見、
　　鼻に香をかぎ、耳に湯音を聴き、口に茶を味ひ、手足格を正し、
　　五根清浄なる時、意自ら清浄なり。畢竟、意を清くする所なり。
　　我は二六時中茶の湯の心離れず、全く慰み事にあらず。又、道具
　　は、たけだけ相応にするものなり。』　　　　　（葉隠第二巻聞書の二）

tea one's mouth is cleansed; and by handling the tea utensils one's sense of touch is cleansed. When thus all the sense-organs are cleansed, the mind itself is cleansed of defilements. The tea-cult is after all a spiritual discipline, and my aspiration for every hour of the day is not to depart from the spirit of the tea-cult, which is by no means a matter of mere entertainment."*

In one of Rikyū's poems we have this:

"While the *roji* is meant to be a passageway
Altogether outside this earthly life,
How is it that people only contrive
To besprinkle it with the dust of mind?"

Here as in the following poems he refers to his own state of mind while looking out quietly from his tea-room:

"The court is left covered
With the fallen leaves
Of the pine-tree;
No dust is stirred,
And calm is my mind!"

"The moonlight
Far up in the sky,
Looking through tile eaves,
Shines on a mind
Undisturbed with remorse."

It is indeed a mind pure, serene, and free from disturbing emotions that can enjoy the aloneness of the Absolute:

"The snow-covered mountain-path

利休の歌の一つにこういうのがある。

　　　露地はただ
　　　浮世の外の道なるに
　　　心の塵をなぞ散らすらむ

　つぎの歌では彼は茶室から静かに外を眺める自分の心境を述べている。

　　　庭の面は
　　　払ひもあへぬ松の葉に
　　　なかなか塵の
　　　見えずもあるかな

　　　軒端もる
　　　天照る月のみかげにも
　　　心晴れては
　　　恥づべくもなし

　それはじつに、純粋にして静寂な、もろもろの情感に妨げられずに、「絶対なるもの」の孤独を味いうる心である。

　　　岩伝ふ

Winding through the rocks
Has come to its end;
[Here stands a hut,
The master is all alone;]
No visitors he has,
Nor are any expected."

In a book called *Nambō-Roku* which is one of the most important, almost sacred, text-books of the tea-cult, we have this passage, showing that the ideal of the cult is to realise a Buddha-land of Purity on earth on however small a scale and to see an ideal community gathered here however temporary the gathering and however few its members:

"The spirit of *wabi* is to give an expression to the Buddha-land of Purity altogether free from defilements, and therefore in this *roji* and in this thatched hut there ought not to be a speck of dust of any kind; both master and visitors are expected to be on terms of absolute sincerity; no ordinary measures of proportion or etiquette or conventionalism are to be followed. A fire is made, water is boiled, and tea is served: this is all that is needed here, no other worldly considerations are to intrude. For what we want here is to give full expression to the Buddha-mind. When ceremony, etiquette, and other such things are insisted on, worldly considerations of various kinds creep in, and master and visitors each feel inclined to find fault with the other. It becomes thus more and more difficult to come across such ones as fully comprehend the meaning of the tea-cult. If we get Jōshū* for master and Bodhi-Dharma the first Zen patriarch for a guest and Rikyū and myself pick tip the dust in the *roji*, would not such a gathering be a happy one indeed?. . ."

We see how thoroughly imbued with the spirit of Zen is this statement made by one of the chief disciples of Rikyū.

A special chapter will be devoted to the elucidation of the concept *sabi* or *wabi* which is enumerated as a fourth constituent of tile tea-cult. In fact, this

雪の細道
あとたえて
訪ふ人もなし
待つ人もなし

　茶の湯の最も重要な、ほとんど神聖視されている教典の一つである「南方録」＊という書に、茶の目的は小規模ながらこの世に清浄無垢の仏土を実現し、一時的の集り、少数の人ながら、ここに理想社会をつくることだという意味の一節がある。

　『侘の本意は清浄無垢の仏世界を表はして、此露地草庵に至りては塵芥を払却し、主客ともに直心の交りなれば、規矩寸尺式法等あながちに云ふべからず。火を起し湯を沸し茶を喫する迄の事也。他事有るべからず。是即ち仏心の露出する所也。作法挨拶に拘る故、種々の世間の義に堕して、或は客は主の過ちを伺ひ譏り、主は客の過ちを嘲る類になりぬ。此仔細熟得悟了する人を待つに時なし。趙州（じょうしゅう）を亭主にし、初祖大師を客にして、休居士と此坊が露地の塵を拾ふ程ならば、一会（え）は調ふべきか。』

（南方録、滅後書）

　この利休高弟の一人の手になる文章に禅の精神のふかく染み透っていることが判る。
　茶の湯の第四の構成分子に算えられるさびまたはわびの概念を説明するためには、とくに一章を割きたい。事実、これは茶を作りあ

is the most essential factor making up the cult, without which there cannot be any *cha-no-yu* whatever, and it is also on this idea that Zen enters into a closer relationship with it.

2

I have used the term tranquillity for the fourth element constituting the spirit of the tea-cult, but it may not be a good term for all that is implied in the Chinese character "*Jaku*" (*chu*). *Jaku* is *sabi* in Japanese, but *sabi* contains much more than tranquillity. Its Sanskrit equivalent *santi*, it is true, means but *sabi* contains much more than tranquility "peace," "serenity," and *jaku* has been frequently used in Buddhist literature to denote "death" or "Nirvana." But as the "poverty," "simplification," "aloneness," and here *sabi* becomes synonymous with *wabi*.

To appreciate poverty, or to accept whatever is given, a tranquil mind is needed, but in both *sabi* and *wabi* there is a suggestion of objectivity. Just to be tranquil is not *sabi*, nor *wabi*. There is always something objective which evokes in one a mood to be called *wabi*. And *wabi* is not merely a psychological reaction to a certain pattern of environment. There is a principle of estheticism in it, and when this is lacking poverty becomes indigence, and aloneness ostracism or inhuman unsociability. *Wabi* or *sabi*, therefore, may be defined as an esthetical appreciation of poverty; when it is used as a principle of art, it is the creating or remodeling of an environment in such a way as to awaken the feeling of *wabi* or *sabi*. Nowadays as these terms are used, we may say that *sabi* applies more to the individual objects and environment generally, and *wabi* to the state of life ordinarily associated with poverty or insufficiency or imperfection.

Shukō, a disciple of Ikkyū and tea-master to Yoshimasa used to teach his pupils with the following story as regards the spirit of the tea-cult.

A Chinese poet happened to compose this couplet:

げる最も本質的な要素で、それなくしてはなんら茶の湯はありえない。そしてまた、この観念の上に立ってこそ、禅は茶とさらに密接な関係に入り込むのである。

二

　茶の湯の精神を組み立てる第四の要素に自分は "tranquillity"（静寂）という語を用いたが、これは漢字の「寂」という文字に含まれるいっさいを表すに適した用語ではないかも知れぬ。寂は日本語のさびである。が、さびは静寂より内容が広い。寂にあたる梵語の Śānti は事実「静寂」「平和」「静穏」を意味し、寂はしばしば仏典では「死」または「涅槃（ねはん）」を指すために用いられてきた。しかし、この語が茶の湯に用いられる時には、その指すところは「貧困」「単純化」「孤絶」などにちかく、ここにさびはわびと同意語（シノニム）となる。

　貧困を味うために、あるいは、与えられしものをそのままに受容れるためには静かな心が要る。が、さび・わび両者には対象性が暗示される。わびという気分（ムード）を引き起こすなにか対象物がいつも存する。わびに単にある型の環境に対する心理的な反動ではない。そこには美的指導原理が存し、これを欠けば貧乏はただの貧困となり、孤絶はオストラシズム（訳註、貝殻追放、より絶交、排斥の意）や非人間的な非社会性となる。ゆえにわびやさびを定義して貧乏の美的趣味となすことができよう。これを芸術の原理として用いる場合には、わびやさびの感情を目覚ますような環境をつくりだすこと、または、摸造することである。今日この語を用いる場合には、さびはいっぱんに個々の事物や環境に、わびは通常、貧乏、不十分あるいは不完全を連想させる生活状態に適用される。

　一休の弟子で足利義政の茶匠であった珠光＊は、茶の湯の精神に関して弟子に教えるのによくつぎの話をもってした。

　ある中国の詩人がたまたま次の一聯を作った。

"In the woods over there deeply buried in snow,
Last night a few branches of plum-tree burst out in bloom."

When he showed this to his friend, the latter suggested to alter "a few branches" into "one branch." The author followed the friend's advice praising him to be his "teacher of one character." A solitary branch of the plum in bloom among the snow-covered woods—here is the idea of *wabi*.

On another occasion Shuko is reported to have said this:

"It is good to see a fine steed tied in the straw roofed shed. Being so, it is also specially fine to find a rare object of art in an ordinarily furnished room."

This reminds one of the Zen phrase, "To fill a monk's tattered robe with a cool refreshing breeze." Outwardly, there is not a sign of distinction, appearances all go against the contents which are in every way priceless. A life of *wabi* can then be defined thus; an inexpressible quiet joy deeply hidden underneath sheer poverty; and the tea-cult tries to express the idea artistically.

But if there is anything here betraying a trace of insincerity, the whole thing is utterly ruined. The priceless contents must be there in a most genuine manner, they must be as if they were never there, they must be rather accidentally discovered. In the beginning, no suspicions of the presence of anything extraordinary, yet something attracts, a closer approach, and a tentative examination and behold a mine of solid gold glitters from among the unexpected. But the gold itself remains ever the same whether discovered or not. It retains its reality, that is, sincerity to itself, regardless of accidents. *Wabi* means to be true to itself. A master lives quietly in his unpretentious hut, a friend comes in unexpectedly, tea is served, a fresh spray of flowers is arranged, and the visitor enjoys a peaceful afternoon charmed with his conversation and entertainment. Is this not real tea-cult?

Parenthetically, some may ask; "In these modern times how many of us are situated like the tea-master? It is nonsense to talk about leisurely entertainment. Let us have bread first, and less working hours." To speak the

前林深雪▸裡　　昨夜数枝開▸

　彼がこれを一友に示したところ、その友人は「数枝」を「一枝」と変えたらといった。詩人は友の助言にしたがい、彼を「梅花一字の師」であるとほめた。雪ふかき森のうちに開いた梅花の一枝——ここにわびの観念がある。

　またあるとき、珠光はつぎのようにいったと伝えられている。

　　『藁屋に名馬を繋いだのを見るのはよいものだ。そのように、ふ
　　つうの室に稀な品を見つけるのも、格別なことだ』

　これは『破襴衫裡 盛▸清風▸』という禅語を想起させる。外面上、際だった様子はみえないが、外形とはことごとく反対に内容はどの点からみても評価もできない『無価の宝』だ。そこでわびの生活はかように定義されよう。貧乏のうちに深く蔵されているところの、言葉では表わしがたい静かなよろこび、と。茶の湯はこの観念を芸術的に表現しようというのである。

　しかし、茶室に不誠実の痕を示すような事物があればいっさいはまったく破滅する。価もつけられぬような調度品がきわめて純然たるままそこになければならぬ。そこになかったかのごとくに在らねばならぬ。たまたま発見されるのでなければならぬ。初めはなにも変った物の在ることに気づかない。が、なにかしら心引かれる、さらに近よって、試すように見調べる、すると思いがけないところに純金の鉱脈がきらめく。しかし、黄金そのものは発見されようとされまいと依然として同じところに在るのだ。それは偶然性にかかわりなくその真実在を、すなわち己に対する誠実を失わぬ。わびは己の本性に忠実なる意味である。茶人は飾り気ない小庵に静かに住み、思いがけなく客が訪れると、茶を点て、新しい花を生け、客は主の話と饗応に感じ入って、静かな午後を楽しむ。これが真の茶の湯ではないか。

　つぎのような問をはさむ人があるかもしれぬ。『現代の世にこの茶人のような境遇の人は何人あろうか。暢気にもてなしのことなぞ

truth, however, we so-called moderners have lost leisureliness, there is no room in our worrying hearts for really enjoying life except running after excitements for excitement's sake, just to keep the inner worries temporarily suffocated. The main question is whether life is meant for leisurely and cultural enjoyments, or for pursuing pleasures and sensational excitements. When the question is settled, and if it is necessary, let us negate the entire machinery of modern life and start a new one. I hope our destination is not the enslaving of ourselves all the time to our material wants and comforts.

Another tea-master writes:

"From Amaterasu Ōmikami* starts the spirit of *wabi*. Being the great ruler of this country, he was free to erect the finest possible palaces inlaid with gold and silver and precious stones, and nobody would dare to speak ill of him, and yet he lived in a reed thatched house and lived on unpolished rice. In every possible way, besides, he was self-sufficient, modest, and ever-striving. He was truly a most excellent tea-master, living a life of *wabi*. . . ."

It is interesting to see that this writer regards Amaterasu Ōmikami as the representative tea-man who lived a life of *wabi*. This, however, shows that the tea-cult is the esthetic appreciation of primitive simplicity; in other words, that the cult is an esthetic expression of the longing which most of us seem to feel in the depths of our hearts to go back to Nature as far as our human existence would permit and to be at one with Nature.

From these statements the concept of *wabi* I think is becoming clearer. Sōtan was a grandson of Rikyū and from him we can say in a way real *wabi* life starts. He explains that *wabi* is the essence of the tea-cult, corresponding to the moral life of the Buddhists:

"It is a great mistake indeed to make an ostentatious show of *wabi* while inwardly there is nothing consonant with it. Such people construct a tea-room as far as appearances go with all that is needed for *wabi*; much gold and silver is wasted for the work; rare objects of art are purchased with the money realized by the sale of their farm—and this just to make a display of them before visitors. They think a life of *wabi* is here. But far from it. *Wabi*

語るのは馬鹿げている。まずパンを与えよ、そして労働時間の短縮を。』しかし、じつを言えば、われわれいわゆる現代人は閑暇を失っている。悶える心には真に生を楽しむ余裕はなく、ただ刺激のために刺激を追って、内心の苦悶を一時的に窒息させておこうとするにすぎない。主要な問題は生活はゆったりした教養的享受のためにあるのか、快楽と感覚的刺激を求めるためにあるのか、どちらだろうかという点である。この問題がきまった上で、必要ならば、われわれは現代生活の全機構を否定して新しく始めてもいい。われわれの目的は終始、物質的欲望と慰安の奴隷となっていることではない。

　また、別の茶人＊は書いている。

　『天下の侘の根元は、天照御神にて、日（本）国の大主にて、金銀
　珠玉をちりばめ、殿作り候へばとて、誰あつて叱るもの無之候に、
　かやぶき・黒米の御供、其外何から何までも、つつしみふかく、
　おこたり給はぬ御事、世に勝れたる茶人にて御入候。……』

（石州流「秘事五ヶ条」）

　この筆者が天照大神をわび住居をする代表的な茶人と見なしているのに面白い。しかし、これは茶の湯が原始的単純性の美的鑑賞であること、換言すれば、茶は人間の生存が許しうるところまで自然に還って、自然と一つになりたいという、われわれの心奥に感じる憧憬の美的表現であることを示している。

　これらの文句からわびの概念がしだいに明瞭になってくると思う。宗旦は利休の孫で、真の侘び生活は彼からでているといってよい。彼はわびは茶道の真髄で、仏教徒の道徳的生活にあたると説いている。

　『侘の一字は茶道に於て重じ用ひて持戒となせり。然るを俗輩陽
　の容態は侘を仮りて、陰には更に侘る意なし。故に形は侘びたる
　一茶斎に許多の黄金を費耗し、珍奇の磁器に田園を換へて賓客に
　衒ひ、此を風流なりと唱ふるは抑何の謂ぞや。それ侘とは物不足
　して一切我意に任せず蹉跎する意なり。侘傺などと連続して離騒
　の註に、侘は立也、傺は住なり。憂思失┐意住立而不┐能┐前とい

means insufficiency of things, inability to fulfill every desire one may cherish, generally a life of poverty and dejection. To halt despondently in one's course of life because of his inability to push himself forward—this is *wabi*. But he does not brood over the situation. Those who really know what *wabi* is, are free from greed, violence, anger, indolence, uneasiness, and folly. He has learned to be self-sufficient with insufficiency of things. He does not seek beyond his means. He has ceased to be cognizant of the fact that he is in tight circumstances. If however he should still abide with the idea of poverty, insufficiency, or wretchedness of his conditions generally, he would no more be a man of *wabi* but a poverty-stricken person. Thus *wabi* corresponds to the Pāramitā of Morality as observed by the Buddhists. . . ."

In *wabi* estheticism is fused with morality or spirituality, and it is for this reason that the tea-masters declare the cult to be life itself and not merely a thing for pleasure, however refined this may be. Zen is thus directly connected with the tea-cult, indeed most ancient tea-masters studied Zen in real earnest and applied their attainment in Zen to the art of their profession.

Religion can sometimes be defined as a way of escape from the humdrumness of this worldly life. Scholars may object to this, saying that religion aspires not to escape but to transcend life in order to reach the Absolute or the Infinite. But, practically stated, it is an escape where one finds a little time to breath and recuperate. Zen as a spiritual discipline does this too, but as it is too transcendental as it were and inaccessible for ordinary minds, the tea-masters who have studied Zen have devised the way to put their understanding in practice in the form of the tea-cult. Probably in this too a great extent their esthetic aspirations asserted themselves.

When *wabi* is explained as above, readers may think that *wabi* is more or less a negative quality, and that its enjoyment is meant for people who have proved a failure in life. This is true to a certain extent. But how many of us are really so healthy as not to need medicine or a tonic of one kind or another at some time in their lives? And then every one of us is destined to pass away. Psychology tells us many cases of active businessmen strong

へり。又、釈氏要覧に、獅子吼菩薩問少_欲知_足有_何差別_仏言少_欲者不_取知_足者得_少不_悔恨_とあるを合せて、侘の意と字訓とを見れば、其不自由なるも不自由なりと思ふ念を不_生、不足も不足の念を起さず。不調も不調の念を抱かぬを侘なりと心得べきなり。其不自由を不自由と思ひ、不足を不足と愁ひ、調はざるも調はざると訴訟へなば、是侘に非ずして実の貧人と云ふべし。一切如_此の念に流到せざる時は、堅固に侘の意を守りて、助仏戒を保つに等し。』　　　　　　　（茶禅同一味、又は禅茶録）

　わびは美と道徳や精神性とが鎔け合っているから、この理由で茶人は茶の湯を生活そのものとなし、いかにこれが洗煉されようとも、たんなる遊芸とはせぬのだ。禅はかくして直接茶と関連する。事実、多くの昔の茶人は真面目に禅を修め、禅にえたるものをその専門の技に応用した。

　宗教は時とすればこの世俗の無味単調から遁れる道と定義することもできよう。学者はこれに反対して、宗教は「絶対境」または「無限」に到達するために生を逃避するのではなくて生を超越することを求めるのだというかもしれぬ。しかし、実際上からいえば、宗教も暫時息をついて恢復できるようなところへの逃避である。禅は精神的鍛錬としてはこの事もするが、いわば超越的すぎて、普通の心ではいたれぬところがあるから、禅を修めた茶人たちは茶の湯の形でその了得したところを実行する途を工夫したのである。おそらくはここに彼らの美的思慕（エステチク・アスピレーション）が現れることも大きかったのであろう。

　わびを上述のように説明すると、読者はわびは多少消極的性質のものであり、人生失意の人の楽しむものと考えるかもしれぬ。これはある程度事実である。しかし、その生涯のある時期に一、二の薬剤や清涼剤・刺激剤を必要とせぬほどに真に壮健な人が幾人とあろうか。しかも誰もはみな死ぬように定められてある。心理学は身心ともに強壮な活動的実業家が隠退すると急に衰える例を多く語って

physically and mentally who will suddenly collapse when they retire. Why? Because they have not learned to keep their energy in reserve, that is to say, they have never become aware of a plan to retreat while still working. The Japanese fighting men in those days of strife and unrest when they were most strenuously engaged in warlike business realized that they could not go on with their nerves always at the highest pitch of vigilance and, therefore, that they ought to have a way of escape sometime and somewhere. The tea-cult must have given them exactly what they needed. They retreated for a while into a quiet corner of their unconscious symbolized by the tea-room no wider than ten feet square. And when they came out of it, they felt not only refreshed in mind and body, but had very likely their memory renowned of things which were of more permanent values than mere fighting.

What follows is the story of a teaman who had to assume the role of a swordsman and fight with a ruffian.

Toward the end of the seventeenth century, Lord Yama-no-uchi, of the province of Tosa, wanted to take his teamaster along with him on his official trip to Yedo, the seat of the Tokugawa Shogunate. The teamaster was not inclined to accompany him, for in the first place he was not of the samurai rank and knew that Yedo was not a quiet and congenial place like Tosa, where he was well known and had many good friends. In Yedo he would most likely get into trouble with ruffians, resulting not only in his own disgrace but in his lord's. The trip would be a most risky adventure, and he had no desire to undertake it.

The lord, however, was insistent and would not listen to the remonstrance of the teamaster for this man was really great in his profession, and it was probable that the lord harbored the secret desire to show him off among his friends and colleagues. Not able to resist further the lord's earnest request, which was in fact a command, the master put off his teaman's garment and dressed himself as one of the samurai, carrying two swords.

いる。なぜか。彼らが精力を貯えておくことを知らなかったからである。すなわち活動最中において、退いて顧みるということに気づかなかったからである。戦国時代の武士は兵馬の事に奮然したがいながらも、油断なく緊張しきった神経をつづけてゆくことはできないこと、したがって、いつかどこかで逃避の道をもたねばならぬことを悟っていた。茶の湯が彼らの必要としたものを的確に与えたに違いない。彼らは四畳半の茶室によって象徴される、静かな「無意識」の一隅に暫時退くのであった。そこからでた時には、心身爽快の思いがするばかりでなく、たんなる争闘よりも永久的な価値ある事柄に関して記憶を新たにしたことであったろう。

　終りに、一人の悪徒と必死の争闘をすることとなった際、武士に変じたある茶人の話を誌しておこう。*この話は、「無意識」というものがいかなる種類の芸術技法をつかう場合にも、実際的な出来事を処理する場合にも、その赴くままに任せられれば驚異を働かすという真理、悟りという禅体験の機会となる「無意識」なるものの目ざめが、芸術活動の完成の基になっているという真理を明らかにするのである。一つの直覚が無意識の神秘のなかへ深く入りこむ時に、われらは観念の創りかた、一連の行動のだしかた、不断に変化する環境に応じてその原則を整えてゆく法をおのずから知るのである。あきらかにこの種の「無意識」はたんに生理学的乃至心理学的概念ではない。それは最もふかい意味で創造的なるものである。
　十七世紀の末近いころ、土佐ノ国の大名山ノ内侯が江戸に参観する際、自分の茶の宗匠を連れてゆこうと思った。宗匠はお伴したくなかった。第一彼は士分の者ではなかったし、江戸は土佐のように静かな自分の性の合ったところではなかった。土佐でこそ自分は人にもよく知られ多くの知己もあった。江戸に行けばなにか悪党と面倒をひき起して、自分のみならず主家の体面に関わるような事になりそうな気がした。そうとすればこの旅ははなはだ冒険になるので、

While staying in Yedo, the teamaster was mostly confined in his lord's house. One day the lord gave him permission to go out and do some sightseeing. Attired as a samurai, he visited Uyeno by the Shinobazu pond, where he espied an evil-looking samurai resting on a stone. He did not like the looks of this man. But finding no way to avoid him, the teaman went on. The man politely addressed him; "As I observe, you are a samurai of Tosa, and I should consider it a great honor if you permit me to try my skill in swordplay with you. "

The teaman of Tosa from the beginning of his trip had been apprehensive of such an encounter. Now, standing face to face with a *ronin* of the worst kind, he did not know what to do. But he answered honestly:

"I am not a regular samurai, though so dressed; I am a teamaster, and as to the art of swordplay I am not at all prepared to be your opponent." But as the real motive of the *ronin* was to extort money from the victim, of whose weakness he was now fully convinced, he pressed the idea even more strongly on the teaman of Tosa.

Finding it impossible to escape the evil-designing ronin, the teaman made up his mind to fall under the enemy's sword. But he did not want to die an ignominious death that would surely reflect on the honor of his lord of Tosa. Suddenly, he remembered that a few minutes before he had passed by a swordman's training school near Uyeno park, and he thought he would go and ask the master about the proper use of the sword on such occasions and also as to how he should honorably meet an inevitable death. He said to the *ronin*.

彼は少しも引受けたくなかった。

　しかし、主君はしきりに随従を説いて、宗匠の異存を聴き入れようとしなかった。というのはこの者はその道で実際すぐれていたからだ。おそらくは主君は彼を大名仲間に誇示しようという密かな野心を懐いていたのであろう。主君の懇望に、それは事実上命令だが、この上逆らい難く、宗匠は自分の茶人衣裳を脱いで大小を携える侍姿になった。

　江戸滞留中、彼は多く主人たる人の屋敷内に閉じ籠っていた。ある日、主君は彼に外へ見物にゆく許しを与えた。侍の風をして宗匠は上野不忍池の畔を訪れたが、そこで石に掛けて休んでいる風体の悪い侍を見つけた。彼はこの男の顔つきが気にいらなかった。しかし、避けようもないので進んで行った。男はていねいに彼を呼びかけて『貴殿は土佐の侍と、お見受けするが、一手合せてお手並拝見できればかたじけないと存じます。』

　土佐のこの茶匠は旅の始めから、こういった邂逅を心配していたのだった。いま、最も質の悪い浪人とぶつかって、彼はどうしていいか判らなかった。しかし、正直に答えた。

『私はこういう服装はしているが正しい士分ではない。茶の湯の稽古を職としているもので、刀の技にかけてはとうてい貴殿のお相手ができようとは思いません。』しかし、浪人の真の腹は十分その弱点を知り抜いたこの犠牲者から金を強請ることにあったから、彼は土佐の茶匠にいっそう強くせまってきた。

　浪人の悪企みの爪牙からのがれられぬと観念した茶匠は敵の刃にたおれる覚悟をした。しかし、彼は藩公の名を傷つけるような犬死はしたくなかった。不意に彼は、いましがた、上野の近くのある剣道指南の道場の前を通ったことを想い出した。そこで彼はその師範のところへ行って、こういう場合の刀の正しい使い方と遁れられぬ死の立派な遂げかたとについて尋ねたいと思った。彼は浪人にいった。

"If you insist so much, we will try to skill in swordsmanship. But as I am now on my master's errand, I must make my report first. It will take some time before I come back to meet you here. You must give me that much time."

The *ronin* agreed. So the teaman hastened to the training school referred to before and made a most urgent request to see the master. The gatekeeper was somewhat reluctant to acquiesce because the visitor carried no introductory letter. But when he noticed the seriousness of the man's desire, which was betrayed in his every word and in his every movement, he decided to take him to the mater.

The master quietly listened to the teaman, who told him the whole story and most earnestly expressed his wish to die as befitted a samurai. The swordsman said, "The pupils who come to me invariably want to know how to use the sword, and not how to die. You are really a unique example. But before I teach you the art of dying, kindly serve me a cup of tea, as you say you are a teaman." The teaman of Tosa was only too glad to make tea for him, because this man in all likelihood the last chance for him to practice his art of tea to his heart's content. The swordsman closely watched the teaman as the latter was engaged in the performance of the art. Forgetting all about his approaching tragedy, the teaman serenely proceeded to prepare tea. He went through all the stages of the art as if this were the only business that concerned him most seriously under the sun at that moment. The swordsman was deeply impressed with the teaman's concentrated state of mind, from which all the superficial stirrings of ordinary consciousness were swept away. He struck his own knee, a sign of hearty approval, and exclaimed,

"There you are! No need for you to learn the art of death! The state of mind in which you are now is enough for you to cope with any swordsman. When you see your *ronin* outcast, go on this way: First, think you are going to serve tea for a guest. Courteously salute him, apologizing for the delay, and tell him that you are now ready for the contest. Take off your

『それほど強ってといわれるなら、おたがいに武道の腕を試そう。しかし、私は主君の御用を帯びているからまず復命しなければならぬ。ここに立戻って貴殿と会うまでには幾らかの暇もかかろう。それだけの余裕はぜひ戴きたい。』

　浪人は承知した。そこで宗匠は急いで前述の道場に行って、その先生に火急にお会いしたいと申し入れた。門番は彼が紹介状を持っていないのでその頼みを聴き入れることに多少躊躇したが、彼のどの言葉にも、どの身の挙動にも、客の望みの由々しさがおのずと表われているのを読んで、主人のところへ通そうと意を決した。

　主(あるじ)は宗匠が一部始終を語るのを、ことに、侍らしい死にかたをしたいと真剣に述べるのを、静かに耳を傾けて聴いた。この剣士はいった。『私のところへくる弟子たちがいつも知りたがるのは、刀の使いかたであって、死にかたではありません。貴方はまことに特殊な例です。だが、貴方に死にかたを御教示する前に、御茶人ということですから、一服点てて戴きましょうか。』土佐の茶人にとっては、これがおそらくは心ゆくまで茶の湯を行なえる最後の機会(チャンス)と思えばこの家の主のために茶を点てることは願ったり叶ったりといってよかった。剣士はじっとこの茶人が茶の湯の事にしたがうのを見守った。宗匠は自分の悲劇の近づいているのもまったく忘れ、静かに茶の仕度をすすめ、茶の湯の順序をことごとく仕通した。まるで、いまその一事(ひとこと)が陽の下においてわが身に最も由々しいかかわりがある唯一の仕事ででもあるかのようだった。剣士は普通意識の皮相な擾(さわ)がしさをことごとく一掃した茶人の集注的な心境に深く感銘した。彼は膝を打って心から同感の意を表した。

『その通りです。死ぬ技などおぼえる必要はありません。貴方のただいまの御心境はいかなる剣士と闘っても十分です。無法な浪人とお会いになったら、こういう風におやりなさい。まず、自分は客に茶を点てているのだと考えるのですね。鄭重に彼に挨拶をして、遅参をわび、勝負をする仕度がまったくできたことをお告げなさい。

haori [outer coat], fold it up carefully, and then put your fan on it just as you do when you are at work. Now bind your head with the *tenugui* [corresponding to a towel], tie your sleeves up with the string, and gather up your *hakama* [skirt]. You are now prepared for the business that is to start immediately. Down your sword, lift it high up over your head, in full readiness to strike down the opponent, and, closing your eyes, collect your thoughts for combat. When you hear him give a yell, strike him with your sword. It will probably end in a mutual slaying." The teaman thanked the master for his instructions and went back to the place where he had promised to meet the combatant.

He scrupulously followed the advice given by the swordmaster with the same attitude of mind as when he was serving tea for his friends. When, boldly standing before the *ronin*, he raised his swords, the *ronin* saw an altogether different personality before him. He had no chance to give a yell, for he did not know where and how to attack the teaman, who now appeared to him as an embodiment of fearlessness, that is, of the Unconscious. Instead of advancing toward the opponent, the *ronin* retreated step by step, finally crying, "I'm done, I'm done!" And, throwing up his sword, he prostrated himself on the ground and pitifully asked the teaman's pardon for his rude request, and then hurriedly left the field.

As to the historicity of the story I am in no position to state anything definite. What I attempt here to establish is the popular belief underlying the story cited here and others of similar character; this is that, underneath all the practical technique or the methodological details necessary for the mastery of an art, there are certain intuitions directly reaching what I call Cosmic Unconscious, and all these intuitions belonging to various arts are not to be regarded as individually unconnected or mutually individually unrelated, but as growing out of one fundamental intuition. It is indeed firmly believed by Japanese generally that the various specific intuitions acquired by the swordsman, the teamaster, and masters of other branches of art and culture are not more than particularized applications of one great

羽織を脱いだらこれを注意して畳み、貴方がお茶にかかる時なさるように、その上に扇子をお置きなさい。さて鉢巻をして、襷をかけ、袴の股立（ももだち）をお取りなさい。これですぐ仕事を始めてよいだけの仕度ができました。刀を抜いて頭の上にたかく上げて相手を打ち倒す用意をし、眼を閉じて闘うために心をお鎮めなさい。相手の掛声を聞いたら、その刀で相手を打つのです。おそらくこれは相打ちに終るでしょう。』茶人は主人の教えを厚く謝して、相手と会う約束をした場所に立ち戻った。

　彼は剣士の与えた忠告を周到に守って、自分の友人に茶を点てるときと同じ心構えをとった。彼が浪人にむかって太刀をかざして立ったとき、浪人は目前にまったく別の人格を見た。彼は掛声を掛ける機（おう）がなかった。どこからどう、この茶人に打って掛っていいか判らなかった。茶人はいまや彼には「無畏」の、すなわち、「無意識」の体現者として現れた。浪人は相手の方に進むかわりに、一歩一歩後退（あとずさ）って、ついに叫んだ。『参った、参った。』そして、太刀を投げ、身を地に平伏して、無体な願いひらにお許し下さいといって、急いでその場を立ち去った。

　この話の史的根拠について、自分は確定した事を述べる地位にない。自分がここで確実にさせておきたいことは、ここに引いた話や同じような性質の話の基をなす一般的の信念である。それは、一芸の熟達に必要なあらゆる実際的な技術や方法論的詳細の底には、自分のいわゆる「宇宙的無意識」に直接到達するある直覚が存し、各種芸術に属するこれらの諸直覚はすべてみな、個々無関連な、相互に無関係なものと見なすべきものではなく、一つの根本的な直覚から生ずるものと、見なすべきものだということである。剣士・茶人そのほかの各種芸道の師匠たちが了得したいろいろな専門的な諸直覚は、要するに、一つの大きな体験の各特殊な応用にすぎないとは、事実、日本人一般からかたく信じられているところである。日本人

experience. They have not yet thoroughly analyzed this belief so as to give it a scientific basis; but the experience is acknowledged to be an insight into the Unconscious itself as source of all creative possibilities, all artistic impulses, and particularly as Reality above all forms of mutability beyond the *samsara*-sea of birth-and-death. The Zen masters, ultimately deriving their philosophy from the Buddhist doctrine of *Śūnyatā* and *prajñā*, describe the Unconscious in terms of life, that is, of birth-and-death which is no-birth-and-death. To the Zen masters, thus, the final intuition is the going beyond birth-and-death and attaining the state of fearlessness. His *satori* is to mature to this, when wonders are accomplished. For the Unconscious then permits its privileged disciples, masters of the arts, to have glimpses of its infinite possibilities.

はこの信念を徹底的に分析して、それに科学的な基礎を与えるよう
には、まだしていないが、この根本的な体験をもって、一切の創造力、
芸術的衝動の根源、とくに、死生の海をこえて一切の無常の形のな
かにある「実在」たる「無意識」そのものへの洞徹であると認めて
いる。禅匠たちは究極においてその哲学を仏法の 空 および 般 若
（智慧）の説から得て、生命、すなわち「生死なき生死」という語
をもって、この「無意識」を説く。禅匠にとっては、それゆえに最
後の直覚というのは生死を超越することであり、無畏の境に到達す
ることである。彼の「悟り」がこの点にまで熟してきたとき、もろ
もろの驚異がなし遂げられる。「無意識」は、そのとき、その特権
ある弟子たち、諸芸の師匠たちに、その無限の可能性に対し瞥見を
許すからである。

N O T E S

第1章

p. 10　原書には以下の文章がある。

I do not think it necessary to make any specific reference to Japanese writers, ancient or modern, who indeed know too well all about the facts of Zen influence on the Japanese people.

第2章

p. 34　原書の註に Fujiwara Sadaiye (1162–1241)とある。

P. 34　原書の註に Fujiwara Iyetaka (1158–1237)とある。

p. 46　原書の註にCf. Takuan on "Immovable Intelligence," p. 112 et seq., of the present workとある。

p. 52　原書の註に These *mondo* of Tōshū, Seccho's poetical comments, and Jōshū's "No-discrimination" are taken from the *Hekigan-shū,* a Zen text-book. The *Hekigan* is a kind of sealed book for ordinary readers.とある。

第3章

p. 72　原書の註に以下の文章がある。

The idea that both friends and enemies when dead are to be equally treated with respect originates from Buddhism; for it teaches that we are all of the same Buddha-nature and that while living in this world of particulars we may espouse a variety of causes and principles, but these controversies vanish when we pass from these

A portrait of Ikkyū Zenji.
一休禅師肖像。

A statue of Takuan Zenji.
沢庵禅師木像。

individual existences to the other shore of transcendental wisdom. From the samurai point of view, the idea of loyalty and sincerity is emphasised more than anything else; enemies are faithful to their cause as we are to our own, and this sentiment when genuine is to be revered wherever and however displayed. Hence one monument dedicated to the spirits of friends and foes. The Shimadzu family erected a great stone monument at Koya for all those fallen in the Korean war of 1591–8. This was no doubt due to the spiritual influence of Shimadzu Nisshinsai (1492–1568), who was one of the greatest scholar-barons of the feudal days. It is interesting to observe that Shimadzu Yoshihiro, one of Nisshinsai's grandsons, started for his ill-behaved subjects a novel form of punishment known as *tera-iri*, "entering into the Buddhist monastery." The offenders, while in the monastery, were made to study the Confucian texts under the personal superintendence of the presiding monk. When they made decided progress in their understanding of the classics, they were restored to their original status.

p. 84 原書の註に以下の文章がある。

When Bokuden was crossing Lake Biwa on a row-boat with a number of passengers, there was among them a rough-looking samurai, stalwart and arrogant in every possible way. He boasted of his skill in swordsmanship saying that he was the foremost man in the art. The fellow-passengers were eagerly listening to his blatant talk while Bokuden was found dozing as if nothing were going on about him. This irritated the braggart very much. He approached Bokuden and shook him, saying, "You also carry a pair of swords, why not say a word?" Answered Bokuden quietly, "My art is different from yours; it consists in not defeating others, but in not being defeated." This incensed him immensely.

"What is your school then?"

"Mine is known as the *muteḳatsu* school" (which means to defeat the enemy "without hands," that is, without using a sword).

"Why do you then carry a sword yourself?"

"This is meant to do away with selfish motives, and not to kill others."

The man's anger now knew no bounds, and exclaimed in a most impassioned manner, "Do you really mean to fight me with no swords?"

"Why not?" was Bokuden's answer.

The braggart-samurai called out to the boatman to row towards the nearest land. But Bokuden suggested that it would be better to go to the island farther off because the mainland might attract people who were liable to get somehow hurt. The samurai agreed. The boat headed towards the solitary island at some distance. As soon as they were near enough, the man jumped off the boat and drawing his sword was all ready for a combat. Bokuden leisurely took off his own swords and handed them to the samurai on the island when Bokuden suddenly took the oar away from the boatman, and applying it to the land gave a hard back-stroke to the boat. Thereupon the boat took a precipitous departure from the island and plunged itself into the deeper water safely away from the man. Bokuden smilingly remarked, "This is my 'no-sword' school."

Another interesting and instructive anecdote is told of Bukokuden whose mastery of the art really went beyond mere acquiring proficiency in sword-play. He had three sons who were all trained in swordsmanship. He wanted to test their attainments. He placed a little pillow over the curtain at the entrance to his room, and it was so arranged that a slight touch on the curtain which had to be raised when entering would make the pillow fall right on one's head.

Bukokuden called in the eldest son first. When he approached he noticed the pillow lying on the curtain, so he took it down and after entering placed it back in the original position. The second son was now called in. He touched the curtain to raise it, and as soon as he saw the pillow coming down, he caught it in his hands, and then carefully put it back where it was. It was the third son's turn to touch the curtain. He came in brusquely and the pillow fell right on his neck. But he cut it in two with his sword even before it came down on the floor. Bukokuden passed his judgment;

"Eldest son, you are well qualified for swordsmanship. "So saying, he gave him a sword. To the second son he said, "Train yourself yet assiduously;" but the youngest was most severely reproved, for he was pronounced to be a disgrace to his family.

p. 86　原書の註に以下の文章がある。

Date Masamune's interview with his Zen monk took place in the following manner. Masamune whose poems on Mount Fuji are else-where quoted was a great student of Zen. When he wished to have a good abbot for his Zen temple where his ancestral spirits were enshrined, he heard of a certain monk residing in an insignificant country temple, who was recommended to him. Wishing to test his attainment, he invited the monk to his castle in Sendai. The monk whose name was Rin-an accepted the invitation and, on the day agreed upon, came up to the city. He was at once ushered into Lord Masamune's residence. After walking through a long corridor, he was told that the Lord was waiting in one of the adjoining rooms. He opened the sliding door to enter the room, but nobody was there; so passing through it he went into another room at the back of it, still nobody greeted him. Feeling strange, he proceeded further on, and when he opened the door, Lord Masamune unexpectedly welcomed him with a drawn sword with which he seemed ready to strike the monk, saying, "What would you say at this moment of life and death?" The monk did not seem to be at all frightened with this most extraordinary way of greeting on the part of his Lord. For Rin-an lost no time to step forward underneath the sword and taking hold of Masamune's waist gave him a severe shaking. The great war-god and the lord of the entire northeastern provinces of Japan then exclaimed, "What a dangerous trick you play!" The monk retorted pushing him away, "O this pretentious man!"

In olden times many such encounters took place between Zen monks and feudal lord who wanted personally and in realistic manner to test the former with regard to their Dhyāna practice and Zen understanding. Being warriors who had to face death any moment even in their supposendly peaceful home life, they were to be trained in this objectively and not scholastically. They did not want philosophy or religion so called, they wanted only some practial guide immediately effective in their professional life. Zen was the very thing they needed.

p. 92　原書の註に以下の文章がある。

The love of the cherry-blossoms among the Japanese seems to be their second nature. There was once, in the Koishikawa dungeon in the days of the Tokugawa régime, a woman prisoner who was destined to be executed before the spring. She used to look out from her window and observing a cherry-tree wished to see it bloom. When the sentence was given, she expressed her intense desire to see the tree in bloom before she parted forever from this earth. The jailer was a kind-hearted man and understood *fūryū* and granted her last wish. It is said that the woman met her death in the happiest mood of spirit. The cherry came to be know later by her name, Asatsuma.

p. 132 原書の註に以下の文章がある。
To Western readers this may sound strange, but in Japan people often keep a kitten tied for a while at least, before she becomes used to the new surrounding.

p. 134 原書の註に以下の文章がある。
Takuan's letter continues further on becoming more or less technical and is cut short here.

第4章
p. 150 原書の註に Hiromasa Takano とある。

第5章
p. 164 原書の註に論語 "Saying of Confucious," 孟子 Works of Mencious, 大學 "Great Learning," and 中庸 "Doctrine of the Means." とある。

p. 166 原書の註に易経 (*yi-ching*), Book of Change; 書経 (*shu-ching*), Book of Annals; 詩経 (*shin-ching*), Book of Odes; 春秋 (*ch'un-ch'in*), Spring and Autumn; 礼記 (*li-chin*), Record of Rites. とある。

p. 176 原書の註に無極 "Limitless," 太極 "Great Limit," 太虚 "Great Vacinity." とある。

第6章
p. 192 原書の註に Returned from China in 1267. とある。

p. 196 原書の註に A Zen master of the T'ang Dynasty, 720–814. とある。

p. 210 原書の註に By Nakano Kazuma in the *Hagakure*. とある。中野数馬のことである。

p. 212 原書の註に An old Chinese Zen master who is reputed for his saying, "Have a cup of tea." とある。

p. 218 原書の註に The Ōmikami is really the sun goddess in Japanese mythology, but the writer seems to understand her to be a male deity. とある。

日本文註

第2章
p. 45 夢窓疎石（1275-1351）。後醍醐天皇、足利尊氏らの帰依を受けた。甲斐恵林寺、京都臨川寺、天竜寺などの開山。京都の西芳寺（苔寺）や天竜寺などの庭園の作者としても有名。

第3章
p. 67 兀庵普寧（1197-1276）。1260 年に来日。博多聖福寺、京都東福寺を経て鎌倉建長寺に入り、時頼の帰依を受ける。時頼の死後、1265 年に帰国。

p. 69 無学祖元禅師(1226-86)のこと。1279 年に来日。1282 年に時宗は円覚寺を建立し、禅師を開山に迎えた。

p. 77 「葉隠」は江戸時代中期に、主君亡きあと出家した鍋島藩の元藩士・山本常朝の語りを、藩士・田代陣基が七年ものあいだ聞き書きし、まとめあげたもの。

p. 79 柳生但馬守宗矩（1571-1646）。二代将軍秀忠、三代将軍家光の兵法指南。初代大目付。一万二千五百石の大名。著書に「兵法家伝書」がある。

p. 79 大道寺友山（1639-1730）。江戸時代前期−中期の兵法家。

p. 83 塚原卜伝(1490-1571)。戦国時代の剣術家。将軍足利義輝や北畠具教の師となる。

第4章
p. 113 以下の訳文が削除されている。「ある禅の著書に、その梗概を記した。原文を完訳すると長いため、ここでは要約したが、重要なすべての考え方は失われていない。」（編集部訳）

p. 115 「この段階を沢庵は無明住地煩悩といっている。無明住地煩悩 無明とは、明に
なしと申す文字にて候。迷を申し候。その五十二位の内に、物毎に心の止る所を、
住地と申し候。住は止ると申す義理にて候。止ると申すは、何事に付ても其事
に心を止るを申し候。貴殿の兵法にて申し候はば」の個所は訳者が追加したもの
である。

p. 121 「荘子」に次の話が載っている。
南海の帝を儵と為し、北海の帝を忽と為し、中央の帝を渾沌と為す。儵と忽と
時に相与に渾沌の地に遇う。渾沌、之を待つこと甚だ善し。儵と忽と渾沌の徳
に報いんことを謀る。曰く、「人皆七竅有りて、以て視聴食息す。此独り有る
こと無し。嘗試みに之を鑿せん」と。日に一竅を鑿し、七日にして渾沌死す。

p. 133 「慈円の歌に、『柴の戸に匂はん花もさもあらばあれ、ながめにけりな恨めしの
世や。』とあり。花は無心に匂ひぬるを、我は心を花に止めて眺めけるよと、
身のこれに染みたる心が恨めしとなり。」の個所は訳者が追加したものである。

p. 135 「沢庵和尚の書翰はなお続くが多少、専門技術的になるからここでは略する。」
の個所は訳者が追加したものである。

p. 143 仏光国師（無学祖元）のこと。

p. 145 上泉伊勢守信綱（1508-1577）。姓は「こういずみ」とも読まれる。また神陰流
は新陰流とも称す。

第6章

p. 213 「南方録」は利休の弟子、南坊宗啓が、千利休のおりにふれての談話や所伝を
記録したものとして、茶の湯の教典とされてきた。

p. 215 村田珠光(1423-1501)。室町 – 戦国時代の茶人。四畳半草庵のわび茶を創始した。
茶祖、茶の湯の開山とされる。

p. 219 片桐石州（1605-1673）。江戸初期の茶人。大和の国小泉の藩主。千宗旦や小堀
遠州らとの交流の中で、茶の湯の研鑽を積み、四代将軍家綱の茶道師範となった。

p. 223 「この話は」に始まる解説は、英語原文にはない。

鈴木大拙 1870年-1966年

明治、大正、昭和時代の仏教学者かつ思想家。1870年10月18日、石川県金沢市に生まれる。本名は貞太郎。東京帝国大学に学び、鎌倉円覚寺の今北洪川に、その没後は釈宗演に師事。1897年アメリカに渡り、「大乗起信論」の英訳、「大乗仏教概論」の英文出版などをおこなう。11年間滞米し、1909年に帰国後、学習院教授、大谷大教授などになる。1911年アメリカ人のビアトリス・レーンと結婚。1921年には英文雑誌「イースタン・ブディスト」（*The Eastern Buddhist*）を創刊。1936年には、イギリスとアメリカの大学で「禅と日本文化」を講じた。1945年鎌倉東慶寺に松ヶ岡文庫を設立。1949年文化勲章受章。同年、ハワイ大学の第2回東西哲学者会議に出席、その後、アメリカの大学やヨーロッパで大乗仏教思想、とくに禅思想を広く世界に紹介した。1963年に「教行信証」全6巻の英訳を完成させる。1966年、7月12日、95歳で死去。代表作に「禅と日本文化」「日本的霊性」「禅の研究」など。和文著作約100冊、英文著作約30冊があり、「鈴木大拙全集」「鈴木大拙選集」も刊行されている。それらの執筆の中で、仏教の幅広い独目の研究だけでなく、日本文化、老荘思想、神秘思想、深層心理学などの本質も解説した。

北川桃雄 1899年-1969年

美術史家、美術評論家。東京生まれ。1924年京都帝国大学経済学部卒業。1941年東京帝国大学文学部美術史科卒業後、共立女子大教授となる。著書に「室生寺」「夢殿」「石庭林泉」「古塔巡歴」「いかるがの里・法隆寺」「敦煌美術の旅」など。

（対訳）禅と日本文化
Zen and Japanese Culture

2005 年 12 月 20 日　第 1 刷発行

著　者	鈴木大拙
訳　者	北川桃雄
発行者	富田 充
発行所	講談社インターナショナル株式会社
	〒 112-8652　東京都文京区音羽 1-17-14
	電話　03-3944-6493 （編集部）
	03-3944-6492 （マーケティング部・業務部）
	ホームページ　www.kodansha-intl.com
印刷・製本所	大日本印刷株式会社

落丁本・乱丁本は購入書店名を明記のうえ、講談社インターナショナル業務部宛にお送りください。送料小社負担にてお取替えします。なお、この本についてのお問い合わせは、編集部宛にお願いいたします。本書の無断複写（コピー）、転載は著作権法の例外を除き、禁じられています。

定価はカバーに表示してあります。